Costume Society of America Series

PHYLLIS A. SPECHT, SERIES EDITOR

A Perfect Fit

The Garment Industry and American Jewry,
1860–1960

EDITED BY GABRIEL M. GOLDSTEIN AND ELIZABETH E. GREENBERG

FOREWORD BY SYLVIA A. HERSKOWITZ

PUBLISHED FOR YESHIVA UNIVERSITY MUSEUM

TEXAS TECH UNIVERSITY PRESS

This book is typeset in Monotype Haarlemmer. The paper used in this book meets the minimum requirements of ANSI/NISO Z39.48-1992 (R1997). ∞

Design and typesetting by Janis Owens, Books By Design, Inc. and project management by Nancy Benjamin, Books By Design, Inc.

Library of Congress Cataloging-in-Publication Data
A perfect fit : the garment industry and American Jewry (1860-1960) / edited by Gabriel Goldstein and Elizabeth Greenberg ; foreword by Sylvia A. Herskowitz.
     p. cm. -- (Costume Society of America series)
   "Published for Yeshiva University Museum."
   Includes bibliographical references and index.
   Summary: "Investigates the U.S. fashion industry's nineteenth-century origins and the role of American Jews in creating, developing, and furthering the national garment industry from the Civil War forward"--Provided by publisher.
   ISBN 978-0-89672-735-9 (hbk. : alk. paper) 1. Clothing trade--United States--History. 2. Jews--United States--History. 3. Jewish businesspeople--United States--History. I. Goldstein, Gabriel M. II. Greenberg, Elizabeth, 1972- III. Yeshiva University. Museum.
   HD9940.U4P47 2012
   338.4'7687097309041--dc23
                     2011047039

Printed in Korea
12 13 14 15 16 17 18 19 20 | 9 8 7 6 5 4 3 2 1

Texas Tech University Press
Box 41037
Lubbock, Texas 79409-1037 USA
800.832.4042
ttup@ttu.edu
www.ttupress.org

Title page photo credits:
Upper left image:
Dress (*left*), Pattullo-Jo Copeland, ca. 1960. Courtesy Yeshiva University Museum.
Dress (*right*), Pauline Trigére, 1960. Courtesy Yeshiva University Museum.
Upper right image:
Cocktail dress, Nettie Rosenstein, ca. 1949. Courtesy Yeshiva University Museum.
Center image (cover and title page):
Model wearing sequin sweater-blouse dinner costume from Hattie Carnegie. Photograph by John Rawlings, from the February 1, 1945, issue of *Vogue*, p. 118. Rawlings / Vogue / Condé Nast Archive. Copyright © Condé Nast.
Background image (cover and title page):
World War I Uniform Factory, ca. 1917. Courtesy YIVO Institute for Jewish Research.

Contents

Contents
vi

List of Illustrations

Acknowledgments

The publication of this volume is the final stage in an exhibition project that first began more than fifteen years ago. Yeshiva University Museum's exhibition A *Perfect Fit: The Garment Industry and American Jewry, 1860-1960*, was the largest and most complex project ever presented by this institution. When planning the publications to accompany the exhibition, we realized that we would need to divide and conquer. The exhibition was accompanied by a beautifully designed exhibition catalogue, summarizing the exhibition's themes and contents and presenting a visual array of the fascinating and beautiful artifacts featured in the exhibition. A more complete multidisciplinary analysis of the many topics discussed in the exhibition deserved a more thorough treatment, and we decided to present this research in a multi-author volume.

We immediately realized that the multi-author volume would take some time to complete; it has taken us longer than we might have ever have imagined, but we are delighted to see it completed and enthusiastic about its contents and quality. We very much hope that it will serve to make the exhibition's contents and overall themes available to a broad readership, and that this volume will encourage new research and considerations of these topics. We express our gratitude to the authors whose essays are featured in this volume. We applaud their research and analysis, and thank them for their patience and encouragement during the several years that it took to bring this project to completion.

This volume is based on and includes much of the thematic, historical, and artifact research conducted in conjunction with the exhibition. We are especially grateful to the insights and efforts of the core members of the curatorial team—Phyllis Dillon, Exhibition Associate Curator, and Mary (Kiplok) Vens, Exhibition Curatorial Associate, who worked alongside us on all aspects of the exhibition project. Together, during the heady and crazed months before the exhibition opened, the four of us formed a semi-formal seminar group to analyze the potential of this volume, to imagine its contents and authors, and then worked as a group to discuss first drafts of the essays and how they might best be—to use a fashion metaphor—sewn together into a stylish ensemble. We then chose the accessories that would strengthen the entire presentation.

Given the time it's taken to bring this volume to fruition, there are many people to thank for their contributions. In 2005, Ari Sclar ably served as the Managing Editor at the point when almost all of the essays were first drafted, and we thank him for his insights and efforts. The final stages in the manuscript and publication process and the overall completion of this project have only been possible due to the talent, patience, and determination of Jessica Goldring, Managing Editor. We are especially indebted to her for enabling us to reach the finish line. Jody Heher, Yeshiva University Museum's Associate Director for Administration, coordinated the final steps of the publication process, with her usual grace, patience, and attention to detail.

This publication and the overall exhibition project have been in many ways an oversize endeavor for Yeshiva University Museum, a midsize institution that has reached far to accomplish such ambitious goals. We express our thanks to all members of the Yeshiva University Museum staff—both past and present—for their creativity, encouragement, and hard work: Ilana Benson, Rachelle Bradt, Eleanor Chiger, Judy Dick, Katharina Feil, Tova Geller, Randi Glickberg, Sara Gruenspecht, Jody Heher, Aliza Mainzer Hughes, Rachel Lazin, Zachary Levine, Aliza Klieman Marriott, Sasha Semach, Reba Wulkan, and Mary Vens. Special recognition to Sylvia Herskowitz, Director Emerita, and Jacob Wisse, the Museum's current Director, for their leadership, and also to Bonni-Dara Michaels, the Museum's Collections Curator, who is the only individual to have worked at the Museum at every stage in this project— from the very first steps until today. We also express our thanks and recognition to June Burns Bové, Yeshiva University Museum's Adjunct Curator of Costume and Textiles and the exhibition's Chief of Costume Installation; June has taught both of us, the Museum, and all of her students and colleagues so very much about the care, presentation, and significance of costume, and her talent and hard work ensured the beauty of the display as seen in the exhibition photographs.

This publication has greatly benefited from the insights and generous support of Sybil Kahn and the Kansas City Garment Industry History Project. As we worked on preparing this volume, Sybil encouraged us to consider Kansas City and midwestern manufacturing centers, and she rightly pointed out that a national story demanded a national analysis. Sybil also served as an able matchmaker, introducing us and enabling us to work with both Laurel Wilson and Jessica Goldring. We thank Sybil for strengthen-

ing the volume and for helping us bring an important part of American manufacturing history to life through its contents.

A more complete list of the many individuals who assisted with the many years of planning and research for the exhibition may be found in the Foreword to the exhibition catalogue; they are too numerous to be mentioned here, but we thank them and recognize that the many aspects of this project have only been possible due to their efforts, sound advice, and encouragement.

We are delighted to be able to publish this volume with Texas Tech University Press as a part of the Costume Society of America series. Our thanks to Judith Keeling, Editor-in-Chief, Texas Tech University Press; Joanna Conrad, Managing Editor, Texas Tech University Press; and Nancy Benjamin, Project Manager, and Janis Owens, Designer, Books By Design, for their guidance, leadership, and professionalism. Thanks also to the Costume Society of America and Phyllis Specht, CSA Series Editor. We thank Sharon Johnson for ably handling the indexing of the volume and express our appreciation to Gretchen Fenston and Leigh Montville of Condé Nast for their assistance with the cover image.

Planning for the exhibition first began in 1996. The exhibition project was supported by both planning (1999) and implementation (2003) grants from the National Endowment for the Humanities, and we are especially proud that the NEH designated this project as a "We the People" initiative. We are very grateful to the NEH and its staff for their generosity, guidance, and encouragement. The project also received programmatic support through a "Museums for America" grant from the Institute for Museum and Library Services, enabling Yeshiva University Museum to take significant steps forward in many areas. Numerous foundations and individuals generously supported the project, many of them garment industry leaders or families with multigenerational connections to the industry. Major exhibition project sponsors include Halina and Samson Bitensky; The Coby Foundation, Ltd., New York; Anonymous; the Jesselson Family Foundation; Levi Strauss Foundation; Fritz and Adelaide Kauffman Foundation; The David Berg Foundation; Robert and Tracey Pruzan; George Feldenkreis, chairman and CEO, Perry Ellis International; Lynn and Sy Syms; Andrew Rosen, founder and president, Theory; Terry Lundgren, Federated Department Stores, Inc.; and Laura and John Pomerantz. Please see the exhibition catalogue for a more complete listing of exhibition supporters.

Our final thanks are reserved for our families, who have patiently stood by us over the years and whose smiling faces continuously encourage us, even as we have found ourselves inundated by Civil War uniforms, hoopskirts, corset patents, Federation fundraising awards, and barbecue aprons. Our grandparents and great-grandparents in the garment industry gave us inspiration and a sense of pride in our heritage. Our children give us hope for a future of both style and substance.

Gabriel M. Goldstein and Elizabeth E. Greenberg

Cocktail dress, Nettie Rosenstein, ca. 1949.
Rosenstein designed high-price wholesale dresses for upscale retailers. Although she catered to wealthy customers, Rosenstein's popular designs were widely copied and influenced American lifestyle at all price points. She has been credited with popularizing the "little black dress" in America, and was especially renowned for designing both of Mamie Eisenhower's inaugural ballgowns (1953 and 1957).

Courtesy Yeshiva University Museum.

Foreword

When work started on the exhibition *A Perfect Fit: The Garment Industry and American Jewry*, everyone—academics, museum professionals, and the general public—felt it was a great idea whose time had come. Some expressed surprise that the topic had not been explored before; many happily volunteered the names of family members who had worked in the garment trades.

This enthusiastic reaction to the exhibition was later echoed in the overwhelming response of those who attended the exhibition's opening in December 2005. When asked to raise their hands if they had relatives who were in the "business," a majority of hands went up. This included the four speakers of the evening: Bruce Cole, chairman of the National Endowment for the Humanities; Brent Glass, director of the Smithsonian National Museum of American History; Bruce Slovin, president of the Center for Jewish History; and Ted Mirvis, vice-chair of the Museum Board and the evening's chair, whose idea it was to ask the question in the first place.

All in all, the overwhelmingly affirmative reaction to our topic and the unprecedented attendance figures and tour requests confirmed for us the relevance and timeliness of the exhibition's theme: the enormous role that American Jewry has played in the germination, growth, and development of one of the largest, most profitable, and most influential industries in this country—the garment industry.

Who knew, until they toured the exhibition, that most of the more than 200,000 German Jews who immigrated to the United States between 1825 and 1875 found work as peddlers and small shopkeepers, many in the rapidly expanding West? Or that the massive demand for uniforms for both North and South in the Civil War was the impetus for manufacturers like Fechheimer of Cincinnati to develop standardized sizes for menswear? Or, jumping ahead to the fabled era of the silver screen, that a designer like Adrian, whose dramatic silhouettes created the images for movie greats like Greta Garbo and Joan Crawford, was born Adolph Greenberg, and Gene Autry's tailor, dubbed the "King of Cowboy Couturiers," was Nudie Cohn from Kiev.

For visitors of a certain age, for whom the initials ILGWU and ACWA still mean something, it was fascinating to learn that Sidney Hillman, leader of the Amalgamated Clothing Workers of America, had been a Lithuanian Yeshiva student before joining the Bund, and came from a distinguished rabbinical family.

As someone who is familiar with today's Jewish community and its fundraising practices, I smiled to myself when I saw the 1898 letter from Ab. Kirschbaum, owner of Vitals Brand Clothing on Philadelphia's Market Street, to one of his suppliers that he enclosed with five tickets for the United Hebrew Charities Benefit. *Plus ça change . . .*

These personal gleanings from an exhibition of more than 320 objects offer some idea of the amount of research that was conducted. Our planning first began in 1996, and for the ensuing years the team of curators and researchers crisscrossed the country locating, investigating, and examining collections in universities, corporate archives, industry workrooms, synagogues, museums, libraries, Jewish communal organizations, and private collections.

We actually gathered—and learned—much more than we needed for the exhibition. A good deal of it was economic, political, and technological history, touching on topics like immigration policies, the Industrial Revolution, the rise of organized labor and the unions, the Depression, and World War II. Truth to tell, what we displayed in our three galleries was really the "showroom samples"—costumes chosen for their visual impact, videos and photographs that captured the spirit of an age, advertisements and posters that defined changing tastes and standards. Even before we created the exhibition, we knew we would want to publish the scholarship that would be amassed, hence this volume.

Sylvia A. Herskowitz
Director Emerita,
Yeshiva University Museum

A Perfect Fit

The Garment Industry and American Jewry, 1860–1960

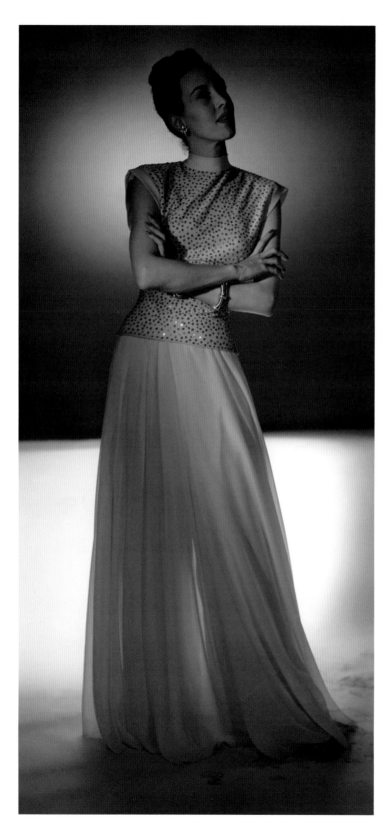

Model wearing sequin sweater-blouse dinner costume from Hattie Carnegie. Beginning with at-home piecework in the early nineteenth century, textile and garment manufacturing offered women a place in the industrial workforce. For generations, Jewish women in central and eastern Europe had been involved in a variety of commercial enterprises; frequently, Jewish women ran family businesses, allowing men to concentrate on traditional study of religious texts. The twentieth century offered even greater opportunities as women not only found employment in the garment industry, but also excelled as leaders, exerting tremendous influence on American dress and lifestyle. With their increased sensitivity to issues of fit and to the nuances of clothing's appropriateness, care and wear, they figured prominently in multiple dimensions of the industry, including manufacturing, fashion design, style forecasting, marketing, and journalism.

Born Henrietta Kanengeiser in Vienna in 1889, Hattie Carnegie started as a milliner and eventually presided over an $8,000,000 fashion industry empire. Carnegie relied on several approaches to build her business. She maintained both custom and ready-to-wear production, sold wholesale to other retailers, imported and sold Parisian models in large quantities, and expanded into accessories, perfume, and cosmetics. While she often turned to Paris for inspiration, she promoted American industry by hiring some of the best young designers of the time (including Norman Norell, Pauline Trigère, and Claire McCardell) and by employing over a thousand people at the height of her success.

Photograph by John Rawlings, from the February 1, 1945, issue of Vogue, p. 118. Rawlings / Vogue / Condé Nast Archive. Copyright © Condé Nast.

Sewn Together

The Garment Industry and American Jewry

GABRIEL M. GOLDSTEIN, ELIZABETH E. GREENBERG, MARY VENS,
AND JESSICA GOLDRING

In understanding how deeply the American garment business is stitched into our national culture and identity, one confronts the role American Jews have played in fashioning together a multibillion-dollar industry from its *schmatte* (rag) trade origins. Threaded through our contemporary panorama of designers and manufacturers, models and moguls, is the saga of nineteenth-century immigrants seeking success in America as tailors, peddlers, pressers, and cutters. Investigating the impact and influence of American Jewry on fashion and American society, *A Perfect Fit* tells a quintessential rags-to-riches story and documents the development of a distinctly American style.

The story of the American garment industry had received scant attention until Yeshiva University Museum presented the comprehensive exhibition *A Perfect Fit: The Garment Industry and American Jewry, 1860–1960* (December 2005–April 2006). This book elaborates on themes explored in the exhibition and places them in historical context. After close to a decade of research and planning, *A Perfect Fit* opened on December 5, 2006, at Yeshiva University Museum. The National Endowment for the Humanities designated it a "We the People"

project "for promoting knowledge and understanding of American society and identity," and it also received the Costume Society of America's Richard Martin Award for Excellence in the Exhibition of Costume (2007).

A Perfect Fit looked at such diverse subjects as the subtleties of fashion design, the formation of communities, the initiation and resolution of social struggles, and the evolution of marketing techniques, and it highlighted formative influences and their role in the story. Items on display included loans from the Smithsonian, the Library of Congress, a European private collector, and the corporate archives of such well-known manufacturers as Hickey Freeman and Levi Strauss & Co. The exhibition housed more than one hundred mannequins dressed in American clothing from across the époques. Artifacts as varied as World War II armaments, Roy Rogers's cowboy suit, nineteenth-century sewing machines, Pauline Trigère's factory time card clock, historic film footage from turn-of-the-century New York, and golden-era films were on display. An interactive computer installation compiled and catalogued personal histories. While some contributors to this volume have selected their own

Yiddish theatre poster, *Schmattes* (Rags), performed December 6, 1921. The massive influx of Yiddish-speaking immigrants greatly enriched New York's cultural life. Popular Yiddish theatre, music, and literature were often inspired by garment industry themes.

Courtesy Kanof Yiddish Theatre Poster Collection, American Jewish Historical Society.

visual material, most of the images in the book were taken from the exhibition. In addition, the exhibition insert provides a guided walk-through of the galleries.

This volume offers in-depth and specific case studies that either emerged from the exhibition or could be touched upon only briefly in a museum setting. Essays address the development of menswear; the early film industry and its relationship to American fashion; the connection among the American, British, and French fashion industries; the acculturation of Jewish immigrants and its impact on American garment making; advertising history and popular culture; and regional centers of manufacturing. These thirteen essays weave together the voices of the garment industry and facilitate a lively dialogue. Illuminated by images that speak resoundingly to the social, economic, and political ramifications of the clothing trade, they reveal the fabric of American life.

In Chapter 4, "American Jewish Identity and the Garment Industry," Hasia Diner reflects upon the centuries-long tradition of European Jews in the production of clothing through early industrialization. Could it be any surprise then that an emerging American garment industry would be pivotal to Jewish immigration? "A perfect fit," Diner posits, "entwined the Jews, America, and the clothing industry."

Between 1880 and 1920 more than two million Jews came to America, primarily from eastern Europe. From peddlers who crisscrossed the plains of the rapidly expanding republic to the shopkeepers posing in front of their storefronts, from ambitious businessmen to gifted designers and artists, working in the garment trade seemed a secular counterpart to religious faith in linking American Jews to a traditional past and, as Diner observes, to a contemporary cultural identity. Over and over, personal stories gathered during the exhibition illuminated scholarly conclusions:

Feather boas and trimmings have been used on Women's Clothing for many centuries. My family, the Goldbergs, had been in the "feather business" since the middle ages. . . . We came over around 1890 in First Class on ships like the Queen Mary I (it had a kosher kitchen) and built a special building to house feathers—before air conditioning, to keep the feathers cool it had three basements.[1]

In Chapter 5, "The Birth of the Clothing Industry in America, 1815–1860," Michael Zakim explores how ready-made clothing reflected and deepened cultural underpinnings of the garment trade as it came to dominate the textile industry from coast to coast and tailors, seamstresses, cutters, sweaters, and department-store owners became interconnected through "tiers of subcontractors" and "social networks of neighborhood and ethnicity."

By the first decades of the twentieth century, Jewish immigrants had built the New York–based garment trade into a billion-dollar-a-year industry. Against the far-reaching effects of technological advances (such as the sewing machine in 1846) and the advent of menswear manufacture (largely motivated by the Civil War's demand for uniforms), this book investigates the unprecedented success of a Jewish immigrant population who, for the most part, arrived with virtually no economic advantages.

German Jews, the first to immigrate (1820–80), paved the way for their eastern coreligionists and often offered them initial employment. This book pays tribute to two German Jewish families from Bavaria who distinguished themselves in the garment trades. In Chapter 6, "German Jews in the Early Manufacture of Ready-Made Clothing," Phyllis Dillon highlights the contributions of the Fechheimer family, uniform manufacturers in Cincinnati. The story of the Strauss family, world-renowned manufacturers of Levi's jeans, is told by William Toll in Chapter 11, "Acclimatizing Fashion: Jewish Inventiveness on the Other (Pacific) Coast, 1850–1940." Today, the Fechheimer label continues to dress postal workers, sports officials, and members of the military as well as employees of private companies like DHL, and Levi's have become the acknowledged uniform for casual attire all over the world.

Andrew Godley and Nancy Green provide perspectives on Jewish immigrants working in the garment trades in London and Paris. In Chapter 2, "Jewish Immigrants and the Garment Industry: A View from London," Godley focuses on the 2.5 million eastern European Jews who settled in Britain and the United States and emphasizes their entrepreneurial spirit and willingness to take whatever work was available. In Chapter 3, "Jewish Immigrants and the Garment Industry: A View from Paris," Green's summation of the observations of French economist Emile Levasseur offers insights into the sweatshop industry as a vehicle for high profits and sustainable business. Zakim provides detailed accounts of average monthly earnings at all levels of employment and describes how the industry was largely dependent on low wages, piecework, and the delegation of

Uniforms, Fechheimer, catalogue no. 100, 1961. From its early start in uniform production for Civil War soldiers, Fechheimer continued to manufacture uniforms for government services during peacetime.

Courtesy Fechheimer Bros. Co.

ready-made clothing industry encompass geography, economics, the logistics of garment manufacture, and the development of a distinctly American style. By the mid-nineteenth century, the nation's frontiers were rapidly expanding and canals and railroads supplied shops across the country. Department stores offered a huge range of goods to a broad spectrum of shoppers. Special sales, giveaways, newspaper advertisements and window displays helped to entice customers to urban stores. Mail-order catalogues offered an array of products to consumers in smaller towns and rural areas. From nineteenth-century immigrants to twentieth-century Hollywood stars, from blue jeans to ball gowns, *A Perfect Fit* traces the spread of the garment industry from coast to coast and includes stories from several American cities across the country.

The growth of the ready-made industry led to the democratization of American style. Working class and middle class, immigrant and native-born—all aspired to a kind of gentility typified by fashionable clothing. Green comments on the phenomenon of a "classless society where 'everyone dresses as he can and wishes.'"

Rob Schorman, in Chapter 8, "Fitting In: Advertising, Clothing, and Social Identity Among Turn-of-the-Century Jewish Immigrants," explains that "donning stylish dress" became "a form of cultural agency." Clothing helped define an individual's role in society, and a distinctly American fashion lent credence to a sense of belonging and was often one's entrée into American society. Schorman cites articles from the *Yiddishes Tageblatt* and the personal stories of the Jews who immigrated

tasks. Despite these negative aspects of the trade, the ability to offer, in Green's words, a relatively "easy-to-learn subcontracted division of labor" to both those who arrived in America with their skills "*in der hand*" and those who did not was positive and substantial. In this light, the Jewish sense of community becomes an essential component of manufacturing and immigrant life.

Discussions about westward expansion and the simultaneous growth of the

Sweatshop in Ludlow Street tenement, New York, ca. 1889, by Jacob Riis. Riis is famous for his photographs documenting the often atrocious working conditions of sweatshops. Immigrant workers struggling to support their families faced long hours, low pay, and unsafe, unhygienic, cramped workspaces. Social reformers like Riis raised public awareness of such working conditions and contributed to the labor movement's efforts to transform and define new regulations and improve work standards.

Courtesy Library of Congress.

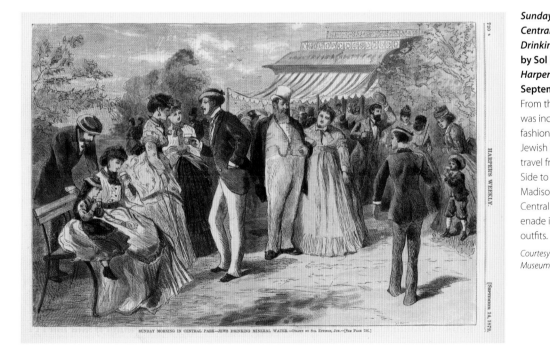

SUNDAY MORNING IN CENTRAL PARK—JEWS DRINKING MINERAL WATER.—DRAWN BY SOL EYTINGE, JUN.—[SEE PAGE 726.]

Sunday Morning in Central Park—Jews Drinking Mineral Water, **by Sol Eytinge, Jun.,** *Harper's Weekly*, **September 14, 1892.** From the early 1870s, it was increasingly fashionable for young Jewish New Yorkers to travel from the Lower East Side to leisure spots like Madison Avenue and Central Park to promenade in their finest outfits.

Courtesy Yeshiva University Museum.

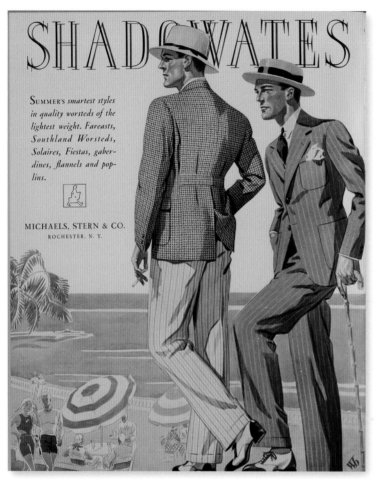

Advertisement in *Apparel Arts*, Michaels, Stern & Co., summer 1934. *Apparel Arts* was a sumptuous menswear trade quarterly first published in September 1931 by David Smart and his brothers, Alfred and John. Arnold Gingrich served as the editor. Smart and Gingrich would go on to publish *Esquire* magazine, showcasing both men's fashion and major literary writers.

Courtesy Special Collections, Gladys Marcus Library at the Fashion Institute of Technology.

through Ellis Island as living documentation of this process.

The manufacture of men's garments was industrialized differently than that of women's. The dark suit became a uniform of respectability. It was available to every American man who wanted one and was especially sought out by the growing middle class. Early production of ready-wear suits was centered in the factories of New York City, but surrounding centers of manufacture also arose to meet the needs of an expanding industrial society. Bernard Smith provides a case study of the ready-made industry in one such city in Chapter 7, "The Ready-Made Menswear Industry of Rochester, New York, 1848–1900." He documents not only the development of menswear manufacture and a vibrant hub for business and labor, but also how families working in the garment trades established social institutions and eventually helped to create a thriving Jewish community. Smith illustrates how a network of about fifty Jewish families incorporated Rochester's congregation, B'rith Kodesh, founded the Hebrew Benevolent Society, and established a parochial school.

In contrast to menswear, when mass production entered the women's garment industry, its transformation was slow and gradual. In Chapter 9, "From Division Street to Seventh Avenue: The Coming of Age of American Fashion," JoAnne Olian traces the development of the New York garment industry from its origins in lower Manhattan to its more fashionable uptown location on Seventh Avenue. Olian investigates ramifications for how women's readywear evolved from independent shops

of skilled dressmakers into a booming industry. She suggests that it was the ability to dress a large number of women in attractive, well-fitting, and affordable clothing that allowed manufacturers and designers to transform American style. By the 1930s, Seventh Avenue was a teeming agglomeration of small factories based in modern skyscrapers, many owned by Jews who had grown up in the business. Until the 1940s, most manufacturers turned out ready-made copies of Parisian couture and American designers toiled in anonymity. But when World War II suspended the influence of Paris, Seventh Avenue's designers and manufacturers demonstrated that Americans could successfully design and mass-produce a range of stylish clothing.

The West Coast's clothing industry evolved from early commercial efforts of Jewish pioneer merchants. Because they had pioneered in the founding of towns and cities all along the Pacific Coast, central European Jewish immigrants created a supply chain of family and friends to transport consumer goods from East Coast and midwestern manufacturers and jobbers to remote mining camps and ranches. Two midwestern case studies are provided in this book. In Chapter 12, "Kansas City's Garment Industry," Laurel Wilson documents the rise and fall of one city's garment industry, and Dillon provides thorough coverage of German Jewish immigrants in Cincinnati, which was known as the "Queen of the West" because of its rich farmlands and industrial opportunities. As

Handbill for "A Summer Style Suggestion," 1908. Washable dresses, skirts, and shirtwaists were practical and convenient, and their mass manufacture allowed for affordable prices. This R. H. Macy & Co. advertisement promises customers that "never have we excelled this season's display of dainty frocks, and never has the price range so nearly met the popular demand." Affordable ready-wear encouraged the equalization of class distinctions.

Courtesy Yeshiva University Museum.

the California garment industry expanded, it increasingly promoted a California lifestyle based on the car, the beach, and outdoor recreational activity. Designers turned to comfortable and easy-wear fabrics like cotton, denim, and gingham, drawing on South America, the Southwest, and the American West for inspiration. William Toll examines the production of outerwear in the Pacific Northwest. He not only provides a detailed account of the dominion of Levi's jeans on American fashion but also tells the stories of other Jewish manufacturers, such as the Hirsch brothers and Harry Weis, who went into business in Portland, Oregon, developing sailcloth into skiwear under the White Stag label.

Film companies were quick to capitalize on the emerging American style. A large number of movie moguls who shaped America's film industry actually began their careers in the garment trades. Hollywood became the center of world movie production and distribution, and the California garment industry, inspired by film fashion, began to have a pronounced influence on American fashion in general. In Chapter 13, "From Seventh Avenue to Hollywood: Fashioning Early Cinema, 1905–1935," Michelle Tolini Finamore investigates how Hollywood soon began to compete with Paris and the silver screen replaced the fashion magazine as an authority on the latest glamour, leisure, and everyday styles.

The garment industry played a crucial role in the early achievements of the American labor movement. Many of the rights that today's American workers take for granted were first won by the garment

Poster for Oppenheim, Collins & Co., ca. 1932. One of the strengths of the American garment industry was its ability to produce fashionable dresses in a vast range of sizes and price points.

Courtesy Warshaw Collection of Business Americana, National Museum of American History, Smithsonian Institution.

Illustration, *Apparel Arts*, summer 1934.

Courtesy Special Collections, Gladys Marcus Library at the Fashion Institute of Technology.

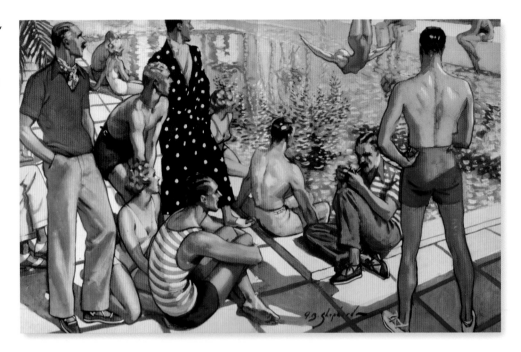

White Stag ski suit, ca. 1940. The firm Hirsch-Weis, based in Portland, Oregon, introduced White Stag skiwear during the Great Depression. In 1929, Harold S. Hirsch, son of one of the company's founders and a member of the Dartmouth ski team, convinced his father to launch a new line of outdoor apparel for skiers. This new line was called White Stag, a translation of the German-Jewish names of the firm's owners.

Courtesy Yeshiva University Museum.

California Fashion Scene, **Matilda Bergman LA Buying Office, winter 1942, and advance spring 1943.** Buying offices acted as consultants to advise retailers about current trends and sometimes produced elaborate merchandising catalogues. "Representation in the California market by the Matilda Bergman Office assures you a 'first' on creations of California's foremost originators of men's wear!"

Courtesy Special Collections, Gladys Marcus Library at the Fashion Institute of Technology.

Glamour of Hollywood **cover featuring Hedy Lamarr, August 1940.**

Courtesy Yeshiva University Museum.

unions; concepts like arbitration and collective bargaining emerged out of their struggles. The unions were also pioneers in developing education and cultural opportunities as well as access to health care and safety and social welfare programs in the decades before the New Deal.

In Chapter 10, "Labor Relations and the Protocol of Peace in Progressive Era New York," Richard A. Greenwald offers insights into the economics of the New York ladies' garment industry sweatshops where workers—the "so-called 'moths of Division Street'—could enter [the industry] at will and with little investment." According to Greenwald, entry-level positions and low technological requirements made low labor costs the defining factor for successful business. Small shop owners "drove industry standards" in "a race to the bottom" and "repeatedly cut wages—sweating labor—to remain competitive."

Most of the industry's owners were Jewish. Although employers and workers shared a common language, history, and culture, employees struggled under social and economic disparity. Hasia Diner addresses how the unique situation resulting from employers and their coreligionist employees coexisting on equal footing motivated unionization. Diner explains that many Jewish workers did not understand why employers in garment making or any of the other Jewish industries should earn higher wages and enjoy a better quality of life. Newcomers believed they were entitled to as good a life as their predecessors who had arrived in America two or three decades before. In Chapter 4, Diner argues that "this internal Jewish class consciousness, this inner conflict of Jews against Jews" was the essential catalyst for unionization in the Jewish trades.

Although the creation of the largely Jewish unions, the International Ladies'

***Strikes, Ladies Tailors, N.Y.*, picket girls on duty, February 1910.** Labor unions recognized the power of public awareness as a tactic for bringing about change. Battles for reform were highly visible, and striking workers became emblematic of the labor movement's reform goals.

Courtesy Library of Congress.

Garment Workers' Union in 1900 and the Amalgamated Clothing Workers of America in 1914, occurred with significantly less employer opposition than unionization in any other heavy industry, some Jewish employers fiercely opposed unionization. It was within this dynamic that several important breakthroughs in labor management relations occurred in the first decades of the twentieth century. The earliest years of the labor movement in the clothing industry saw the organization of unions and efforts to obtain higher wages, better hours, and basic rights for workers. Twenty thousand shirtwaist workers went on strike in the Uprising of 1909; the following year, sixty thousand cloak makers struck in what became known as the Great Revolt. In the wake of the 1910 strike, Jewish representatives of labor and management met with a team of Jewish arbitrators (including Louis Brandeis, who was appointed to the Supreme Court in 1916) to broker an agreement. The resulting Protocol of Peace was a landmark in labor management relations. The protocol established standards for health, safety, and arbitration and influenced all subsequent labor agreements. Extensive attention is given to this topic by Richard Greenwald, who describes how the labor system designed for New York City's garment industry became a model for the nation. Greenwald views the protocols—industrial agreements created by Jews to solve the problems of a predominantly Jewish New York ladies' garment industry—as a profound experiment in industrial relations that influenced the New Deal.

With so many Jews involved in all facets of the garment industry—as owners,

Mourning badge, Cloak and Tailors Union Local 9, April 5, 1911. "We mourn our loss." Unions stressed a sense of brotherhood among workers. After the Triangle Shirtwaist Factory fire, members of the Cloak and Tailors Union donned black mourning badges in memory of fellow workers who perished in the tragedy.

Courtesy UNITE HERE Archives, Kheel Center, Cornell University.

workers, and labor leaders—there was a unique symbiosis between the industry and Jewish life. For many American Jews, family relationships, wholesale and retail connections, economic success, and communal philanthropy were all interconnected. For much of the twentieth century,

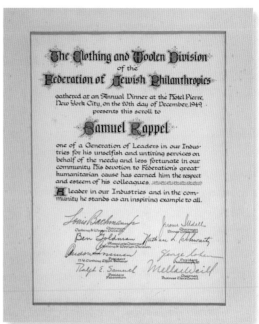

Letter from Ab. Kirschbaum & Co., December 28, 1898. Kirschbaum & Co. actively participated in Philadelphia's Jewish charity networks. This letter on company letterhead promotes a ball benefiting the United Hebrew Charities of the City of Philadelphia.

Courtesy National Museum of American Jewish History, Philadelphia.

Tribute scroll to Samuel Kappel, Annual Dinner of the Clothing and Woolen Division, Federation of Jewish Philanthropies, Hotel Pierre, New York, December 20, 1949. In 1916, Samuel Kappel, a Russian immigrant, founded the Howard Clothing firm that produced menswear for a chain of stores. Kappel used his business success to help raise money for the Federation of Jewish Philanthropies beginning in the 1930s.

Courtesy Elaine Winik.

the American Jewish calendar was punctuated not only by Rosh Hashanah and Passover, but also by buyers' weeks and the new season's inventory.

In the first decades of the twentieth century, American Jews began to have increased opportunities to blend into American society. The garment industry provided a setting in which they could comfortably be identified as Jews, while still achieving economic mobility. Jews in the industry socialized together in both work and personal life. As they moved to the suburbs, they often chose to settle in the same communities. When they went on vacation, they frequented hotels in the

Catskills and Miami Beach, where they could comfortably speak Yiddish, eat Jewish foods, and enjoy Jewish entertainment.

Charity and communal support are fundamental precepts of Judaism, and, as many of these chapters illustrate, the economic success of American Jewish garment industry leaders enabled them to become active contributors to local and world Jewish religious and charitable organizations. For many Jews in the industry, the plight of European Jewish refugees during and after World War II and the founding of the State of Israel heightened their involvement in Jewish philanthropic activities.

We hope that this volume, copublished by Yeshiva University Museum and Texas Tech University as part of the Costume Society of America series, will be enjoyed widely among every audience. A fascinating prism of perspectives, these windows into the American garment industry have relevance well beyond the story of American Jewry. In a broader sense, they speak to the ways numerous minority groups effect cultural change and experience, defining and redefining American life. Among the vibrant cultural contributions and influences of Asian, Latino, and other ethnic American and immigrant groups, workers' rights and the injustices of sweatshop labor persist as social and economic issues. In this light, *A Perfect Fit* provides a framework and paradigm for further study and for other richly visual and accessible examinations of American culture. Like the exhibition, this book investigates topics that are often addressed in isolation: production and consumption; labor and management; haute couture and bargain basement dresses; ethnicity and acculturation; railroads and hoopskirts. We believe that these essays, sewn together, do indeed form a perfect fit.

Dress (left), Pattullo-Jo Copeland, ca. 1960. Jo Copeland's father was a blouse jobber, and she followed him into the clothing business, achieving great success as one of America's best-known designers. After studying at the Art Students League and the New York School of Fine and Applied Art (later Parsons School of Design), Copeland became a designer at Pattullo Modes in the 1920s and a partner in 1938. She was considered a truly American designer, and in her own words focused on "the American woman, whoever she is." Known for her sophisticated designs, particularly her after-five clothes, she tended to use asymmetric draperies, subtle details, and rich fabrics. She also is credited with introducing the two-piece suit worn without a blouse.

Courtesy Yeshiva University Museum.

Dress (right), Pauline Trigère, 1960. Pauline Trigère was born in Paris in 1908, the daughter of Russian immigrants. Her father was a tailor and her mother a dressmaker, providing her with early exposure to the trade. In 1937, she immigrated to the United States, and within ten years she was designing under her own label. She was a master draper, preferring to create her designs by working on live models, rather than on a sketch pad. She was considered an intellectual designer and was noted for her truly original, elegant, and timeless designs, which earned her numerous accolades, including three Coty Awards. Trigère also prioritized practicality—she was one of the first designers to incorporate cotton and wool into eveningwear. In her words, "Practicality has always been very important in my life and my designs. You have to make things functional, but that doesn't mean they can't be attractive." Her clients were loyal, allowing her to stay in business until 1994.

Courtesy Yeshiva University Museum.

Jewish Immigrants and the Garment Industry

2

A View from London

ANDREW GODLEY

Between 1880 and 1914, more than 2.5 million Jews left eastern Europe. Almost 2 million settled in the United States and approximately 150,000 came to Britain. Among the many millions of European immigrants at the time, Jews were the poorest of all arrivals, and most arrived with absolutely nothing. Typically, they hadn't even had enough money to pay for their own ticket.[1] Yet today, the average Jewish household in the United States and in the United Kingdom enjoys a top decile income, a wholly exceptional path of upward mobility in modern, advanced twentieth-century societies like Britain and America.

This exceptional high social status exists to a large extent because half of the employed Jews in Britain, as in America, are today in professional occupations, earning professional salaries. But the professionalization of American and British Jewry is only relatively recent—a third-generation phenomenon. What was truly remarkable about first- and second-generation Jewish immigrants in the West was just how many were entrepreneurs. Between 15 and 20 percent of Jewish immigrant male workers in Britain and the United States were entrepreneurs in the 1880s. In the United

States, that figure rose to approximately 40–45 percent from 1920 to 1940, compared with almost 30 percent in Britain by the 1920s, which rose to 40 percent by the 1950s.[2]

Of course in other societies, Jews had even higher rates of self-employment, but these were typically the by-product of anti-Semitic restrictions on occupational choice, and self-employment under these conditions rarely led to material success. Despite sometimes suffering appalling racial abuse, the Jewish immigrants in America and Britain could, and did, work wherever they wanted, and they could, and did, enjoy the fruits of their economic success. And such economic success across an entire population is without precedent in recent decades. It is no surprise, therefore, that the eastern European Jewish immigrant entrepreneurial success has become the classic stereotype behind academic and policy focus on entrepreneurship as a vehicle for social mobility among ethnic minorities. When they arrived, however, eastern European Jewish immigrants possessed no obvious advantages in moving upward in these new societies in the years before 1914. Many contemporaries, seeing how they had been forced out of "useful"

1921 FALL *American Gentleman* WINTER 1922
Young Men's Fashions

Men's fashion plate, fall 1921–winter 1922. The dark suit became a long-lasting symbol of middle-class respectability. Menswear styles were relatively stable compared to the rapidly changing fashions and trend-based structure of the women's clothing industry.

Courtesy Jewish Museum of Maryland.

trades (like farming) and barred from owning land in anti-Semitic countries of eastern Europe, concluded that they were the most unlikely of all immigrant arrivals to succeed in their new homes of New York, London, and elsewhere.

And despite the extraordinary levels of college attendance among subsequent generations, immigrants themselves possessed no particular advantage in schooling. Contrary to popular myth, levels of literacy were not particularly high. According to Samuel Joseph's compilation of U.S. immigration statistics before World War I, a smaller proportion of eastern

European Jewish arrivals were deemed by immigration officials to be illiterate than for arrivals from Croatia, Hungary, Lithuania, or Poland. But they were far less likely to be literate than arrivals from other European locations, including Italy and Ireland, never mind more obviously literate regions like Britain, Germany, and Scandinavia.[3]

So how can we explain their success? Scholars and commentators have cited a whole spectrum of possible explanations, ranging from the importance of Jewish culture or religion, to anti-Semitism, or the welcoming nature of the British and American mainstreams. Indeed, almost any apparently unique attribute of western Jewry has been used as a potential explanation for such exceptional success. But coincidence is not causation. One vitally important factor that emerges from any serious study of Jewish economic history is almost always overlooked. Luck.

The great fortune of the eastern European Jewish immigrants in London, as in New York and Paris, was that as they moved into the garment industry en masse, the garment industry began to change.[4] It transformed from an industry characterized by appalling conditions of cutthroat competition into a sector that enjoyed moderately good economic returns. For an immigrant trade, this represents quite a remarkable transformation. But what turns this route of modest prosperity into great fortune is the realization that it came through economic forces over which the immigrants had little or no control.

As is well known, the Jewish immigrants more or less took over the garment industries in Britain and the United States. And the reason why the Jews were so prominent in these industries is also not hard to ascertain. These were the worst of trades to move into, and so only the immigrants with the least opportunity for better alternatives entered them. With their limited savings and minimal relevant education, eastern European Jews simply took whatever they could get—and the garment industry was all they could get. And, as menswear increasingly industrialized and moved into larger factories, the typical Jewish tailor in London, as in New York and Paris, was forced into the women's-wear business.

The long hours and unsanitary conditions of the garment industry workshops in the late nineteenth and early twentieth centuries undoubtedly increased occupational disease and reduced lifespan among these first-generation immigrants. But in the midst of their rightful condemnation of these conditions, historians of sweatshops have missed a major point. For while it was true that Jewish entrepreneurs were largely dominant in the clothing industry of the 1900s, especially women's clothing, their very good fortune was that the demand for women's wear changed around that time. From the beginning of the twentieth century, fashion became ever more important. And as the fashion content rose, so did the profit margins. Fashion had always enjoyed some prominence in women's clothing, especially among the well-to-do, but what changed in the years before and after World War I was how fashion became important to the mass of women in countries like Britain and America. Simply stated, fashion became a feature of everyday clothing for most women. And as it did so, it transformed the dynamics of the industry.

Fashion has the twin effect of both increasing the price that consumers are willing to pay for a product (a fashionable skirt, dress, or jacket is more desirable than a basic utilitarian model) and reducing the time a product can be worn (because it is shortly "out" of fashion). So, producers of these newly fashionable goods were able to command higher prices than before and then sell more articles as the earlier models went out of style. Across the women's-wear industry, the net effect was to increase sales and drive up profits. Lucky for some.

But what is yet more important for helping us to understand how the garment industry has so shaped Jewish fortunes in the twentieth century is to know what transpired next. Or perhaps, what failed to happen. For ordinarily when industries become more attractive as a result of new technology or changes in the pattern of demand, the higher profits attract new entrants into the industry, who then bid down profits. But the growing attractiveness of women's wear in America and Britain also coincided with the gathering clouds in Europe. In August 1914, war was declared and the borders tightened in both countries. Apart from a few short years in the early 1920s, no new immigrants were allowed to enter.[5] While this was ultimately tragic for those left behind, for the new entrepreneurs and workers in the burgeoning women's-wear industry, the restriction of immigration proved a boon since it effectively reduced new entrants into the industry to a trickle. With no new entrants, there was little downward competitive pressure on profits.

In the United States, there was a further unanticipated gain for Jewish entrepreneurs in the rag trades. For just as the famed International Ladies' Garment Workers' Union (ILGWU) gained control over the industry, even to the point of ensuring that retail outlets would sell only "union" clothing, the prices consumers paid were forced up. Higher prices translated into higher revenues for firms, and led to higher wages and profits for both Jewish workers and entrepreneurs.

So, from around 1910 until the 1960s, Jewish entrepreneurs enjoyed the great fortune of being incumbents in a growth sector. In addition, they dominated the most profitable segment of the garment trade in Britain and America and experienced industry returns seen neither before nor since. The coincidence of arrival and entry into the garment trade just at the moment of fashion-related structural change presented those early immigrant entrepreneurs with something close to windfall gains.

These gains were locked in after August 1914 when war in Europe closed the borders and restricted the possibility of any future immigrants bidding down their profits. And it was these gains that were reinvested in second- and third-generation education to secure middle-class status and income later in the century. The garment industry therefore played a key role in twentieth-century Jewish history. Indeed, without the transformation of demand and the emergence of fashion as a powerful force in women's wear in Britain and America, along with the restriction of immigration from August 1914 onward, the entire pattern of Jewish social mobility would surely have been more circumscribed and more in keeping with the typical mobility path of all immigrants arriving during the great wave of migration between 1880 and 1914.

3

Jewish Immigrants and the Garment Industry

A View from Paris

NANCY L. GREEN

At the end of the nineteenth century, the French economist Emile Levasseur went to the United States to study the American system of production. He was impressed, and equally so by the American pattern of consumption. The "democratic luxury" of American workers struck him as particular to this classless society where "everyone dresses as he can and as he wishes."[1] Bosses and workers in Central Park looked alike to Levasseur, although he admitted that the cloth of their garments might be of differing quality, a fact only evident to a more practiced eye. (Citing an "indiscreet" corset survey, he also surmised that women sacrificed the quality of their undergarments in order to maintain surface appearances!) Levasseur's guarded appreciation of American clothing habits goes to the heart of the ready-made revolution and the way in which it affected fit, style, consumption, and production.[2]

At the core of this democratization of consumption, as Levasseur correctly understood it, was an expansion of production that fueled the growing ready-made industry. Levasseur identified "*le sweating system*" in Chicago, Boston, and New York as a regime of long hours and low pay endured by a multitude of workers hailing from a variety of European countries— from Germans and Scandinavians to Jews, Italians, and others. He did not single out Jews, noting that Germans had come to the industry long before the eastern European Jews. But, like many other social investigators of the time, he was severe in his castigation of the grueling labor conditions that affected immigrant and (native) women workers alike.

While Levasseur crossed the Atlantic to study American garment workers (among others), similar conditions were emerging in his own backyard.[3] German and Belgian immigrants had worked in the garment trades in Paris since mid-century, and as the ready-made industry grew in the late nineteenth century, eastern European Jews arriving in France entered the women's-wear trade in large numbers.[4] As in New York and London, they became machine workers, cutters, finishers, jobbers, contractors, and ultimately manufacturers, as well as union organizers.

On both sides of the Atlantic, the "Jewish tailor" became a popular stereotype that was used to represent everything from an innate needle talent to evil exploiter or energetic entrepreneur. However, as Yankel Mykhanowitzki, hero of *Les Eaux mêlées*, a

Skirts in comparative perspective: Paris style (top), and New York style, 1953. This drawing appears in Murray Sices's *Seventh Avenue*.

Courtesy Fairchild Publications.

Siegel-Cooper department store, bargain counter, 1897. Throngs of consumers encircle intricately displayed products at the Siegel-Cooper bargain counter. Customers and shop girls alike wear the ubiquitous shirtwaist and skirt, which, in an age of increasing freedom for women, offered comfortable attire for an active, working lifestyle.

Courtesy Museum of the City of New York, Byron Collection.

prize-winning French novel about a Jewish cap maker, complained, imported sewing skills meant little in the face of an industrializing trade: "[S]ometimes he surprised himself, fairly naively, at being bored in the workshop. Only yesterday wasn't the least gesture of his trade a constantly renewed source of pleasure? . . . No: that was in the old days, in the [Russian] days. Now Yankel's work was mechanized."[5] While there were indeed Jewish tailors who brought their skills with them, literally *in der hand* according to the Yiddish expression, the ready-made trade thrived off of a relatively easy-to-learn subcontracted division of labor. Throughout the small workshops of the immigrant quarters, from the Pletzl neighborhood of Paris to the East

End of London, many Jewish immigrants learned to work a sewing machine for the first time, like the greenhorn "Columbus tailors" on the Lower East Side of New York.

Ethnic entrepreneurship mobilized networks of kith and kin in the Pletzl as elsewhere, and this light industry spread throughout the lofts of immigrant neighborhoods. Little capital was needed to set up shop, and the Paris workshops created an ethnic or even familial environment well adapted to immigrant needs. A sense of independence and the possibility of striking out on one's own were appealing for many newcomers. As demand grew, Jewish bosses hired Yiddish-speaking coreligionists directly at the Gare du Nord or Gare de Lyon train stations, offering immediate work and temporary lodging to those who had just arrived. The advantages were obvious: quick access to a first job and working among one's own, where traditions and language were no barriers.

However, the community model of labor market had its limits. Jewish workers sometimes went on strike against their Jewish bosses, demanding higher wages, an end to piecework (the so-called workers' bribe), better working conditions, and more respect. During the interwar years, tensions among the Jewish garment workers in Paris revolved around the specific form of subcontracting prevalent in the industry, as the union debated the role of the *façonniers* (independent pieceworkers). Were they workers or self-employed bosses? Should they be able to join the union or not? In the small workshops, heavily dependent on homework, the line between who was a boss and who was a worker was often

Campement d'Émigrants Juifs à la Gare de Lyon, *Le Petit Journal*, **no. 94, September 10, 1892.** Newly arrived Jewish immigrants at the Paris train station created a flurry of worry in the Parisian press in 1892. The far-right anti-Semitic French press called it shocking; the French Jewish press was concerned for the image of Jews in France. Many eastern European Jewish immigrants in Paris, as in New York and elsewhere, soon found jobs in the garment industry.

Courtesy Bibliothèque Nationale.

Sketch (left), 1928. Many American designers took direction from Parisian high fashion. The Davidows found inspiration in the designs of Chanel, who became a lifelong influence on their work.

Courtesy Special Collections, Gladys Marcus Library at the Fashion Institute of Technology.

Sketch (right), 1950. Known for well-fitting tweed suits, Davidow offered American consumers a "look" derived from Chanel.

Courtesy Special Collections, Gladys Marcus Library at the Fashion Institute of Technology.

blurred. And indeed the industry served as an avenue of social mobility for some while others joined the Yiddish language sections of the French socialist or communist unions.

In 1910, there were an estimated 11,410 Jewish immigrants (over one-third of the community) at work in the Paris garment trade: some 3,500 in men's wear, 2,800 in women's wear, and 1,400 in the fur trade. Another 1,400 were involved in cap making, which became a specialty of the eastern European Jews in Paris.[6] The numbers grew in the interwar years as new waves of Polish Jews came to France, especially as the United States closed its doors with the 1921 Emergency Quota Act and the 1924 Immigration Act.

World War II affected the Paris garment industry in many ways. The penury of materials (wool, silk) had an impact on styles, and the occupying forces stressed the importance of restructuring

and concentrating an industry known for its anarchic, if not archaic, multitudinous units of production. Jewish businesses and shops were Aryanized or simply shut down. (In the process some four thousand sewing machines were confiscated.) Some Jewish workers turned to industrial homework as a survival tactic while in hiding. Others were able to continue to work even in war-production units, where one form of resistance was to sabotage items produced for the German army (making sweater neck holes too small, foreshortening glove fingers, etc.). But for all too many, World War II meant deportation. By December 1943, 1,233 garment firms in occupied France had been closed. It was subsequently estimated that the industry's labor force had declined by 45 percent during the war, largely due to the Shoah.

After World War II, homework and piecework once again provided a way of reentering the labor market for some of the survivors. According to one estimate, approximately 40 percent of those in the ready-made clothing business in Paris in the early 1950s were Jewish as were 60 percent of the cap makers.[7] But two major changes occurred in the 1960s and 1970s that gradually challenged Russian-Polish Jewish predominance in the industry. First, North African Jews (especially from Tunisia) arrived in France after decolonization and thrived on the new niche of sportswear. Then, other new waves of immigrants from Yugoslavia (Serbs), Turkey (Kurds), Cambodia (Chinese), and ultimately China (Wenzhou) and Pakistan also entered this immigrant-friendly and immigrant-dependent industry.

The image of the Jew and the *shmattes* industry has been complex. In France, as in the United States, the Jewish joke is the same: "What is the difference between a tailor and a psychoanalyst? One generation" (or two, for the pessimists). French demographer Michel Roblin, in his work *Les Juifs de Paris*, sought to answer the question of the specificity—or not—of the Jews' role in the Parisian garment industry. Writing shortly after World War II, he chose his words carefully:

[The Yiddish emigration] has played an important role [in various sectors of the garment industry], thanks to which several positive changes have come about. However, this migration did not cast out the French from an occupation they had created several centuries earlier. On the contrary, it accelerated a tendency toward proletarianization which was already underway at the end of the XIXth century.[8]

He, too, pointed out that German garment workers had been in Paris before the Jews,

Fashion sketch of Grubère original, ca. 1945. An "unknown" coat and suit designer originally from Memphis, Abraham Grubère (born Gruber) enjoyed a long career in the garment industry. He worked intermittently for several Seventh Avenue firms, such as Morris W. Haft & Bros., and also ran his own design house, Grubère Inc., which sold models to retailers like Bendels, Franklin Simon, and Hall Bros. Abe Grubère served as president of the Guild of Designers in the 1940s, and was committed to improving educational opportunities in the fashion trades.

Courtesy Yeshiva University Museum.

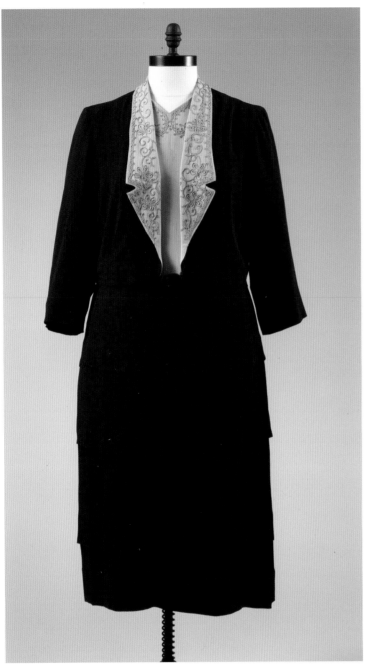

Dress, Puritan Fashions, Maggy Rouff Registered Design, 1950. Copies of French couture—both legal and illegal—were regularly produced for the American market before World War II. After the war, some manufacturers returned to this practice and made lucrative deals with French designers. The Puritan Dress Company, owned by the Rosen family, contracted with designers such as Christian Dior, Jacques Fath, and Maggy Rouff, bringing French high fashion to average women around the country. This dress, made for "a mature woman," sold for about $18 in 1950.

Courtesy Daniel Milford-Cottam.

commenting that "It is fairly certain that no essential transformation of the garment industry, however 'Jewish,' can be especially attributed to Jewish initiative."[9] Perhaps more so than in the United States, pride yet caution has marked French Jewish representation of the role of Jews in the garment industry.

All in all, the view from Paris (like London) confirms that not all Jewish garment workers ended up in New York, that not all garment workers were Jews, and that the American pattern was not unique. In this quintessential form of flexible manufacturing, Jews have never been alone. The unrelenting pursuit of changing fashion has created incessant demand for cheap labor and the hiring of successive waves of immigrant workers by successive waves of ethnic entrepreneurs, before moving offshore altogether. In the meantime, the workshops of immigrant subcontractors, from Jews to Chinese, have dotted the urban landscape for the last century.

American Jewish Identity and the Garment Industry

HASIA DINER

Over the course of a century—from 1820 through the middle of the 1920s—more than three million European Jews immigrated to the United States. This exodus represented about one-third of the continent's Jews. While the sources of the Jewish emigration shifted over time, gradually moving from western to eastern Europe, certain profound similarities characterized that entire one hundred years.

At either end of this span of years, the emigration reflected dwindling economic prospects particularly for young Jews as well as escalating levels of difficulty for Jews. The decline in domestic production, the expansion of large-scale agriculture, and advances in transportation obviated the need for the traditional Jewish occupations at a time when the Jewish population had grown dramatically. These factors set against the sporadic outbreaks of violence against the Jews in various regions made emigration an attractive option. That America functioned as the destination of choice also made 1820 and 1920 quite similar.

So too, the involvement of Jews in the garment trades provided a matter of continuity between the century's start and finish. It bridged the experiences of America's Jews

from the decades before the Civil War until well after World War I. While the industry underwent tremendous change in that century, it functioned consistently throughout as a crucial factor in the American Jewish economy.

Jewish migration, in part, pivoted around garment making. For centuries, Jews in Europe had been involved in the production of clothing. Full families worked first by hand and later in the emerging industrial workshops and factories. Jewish tailors worked with both the finest fabrics and the coarsest. Some of them gathered rags and discarded pieces of cloth, transforming these into wearable garments for the poor. At whatever level they worked, and wherever they did so, the close association between Jews and garment making extended broadly and deeply in world history.[1]

While the Jews' experience in the production of clothing linked their histories before and after migration to the United States, the need and desire of Americans for ready-made clothing (available in a variety of styles and at a price accessible even to the working class) helped stimulate a continuous Jewish migration. Until the 1850s, all sewing was done by hand and

Boy in prayer shawl, Jewish New Year, September 20, 1911. The Lower East Side offered eastern European immigrants an instant community steeped in the cultural and religious traditions of their homelands, where everyone spoke Yiddish and felt at home.

Courtesy Library of Congress.

Prang's Aids for Object Teaching—Tailor, ca. 1874. This lithograph from L. Prang & Co., Boston, shows the division of labor in a tailor's shop. At this time the sewing machine was used for much of the tailoring process, but a significant portion of the work still had to be done by hand. Younger apprentices completed hand-sewing tasks, while a more seasoned tailor cut the fabric. Women seamstresses often worked side by side with men in shops like this one.

Courtesy Library of Congress.

needlework was exactly that. Jews in America, as well as in Europe, threaded their needles and sewed clothes, garment by garment. Well-off women and men could buy from skilled tailors and seamstresses who fashioned custom-made garments. Poorer people purchased secondhand clothing that had been made over after being discarded by their original owners. However, most women did their own sewing and outfitted themselves and their families by their efforts. Out of necessity, Americans made do with a relatively small wardrobe.

In the pre–Civil War era (and more important, in the pre–sewing machine era) the Jews and the making and selling of clothes went hand in hand. This held for both the United States and Europe. Although most American women did their own sewing before the Civil War era, opportunities to make a living in the garment trades beckoned European Jews. As early as the 1820s, Jewish entrepreneurs, mostly from the German states of Bavaria and Posen, sold caps, hoopskirts, cloaks, and other kinds of garments in New York. These merchants, along with various family members who were usually new immigrants eager to find a niche for themselves in the American economy, also produced

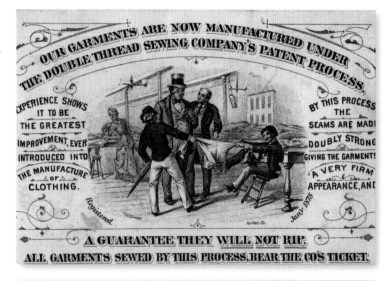

Trade card (front and back), January 1878, A. Levy & Bro. "Our garments are now manufactured under the Double Thread Sewing Company's patent process." Advertisements like this one promoted new inventions and promised quality guarantees to eager American consumers. New technologies and improved production methods increased the speed of manufacture and the durability of garments.

Courtesy The New-York Historical Society.

JEW purchasing old Clothes.

Printed and Published by W. Davison Alnwick.

these garments. By 1855, over 20 percent of employed Polish immigrants in New York, nearly all of whom were Jews, wielded a needle to make a living.[2] In the 1830s, a British traveler wrote disparagingly about the clustering of Jews in the city's second-hand clothing trade, a business concentrated on Chatham Street. "The inhabitants of this street" and the owners of these "slop shops" consisted of "the tribe of Judah: as any body may be satisfied by going into their shops as well on account of their dealings, as their long beards, which reach to the bottoms of their waist."[3]

In most cases in pre–Civil War America, an inextricable relationship connected the selling of clothes by Jews and the making of them, with Jewish peddlers and other itinerant merchants functioning as middlemen. Jewish hawkers, for example, traversed the streets of many American cities selling old clothes and collecting rags

that could then be reused as garments for the poor. A lively trade flourished between the Chatham Street shops and the sale of clothing by Jewish peddlers to the slave populations on southern plantations.

That Jews functioned on both ends of this process deserves to be highlighted. A Jewish economy linked the Jewish tailors, the shopkeepers, the wholesalers, and the peddlers to each other. Each had a role to play, but the peddlers in some ways were the most important, as many Jewish men facilitated their migration to America by peddling.

Peddling had been a Jewish occupation since the Middle Ages, and for hundreds of thousands of young Jewish men who wanted to immigrate to America to make a living, peddling provided a handy way to do so. They learned by word of mouth that so many Americans lived away from commercial hubs (on farms and in mining and logging camps) that a living could be made by going to their homes. The peddlers, who usually began their careers by carrying their goods on their backs and then graduated to a horse and cart, went week after week to the same customers and in the process provided isolated rural Americans with their only reliable link to the marketplace. Among the items for sale, along with pots and pans, eyeglasses, pictures and picture frames, needles, ribbons, buttons, and thread, was clothing of all sorts. The peddlers also told farm families, the women in particular, about the newest styles flourishing in the cities. In fact, they brought them newspaper and magazine advertisements that showed exactly what urban women were wearing. The peddlers thus helped stimulate taste for new items among the people in the hinterlands.

Jewish peddlers, it should be noted, did not just sell on the road to farmers and miners. They also traversed the city streets, selling clothing among other items. Urban Jewish peddlers had a different lifestyle than itinerant Jewish peddlers who spent all week away from Jewish communities, but they functioned in the same way. They carried their goods on their backs, and all sorts of clothing were among those goods. Urban peddlers also functioned at times as purchasers of used clothing, replenishing what they had sold with what they had just bought.

The dense connection between Jews and the making and selling of garments in antebellum America did not end at the borders of New York City. In medium-size and even relatively small towns, this relationship flourished. Seventy percent of all clothing establishments in Indianapolis

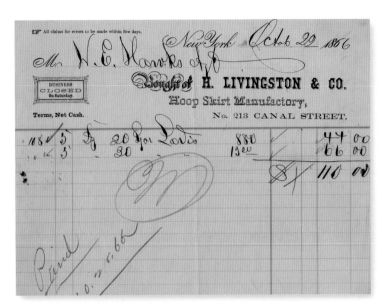

Hoopskirt invoice, October 29, 1866, H. Livingston & Co. As shown on this invoice, H. Livingston & Co. Hoop Skirt Manufactory was closed on Saturdays. Although economic necessities and the requirement for Saturday labor in most garment factory settings meant that many Jewish immigrants had to forgo traditional Sabbath observance, other religiously observant eastern European Jewish immigrants chose to work in small garment industry workshops or to establish their own businesses in order to observe the Sabbath. Rabbi Abraham J. Ash of New York City's Beth Hamedrash Hagodol synagogue also owned a hoopskirt factory.

Courtesy Warshaw Collection of Business Americana, National Museum of American History, Smithsonian Institution.

in 1860 lay in Jewish hands, while a local newspaper of that same decade in Johnstown, Pennsylvania, reported that not a single clothing dealer was a Christian. In Poughkeepsie, New York, hardly a major industrial or commercial hub, eight tailoring and clothing establishments existed in 1850 to serve the local population. Jews owned and worked in six of them. So too in Milwaukee, San Francisco, St. Louis, Columbus, and nearly everywhere immigrant Jews lived, they answered their neighbors sartorial needs by both sewing and selling.[4]

Two events revolutionized the garment industry and furthered Jewish concentration in it: the invention of the sewing machine in 1846 and the Civil War. The first dramatically decreased production time, which meant a tailor could buy a few sewing machines, hire a few workers, and vastly expand the number of dresses or shirts he could sell. The *New York Tribune*, recognizing the power of the machine to change social practice, uttered a prophecy in 1859: "The needle will soon be consigned to oblivion, like the wheel, the loom, and the knitting-needles. The working woman will now work fewer hours and receive greater remuneration. People will . . . dress better, change oftener, and altogether grow better looking."[5]

The Civil War followed on the heels of the invention of the sewing machine. The need for uniforms transformed small stores that had hand-produced garments into workshops and proto-factories that churned out clothing for soldiers. Given the great demand, manufacturers came up with the fixed size as a standard of production.[6] Many Jewish merchants saw the opportunity the Civil War offered in the field of garment making. The war helped transform small garment shops into more substantial enterprises, expanded the number of Jews involved in the field, and tightened the bonds between Jews and this particular enterprise. The fact that Jewish merchants benefited from the need for uniforms did not go unnoticed by some Gentiles who were already agitated by the exigencies of war. In the heat of emotion generated by the conflict, accusations of war profiteering could be heard. For example, Henry Mack of Cincinnati had been a small-scale tailor before the war. He received some generous contracts for uniforms while serving on the Hamilton County Military Committee, the

local draft board; public attention focused on this convergence.[7]

To the invention of the sewing machine and the Civil War, an additional factor must be added to explain why the American garment industry took off by the 1870s. Young women in all parts of the country, both American-born daughters of immigrants and the daughters of longtime Americans, increasingly worked outside the home in the years after school and before marriage. Many worked in factories and department stores while others taught school or mastered the era's other new piece of technology, the typewriter, and helped create the modern office in the emerging corporate bureaucracies. Regardless of where they worked, they needed clothes. Clean and stylish clothing announced their respectability, and since they were no longer sitting at home and sewing, they turned to, and helped shape, the American garment industry. The ancillary development of an advertising industry, which stimulated taste for fashion and whetted the appetites of young women for new and stylish clothing, further made garment making "big business" in the last three decades of the nineteenth century.[8]

Although Chicago, Boston, Baltimore, Cincinnati, Rochester, Cleveland, and a number of other interior cities produced clothing at a dizzying pace, New York overshadowed all others and emerged as the center of the industry. In 1910, it produced 70 percent of the nation's clothing for women and 40 percent for men.[9] It was also the center of the American publishing industry, and the dozens of magazines published in New York and distributed around the country advertised a New York

Sixth Maine Infantry, ca. 1863. Massive need for Civil War uniforms, for both Union and Confederate troops, meant that large-scale orders had to be contracted out. To maintain conformity, specific production regulations were issued.

Courtesy New York Public Library.

Union soldier's uniform, ca. 1861–65.

Courtesy Western Reserve Historical Society.

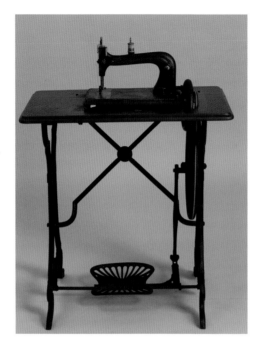

Sewing machine, ca. 1870. This Grover and Baker lockstitch treadle sewing machine was manufactured in Boston for light industrial and domestic use. Machines like this were used by dressmakers, in tailor's shops, or in private homes.

Courtesy Elizabeth Schmeck Brown.

style and a New York look. And New York provided immigrating Jews with an attractive destination.

Jews controlled much of the garment manufacturing done either in apartment workshops known as sweatshops or in the modern factories being developed by the second decade of the twentieth century. Most of the workers in the field were Jews as well. By 1897, 60 percent of employed New York Jews made a living in this industry and 75 percent of the workers were Jews.[10] Initially, most of the employers were Jews who had come to America before the 1870s and fell into the category of German Jews. In reality, they were just as likely to have been from Posen or Lithuania. Nonetheless, they were notable for their "Americanness" and for the fact that they had accumulated enough capital to be able to employ others.

Indeed, one of the most notable characteristics of the garment trade, besides its high concentration of Jews as employers and employees, was the relatively meager capital it took to cross the line from one to the other. Most of the contractors in the garment industry's sweatshops were relatively recent Jewish immigrants, and most came from eastern Europe. They usually worked for contractors before they could enter that group themselves. A contractor received garments from a manufacturer that had been cut but not yet sewn. Then, in his apartment or in a rented loft, the contractor brought together a group of workers, including sewing machine operators, finishers, basters, pocket makers, and pressers. The contractor worked in the same space and at the same tasks as the workers. He, however, if lucky, made a profit from all this, while low pay and horrible conditions were endured by the Jewish immigrant women and men who worked in these shops and constructed the garments that dressed the bodies of American women.

This structure of work and the organization of the industry made garment making very different from most other American industries. The fluid lines between workers and employers, and the low level of capitalization required to go into business "for oneself," made it a unique niche in the American economy. Compounding the uniqueness of the garment industry was the issue of gender, as it was one of the few spots in the American economy where men and women overlapped in jobs. While certain parts of the operation were off-limits to women, such as cutting and pressing (the highest and the lowest prestige jobs, respectively), most women and men labored at the same

Women in a factory, 1910.

Courtesy National Museum of American Jewish History, Philadelphia.

specialty, operating sewing machines. While men earned more, had greater chances for mobility, and participated in the industry for a lifetime, the nature of the garment industry shaped the gendered nature of the east European Jewish migration. Because young women had a chance, with relatively little skill or training, to find sewing work right away, east European Jewish families often sent daughters to America with their fathers as the trailblazers who would pave the way for the rest of the family. Because of the mushrooming of the industry in New York and the need for large numbers of hands, male or female, some east European Jewish women also migrated on their own or with female friends and relatives, and not as part of a nuclear family.

The fact that Jewish women and men worked together in these factories owned almost exclusively by Jews left its mark on Jewish life. For one, Jewish women came to see firsthand the workings of gender inequity. They worked as many hours and produced as many garments of equal quality, yet received less pay. The men had the chance of moving up to become factory owners or, if not that, foremen in larger factories. Women had no such options, and after the unionization of the industry men achieved the leadership positions in the unions, while women did not. Finally, the Jewish women experienced the unwelcome sexual advances of male coworkers, employers, and shop floor managers. The kind of resentment that Jewish women articulated at Jewish men grew in large measure out of the particular conditions of the garment industry. The consciousness Jewish women developed in the garment industry and their resentment against their own men may explain the extraordinary level of trade union activism of Jewish women.[11]

So, too, the garment industry's Jewishness was sui generis. Jews dominated the field from the top to the bottom. From the manufacturers to the contractors to the laborers, they were predominantly Jews, and by early in the twentieth century most were of east European origin. Likewise, in modern factories, such as the Triangle Shirtwaist Company, which women workers preferred, Jewish employers largely hired Jewish workers.[12] Additionally, most east European Jewish immigrant workers in the garment industry worked for other east European Jews. Although the earliest of the immigrants tended to work for German Jews, successful east Europeans became the primary factory owners well before the beginning of the twentieth century.

This had multiple implications for the continued immigration of Jews to the United States into the 1920s and for the development of Jewish community life in America. First among these involved a matter of exquisite timing and the confluence of moment and place. East European Jews, already comfortable with garment making, came to New York precisely as the revolution in clothing production intertwined with increased consumption of fashionable dress. Those twinned revolutions happened in part because east European Jews were on the move to America and were choosing to remain in huge numbers in their port of entry. Had the garment industry not burst out of its preindustrial mode when it did, the east European Jewish migration to America might have looked quite different indeed. But had the east European migration to America not happened when it did, then there is good reason to assume that the revolution in clothing would not have occurred in quite the same way.

As it happened, the two phenomena converged. Two and a half million east European immigrant Jews chose to immigrate to America after the 1870s. Vast numbers of them spent some or all of their working lives in a particular place in the American economy, the garment industry. Here they worked primarily for, and with, Jews. Employers, fellow Jews, had much in common with the workers, be they newly arrived immigrants or those who made up the American Jewish working class. On the one hand, the employer provided a model of mobility because he had not needed vast amounts of wealth to get his start, and this offered workers a sense that they too could aspire to self-employment. There was nothing about the employer—race, religion, ethnicity—that put him in a category unattainable by the workers.

Perhaps of greater significance, though, immigrant Jews entered into an industry where they met their coreligionists on an unequal footing. Unlike, for example, their co-immigrants in steerage who came to America from Italy or Poland and went to work for "others" with whom they shared no common origins and no bonds of communal responsibility, immigrant Jews went to work for other Jews, who had much in common with them. They shared a language and a history, and they understood themselves to have common enemies. From the point of view of the workers, this commonality proved to be a double-edged sword and bred a sense of resentment. They saw no reason why the employers in garment making, or in any of the other Jewish industries, should earn more and live better. They considered themselves entitled to as good a life as other immigrant

Jews who had preceded them to America by only a decade or two or three.[13] The impetus for unionization in the Jewish trades grew in part out of this internal Jewish class consciousness, this inner conflict of Jews against Jews.

Jewish employers were also shaped by the Jewishness of their workforce. While initially they could view the act of giving a friend, relative, or even a fellow Jew a job in a sweatshop as a favor, over time the demands shouted by the women and men in the immigrant community for better wages and better working conditions could not be ignored. The creation of Jewish unions, the International Ladies' Garment Workers' Union in 1900 and the Amalgamated Clothing Workers of America in 1914, took place with dramatically less strife and opposition from employers than did unionization efforts in textiles, steel, automobiles, coal mining, or any of the other heavy industries where employers could answer "nothing" to William Graham Sumner's rhetorical question of 1883, "What social classes owe to each other."[14] Jewish employers could not say this about their Jewish employees. The dramatic strike of 1909 in the shirtwaist industry, known in labor history as "the uprising of the 20,000," in which masses of Jewish women shirtwaist makers went on strike, ultimately ended through the intervention of leaders of the American Jewish community. Jacob Schiff, Louis Marshall, Louis Brandeis, Henry Moskowitz, Abraham Lincoln Filene, and Julius Cohen brought pressure upon the Jewish manufacturers to agree to mediation with the strikers. They reminded them directly that Jews, be they employers or laborers, had to contend with anti-

Sidney Hillman's Membership Book, Amalgamated Clothing Workers of America, 1917–19.

Courtesy UNITE HERE Archives, Kheel Center, Cornell University.

Semitic critics who used the class warfare as ammunition against all Jews. They also reminded them indirectly of the often-cited Talmudic statement that stated that all of Israel had a responsibility to one another.

Certainly some important differences can be cited to distinguish the beginning and end of the long century of Jewish migration to America as it involved the making of clothing. At the start of this era, most of the immigrants hailed from central Europe while by the end, they came from further east. In the matter of production, at the beginning, (mostly) men worked by hand and little separated the shopkeeper from the individual who made the garments

Photo by
Underwood &
Underwood, N. Y.

**World War I uniform
factory, ca. 1917.**

Courtesy YIVO Institute.

and sold them primarily to local buyers. Indeed, by and large, one person did both. At the century's end, however, Jewish women and men sat side by side at sewing machines and churned out garments at a rapid rate. Consumers around the country purchased these skirts and coats, blouses and shirts without knowing who had sewn them. Despite these differences, this century in American Jewish history shared sewing as a common experience. Whether looking at the early decades of the nineteenth century or the early decades of the twentieth century, Jews in America shared a common niche, and a perfect fit entwined the Jews, America, and the clothing industry.

5   The Birth of the Clothing Industry in America, 1815–1860

MICHAEL ZAKIM

In 1818, Henry Brooks opened a clothing store at the corner of Catharine and Cherry Streets in Manhattan, across from one of New York's busiest public markets and two blocks away from the East River wharves. Brooks had sold groceries at the same address—an ideal business location—several years earlier, but retired to an upstate farm in Rye when the War of 1812 interrupted his provisioning trade. With the return of peace, Henry returned to business, albeit not to groceries. Instead, he joined a younger brother, David, in the latter's clothing store on Cherry Street, and while the brothers dissolved their partnership in 1817, each stayed in the trade. Henry moved a few blocks down Cherry to his old location at the corner of Catharine Street, across from Henry Robinson's well-known clothing store. A year later, he bought the building for the not inconsiderable sum of $15,250. By 1825, his business was averaging sales of almost $50,000 per year and Henry opened a second store a short distance away, near James Slip, on the water.[1]

Brooks's decision to sell clothing was spurred by a flood of cheap British textiles that began arriving in America after 1815. They could be bought in small lots directly at auction on the wharves or from import-ers offering improved credit terms. Brooks, like many other ambitious men looking for new opportunities, would hire tailors to cut the cloths up into the desired styles and sizes and then put out the pieces to a wide circle of laborers sewing at home whom he paid by the piece. Finally, he would sell the finished garments to local retail customers or to wholesale merchants coming to the city to restock their own provincial stores. It was a simple business plan that required no giant investment, no corporate structure, and no sublime machines, but which nevertheless effected an industrial revolution in the way Americans got dressed.

Humanity, of course, has been clothing itself ever since the ignominious expulsion from the Garden in the third chapter of Genesis. Alexander Stuart, lecturing before New York City's American Institute in 1844, described the considerable social effort consequently required. "You must," Stuart began, "estimate the value of the grass which sustained the sheep, the labour and support of the shepherd whilst tending the flocks, the labour of the manufacturers in spinning, weaving, dying and dressing the cloth, including the support of their families whilst they were employed in these various processes." To these factors, he

Cutting Garments **(New York, N.Y., 1841) on cutting garments to fit the human form.** An individual fit was achieved by applying universal truths from *Scott and Wilson's Treatise on Cutting Garments* on cutting garments to fit the human form. The work contains fifty diagrams and designs reduced to mathematical principles, accompanied by a periodical report of fashions.

Courtesy The Winterthur Library, Printed Book and Periodical Collection.

added the interest on capital, the profits of the manufacturer, rents, taxes, poor-rates, the cost of transportation, the profits of the wholesale and retail merchants who marketed the cloth, and other incidental charges "which it is not necessary to enumerate."[2]

Until the nineteenth century, many viewed the effort as ending there since the next step in production—in which the cloth was actually turned into clothing—was considered to be so simple, both socially and technically, that writers on political economy ignored it altogether. There was little extra significance or value added in bringing the cloth to an artisan tailor to cut up and then sew into a garment; or in paying a tailor to cut the cloth (using his professional drafting patterns) and taking the pieces home to be sewn up; or in giving the sewing to a more skilled neighbor (in exchange for a future favor in kind); or in both cutting and sewing the cloths at home, particularly if this involved less fitted articles such as shirts or nightgowns made up of less costly mixed cotton fabrics. Until the 1800s, most families utilized all these options in one combination or another, depending on their needs, abilities, and resources.[3]

Men were the first to abandon such household practices and acquire their wardrobe "from the shelf." The change was soon recognized as a signal event in the forward march of civilization. "It used to be one job to seek for the cloth, and another to repair to the tailor, causing not unfrequently great loss of time and much vexation," *Hunt's Merchant's Magazine* enthused in 1848. "We now see everywhere, not only the economist, but the man of

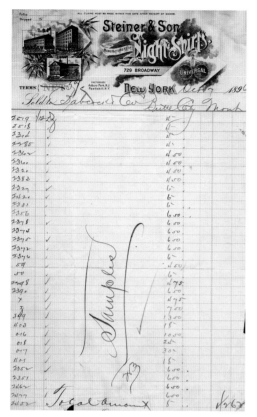

Invoice for nightshirts, Steiner & Son, October 7, 1896.

Courtesy National Museum of American Jewish History, Philadelphia.

revolution (by which canals, steam, and iron integrated a continental market). They overcame one of the central problems of doing business in industrial conditions—bringing the new material abundance to market—by integrating two traditionally distinct enterprises, cloth (dry goods) jobbing, and merchant tailoring. They balanced the exigencies of a local retail and a distant wholesale market, operating at the intersection of the two great trading triangles of the age, where agricultural exports from the South and West met cloth and capital from the North and from Europe. And they connected the individual citizen—in this case, the male consumer, as the manufacture of ready-made women's garments was still decades away—to the ethos of mass production.[5]

A wife writing from Oregon at mid-century described the results: "Your Father has as nice Cloathes as enney man both fine and corse.... It is cheaper to buy them Made up than to Buy the Cloath and Made them." It is no wonder, then, that there were 430 "clothing houses" doing business in New York City on the eve of the Civil War, compared to the twelve "slop sellers" purveying cheap ready-made garments listed in the city's directories just sixty years earlier. In fact, their dramatic business success made clothing merchants the bearers of industrial-age abundance. When the New York Chamber of Commerce published its first *Annual Report* in 1858, it acknowledged the trade's contribution to the city's rise to commercial preeminence. "The appetite grows by what it feeds upon," these merchant princes, long indifferent to such ordinary pursuits, observed of the clothing trade's seemingly limitless elasticity.

fashion, saving his time and his money by procuring the very articles he requires all ready made to his hand."[4] Such savings in "time and money" were made possible by a new type of business that situated itself between cloth maker and cloth wearer. Leaving to others what always had been (and continued to be) the far more complicated effort of producing textiles, clothiers staked out a previously nonexistent position in the developing networks of industrial exchange. They coordinated a textile revolution (the plethora of cheapening fabrics), a social revolution (the rise of wage labor in the cities), and a transportation

"There is no telling the extent it may not reach."[6]

"Tom, Dick, and Harry, here, there, and everywhere" all sought to secure a place in the new economy of affordable male raiment. Joseph Seligman's career was representative of these flush times. The eighteen-year-old son of a Jewish woolens weaver and a mother who managed the family's general merchandise store in Bavaria, Joseph arrived in America in 1837 and settled in Mauch Chunk, Pennsylvania. He became a clerk and cashier and then the personal secretary of Asa Packer, who had recently begun to build his coal empire in the Lehigh Valley. Seligman soon went out on his own and after peddling for a year, paid for the passage of two brothers, William and James, from Europe. In 1840, Joseph and William opened a store in Lancaster, Pennsylvania, while James went south to explore prospects. After the latter returned the next summer with $1,000, all three brothers, now joined by a fourth, Jesse, decided to relocate. They departed from New York with $5,000 worth of general merchandise, landed in Mobile, Alabama, and, after discovering that they had insufficient capital to compete in business there, moved further upstate. Within two years, the Seligmans were operating stores in Selma, Greensboro, Eutaw, and Clinton, in addition to peddling their merchandise throughout the surrounding region. By 1846, however, it was clear that the provincial market could no longer satisfy their ambitions. Clothing would be their ticket out.[7]

William left Alabama to open a clothing store in St. Louis with his brother-in-law, Max Stettheimer, who had previ-

ously sold clothing in Natchez, Mississippi. Jesse went to Watertown, New York, and with a fifth brother, Henry, opened a clothing store. Joseph and James, together with Max Stettheimer's father, Jacob, started a cloth-importing business on Pine Street in New York City. In 1850, Jesse and Henry left Watertown in order to open a clothing store in the boomtown of San Francisco. In California, they were joined by William while Max Stettheimer became a partner in the dry goods (cloth-importing) firm of Seligman & Stettheimer on Pine Street. In 1852, William picked up and moved again, this time to New York, where he began manufacturing clothing for the San Francisco store in addition to selling to the general wholesale trade. The following year another brother, Isaac, was sent to Europe to broker the bullion Jesse was regularly shipping from California, which in 1861 alone totaled no less than one million dollars. With so much money on account, the Seligmans soon moved into banking. In that same year, thanks to Joseph's influence in Republican Party circles, William secured contracts for army uniforms worth 1.5 million dollars. In 1864, the Seligmans closed a circle, both in their family history and in the annals of global exchange, when Max Stettheimer moved back to Germany to open up a European branch of the family bank.

The Seligmans' business career contained all the elements of the industrialization of clothing. Their very entry into the trade was testimony to the modest capital and technical requirements of the business, and their expansion into dry goods addressed the crucial need for a reliable supply of cloth. The move into manufacturing, again resting on the relatively simple production requirements for making a suit of clothes, assured control over styles, terms, and the supply of finished goods to their retail operations in San Francisco. Meanwhile, the move to San Francisco itself merely followed the latest tributary in a network of exchanges governed by the country's commercial tides. The peripatetic pursuit of profits that took the Seligmans from Pennsylvania to Alabama, then to Mississippi, St. Louis, Upstate New York, New York City, San Francisco, and finally back to Europe, was entirely characteristic of clothing's business geography, and of the fluid nature of the industrial market in general.

A "country tailor" subsequently wrote to the *New York Tribune* in 1849 to complain how the "many pleasant and flourishing little villages which a few years ago sustained half a dozen tailors each . . . are now giving a scanty support to less than half the number." Local artisans were hard pressed to compete with city firms, with both their scales of production and their access to metropolitan fashion. In fact, the industry's successful application of mass economies of scale to a person's unique appearance was a milestone in the development of modern culture, putting the men's clothing business firmly at the center of bourgeois life. Daniel Devlin was a well-known agent of this trend. Arriving from Ireland in the 1830s, Devlin settled in Louisville, Kentucky, and promptly opened a clothing business. Ten years later, he moved to New York to manufacture for the family store in Kentucky. Marrying well, he soon owned a five-story establishment on John Street that sought to dominate every branch of the

trade. This included "city retailing" ready-made garments to local shoppers, "wholesaling" ready-mades to clothing merchants around the country, "cutting" cloths in a giant range of sizes and styles for other manufacturers, and "custom" tailoring for individual customers who would also buy their cloths from Devlin. The plurality of separate "departments" made it possible for Devlin to maximize the commercial value of "at least eight millions of white males over fifteen years old," as observers estimated the size of the American clothing market. Local retail sales thus generated the cash that allowed clothiers to balance short-term expenses—salaries, wages, rents, production supplies, and other overhead costs—with the long-term wholesale credit rhythms of annual harvests. In this respect, one could say that the broadcloth suit purchased at an upscale urban "emporium" was joined at the seam with the Iowa farmer's smock and the California miner's denims.[8]

In the early 1850s, Devlin decided to move his operations to Broadway in an ultimate union of mass marketing and polite living. He negotiated purchase of a property kitty-corner from Alexander Stewart's famous Marble Palace, America's first department store. The asking price was over $100,000, a sum that financial sources considered extravagant. Indeed, creditors became notably anxious over Devlin's stubborn insistence on acquiring a Broadway address, fearing that he would quickly run up huge indebtedness if he went through with the move. But as New York's former mayor Philip Hone wrote about the times: "the mania for converting Broadway into a street of shops is greater than ever."

Indeed, the metropolis was becoming as much a subject of consumption as a place to live. *Putnam's Magazine* accordingly noted the "startling . . . number of churches which have been pulled down and displaced to make room for the great business which spreads with such astounding rapidity . . . utterly obliterating everything that is old and venerable." Daniel Devlin sought to put men's dress in the middle of this escalating flow of people, goods, and sales.[9]

So did Henry Brooks's four sons. In 1850, they had changed the name of their father's firm to Brooks Brothers and then built a new store at the corner of Broadway and Grand Street on the former site of the old Whig Party headquarters in an emerging neighborhood of high culture and shopping. The black walnut interiors of the new store dramatically highlighted the golden detail of its interior capitals—like Daniel Devlin's Corinthian columns and Italianate symmetries located a few blocks down the street—and informed a new mid-century aesthetic of business grandiloquence. Brooks Brothers built 100,000 square feet "expressly adapted to the various requirements of the business," while Devlin, who assuaged the worries of his creditors by generating $4,000 a day in sales not long after opening, boasted of his ability to "supply with expedition all wants and all fancies, even to the minute details of a wardrobe." Civil life consequently moved off the street and into the store, where it was organized under the commodity's aegis into standard sizes, "single prices," cash sales, return guarantees, and a plethora of other retail novelties.[10]

Clothiers regularly advertised inventories encompassing tens of thousands of garments in a seemingly limitless permutation of cloths, styles, sizes, and prices. This made it possible for them to furnish "tall men and short men, stout men and thin men, old men and young men, fast boys and slow boys" in a veritable democracy of self-fashioning citizens with cash to spend. But satisfying the varying tastes of both "the Quaker and the dandy" did not rest solely on marketing acumen. The ability to organize an equally extensive workforce of clothing makers was no less essential to business success. The trade, in other words, might have been born of a mercantile constellation of transatlantic and intra-continental exchange dominated by innovative wholesale and retail merchants, but it remained a uniquely labor-intensive project. Devlin & Co. thus required "near 2000 hands!!" to produce its giant inventories, a hierarchy of in-house trimmers, southern-work cutters, vest embroiderers, journeymen sewing surtouts, and subcontracted plain shirtmakers earning what contemporaries acknowledged to be starvation wages. Clothing production was divided between men and women, immigrants and native-born, Germans and Irish, and between the poor and those enjoying a "comfortable existence." All of these workers were integral in matching living and breathing "hands" to the highly variegated production needs of businesses that aspired to furnish all tastes and all budgets. Yet, the fact that these divisions were also the most fundamental social categories of urban life in general suggests how much the clothing business was implicated in the life of the modern city, and how much the modern order, in turn, served its hackneyed needs.[11]

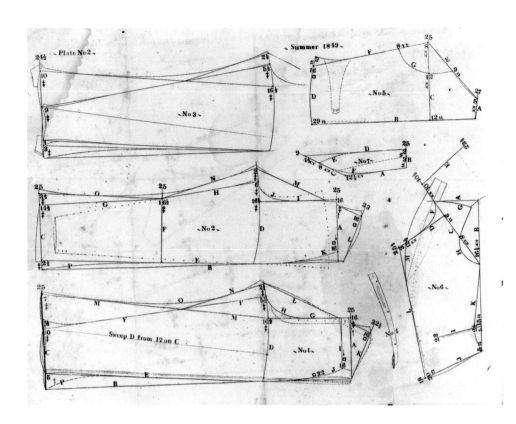

Diagrams for cutting from Samuel and Asahel Ward's Philadelphia Fashions and Tailors' Archetypes, 1849.

Courtesy The Winterthur Library, Printed Book and Periodical Collection.

Cutters worked at the high end of this labor market and the trade journal *Mirror of Fashion* identified them as artists "of great skill and refined taste" who were responsible for the appearance of mankind. This justified salaries that occasionally reached $2,500 a year, turning cutting into a distinct employment category that was dominated by native-born men. Many cutters also drafted garments, superintended construction, and sometimes made partner, such as C. A. Hughes of Arnoux & Son or R. B. Valentine of William Jennings's firm. As such, they were situated between the contractual obligations of a waged employee and the self-conceits of a proud artisan. Cutters were placed in a position to benefit from the fluidity of the industrial market and from the impermanence of traditional labor hierarchies.[12]

But not all cutters were created equal. There was a class that did nothing but cut, and by mid-century they numbered over a thousand in New York City alone. They might have been paid fourteen dollars a week, a not unrespectable income, but they earned this for cutting 150 frocks, an average of less than ten cents per garment, far below custom rates, even in the countryside. These cutters did no designing, no measuring, and had no contact with customers. Instead, they were assigned to the coats, pants, vests, or trimmings department of the large firms, where a foreman was responsible for keeping them supplied with materials and a steady flow of work. They cut from standard patterns placed on the cloth by someone else responsible for generating the maximum number of garments that could be extracted from a given piece of fabric. They worked in a central shop where the continual clip of shears could be deafening and where their pace could be sped up. Indeed, on occasion, they were even given knives, which could cut through several thicknesses of coarse goods at once, in place of the cutter's proverbial shears in an attempt to raise productivity.[13]

Cutting cloth into the constituent parts of a coat or pantaloons required several minutes. Sewing the pieces back together into a garment took far longer. "One cutter will cut as many garments in one week as three hundred persons can make up in the same time" was the contemporary estimate before the advent of the sewing machine in the 1850s dramatically increased productivity, without, however, altering the organization of production. "Oh, my! it is an undertaking," a young diarist agreed, upon being asked to stitch a linen shirt bosom, wrist bands, and sleeves. "I have to pull the threads out and then take up two threads and leave three. . . . The stitches must not be visible to the naked eye. I have to fell the sleeves with the tiniest seams and stroke all the gather and put a stitch on each gather." There were 25,243 stitches in a man's coat, constituting two days of work in "journeymen's hours," according to *Niles' Weekly Register*, for whom such numbers were a part of its tireless campaign for a rationalized system befitting an industrial society. Of these, 782 stitches were required for the basting; 5,500 for the edges; 7,114 for felling edges and faces; 1,982 for the pockets and other out-of-sight places; 3,056 more for the collar; 5,359 for the seams; and 1,450 for the holes. The enumeration broke the activity of sewing down in terms of a

standard denominator—the stitch—which could then be translated into time, into piecework, or into specific tasks.[14]

Most sewing was carried out off the premises in a system of "putting-out" that allowed manufacturers to avoid fixed costs and to adjust the labor force to their variable production needs. They saved money by passing on expenses and risks to their labor force, including the costs of unemployment and of "unused capital," principally in the form of workspace, but also of tools (threads, needles, candles) and even wood for heating one's room. What were inhibiting factors for other large industrial enterprises—the city's lack of a power source, high rents, and endemic social fluidity—were incentives for clothiers as

A fashion plate from Joseph Couts's *A Practical Guide for the Tailor's Cutting-Room*, 1848. The tailor presided over the male renunciation of fashion by allowing men to ignore the fashions without risking the wrong appearance.

Courtesy The Winterthur Library, Printed Book and Periodical Collection.

clothing proved ideally suited to the exigencies of profit-making in the metropolis.[15]

Such sewing was paid by the piece since there was no one to watch the clock. Piecework was also the most effective method of ensuring discipline among an unorganized, heterogeneous, and variously skilled labor force working without direct supervision. Sewers kept themselves working hard on the job in order to maximize the number of garments they could finish in a week because the prices for each piece were set at a level where only persistent effort would earn a decent subsistence. The arithmetic was simple. White or checked cotton shirts, the common variety with five seams in each sleeve, paid six cents each in the mid-1840s. A "common fast seamstress" could make two a day. The swiftest hand could possibly make three if she worked eighteen-hour days. In the best of circumstances, this brought in $1.12 at the end of the week. Rent for a single room in a working-class neighborhood cost four dollars a month in those years. Duck trousers, overalls, and other cheap working clothes paid a little more per piece—eight to ten cents each—but because of the greater intricacy involved in their construction, they generated no greater a weekly wage. On the other hand, provided she had the requisite skills and could convince an employer of the same, a seamstress might receive fine linen shirts with plaited

Max Hoffman's tailor shop on Riggs Avenue, 1920s. This image shows a typical view of a small-scale tailor's shop, with the owner surrounded by the tools of his trade.

Courtesy Jewish Museum of Maryland.

bosoms. These paid fifty cents apiece and could be finished at the rate of about one every two days, well beyond bare subsistence. Likewise, three cloth roundabout jackets, each paying fifty cents, could be made in two days. But all these budgets assumed that one assignment immediately followed upon another. They did not take into account the half a day often required to pick up work or deliver finished goods and then receive one's payment. These figures also presumed maximal productivity and that the "15 to 18 hours of steady work by the best hand" would not be interrupted by children, washing, cooking, other housework, or even illness and exhaustion. They also ignored seasonal layoffs and regular economic downturns, which in the mid-1850s resulted in a deflation of up to 40 percent in sewing prices in the industry.[16]

Putting-out also provided access to the cheapest labor of all, that of domestically bound women. While complaints were often heard in other industries about the transience of female labor—particularly about the unreliability of married women's employment—clothiers made few such noises. In fact, they counted on the family's desire to generate extra cash for household expenses and on the ability of wife and mother to pick up and put down her sewing while caring for children, preparing meals, cleaning house, and otherwise managing the family's domicile. But the same conditions that made waged sewing convenient for some, made it highly problematic for those who needed to earn a living wage. Clothiers consistently exploited this contradiction. Virginia Penny observed in her *Employments of Women* in 1863 that "the nature of [sewing] employment is such that no woman could enjoy health long, who did nothing else, and the wages are so small that anyone must work all the time to make a living; hence the work does not suit any, except those who have homes and have recourse to this as a secondary employment." Meanwhile, the foreman at a large clothing manufactory in New York told Penny, "those [seamstresses] that are dependent on their work for a living, do their work better than those that merely do it for pocket money." Women who needed to support themselves by sewing, in other words, were more disciplined employees. And so, while the wage that women earned for piecework was designed to be supplementary income, the trade preferred primary earners.[17]

It should come as no surprise, therefore, that women organized the earliest labor protests in the clothing industry, beginning in the 1820s. By 1831, female sewers in New York had established the United Tailoresses' Society, a trade union with a constitution, a plan of action, and a strike fund. The Society promoted a feminist critique of labor relations, arguing that the chronically low wages paid to tailoresses were the result of the power structure of American society. They claimed that tailoresses automatically earned less because as women they were barred from assuming responsibility for their households. At the same time, this very subordination is what made women so attractive (that is, so cheap) to the new industrial order. In June 1831, close to two thousand tailoresses answered the Society's call to strike. They demanded higher wages, while also seeking to test their bargaining power as wage earners in the labor market,

Employment notices from the *New York Sun*, September 11, 1835. The penny press was one of the great democratic inventions of the industrial age. As such, it was integral to another great innovation: the city's anonymous labor market.

Courtesy The New-York Historical Society.

to see if it could be used to break the vicious circle of patriarchal authority that controlled their lives. The strike, in fact, provoked far greater controversy because of its implicit goal of equal rights for (working) women than for the explicit demand of improved pay for clothing workers. The *Boston Evening Transcript*, among others, denounced the Society's "unfeminine" ways, advising New York's tailoresses to desist from such politicking and be content with their scissors and pincushions. Male wage earners were also ambivalent about the Society's social agenda, and by 1834 the National Trades' Union prohibited independent organizing on the part of working women in an attempt to retain control over the actions of their wives and daughters.[18]

At the same time, the advanced industrial consciousness of New York tailoresses soon radicalized male employees in the clothing trade, most of whom had been devoting their political efforts to defending journeymen's traditional prerogatives in the master's shop. It was women who first understood that such paternalism offered little protection to any worker in an emerging capitalist system where labor had become a crucial variable in the profit equation, thus undermining all traditional arrangements and mutual obligations. The developing zero-sum confrontation between employers and wage earners over control of production reached a climax in the summer of 1850 when the largest strike to date in New York City's history broke out in the ready-made clothing industry. Thousands of waged journeymen refused to continue working until their pay was brought into line with the rising costs of living and the rising profits of clothiers.

Open-air meetings were organized as were actions against bosses who attempted to bypass the strikers by putting out their work to other sources. Tense confrontations between journeymen tailors on one side and an alliance of employers' men, strikebreakers, and the police on the other, became weekly occurrences. These often developed into running street battles, the most serious of which ended in the beating death of two strikers at the hands of the police on August 5 in front of Frederick Wartz's house on 38th Street (Wartz was suspected of working for a boss under the going rate).[19]

The 1850 strike ended in a general acceptance by city firms of the journeymen's new bill of prices. It was, however, a Pyrrhic victory for most of the city's tens of thousands of waged sewers because a growing number of clothing firms no longer hired their workers directly but preferred a system of so-called farming operations. This system saw firms pay tailors for orders that the tailors then gave out to others to execute. "By this means," the *New York Herald* noted in 1857, "the persons who employ such hands are generally enabled to make a very handsome profit." Journeymen tailors who had failed to reverse or at least control the industrialization of their craft, and who had been left with few prospects for a proprietorship themselves, thus became brokers in labor, claiming a share of the surplus labor they had lost to the capitalist. These "sweaters," the era's leading feuilletonist, George Foster, wrote, barely containing his repulsion, "carry competition to its lowest and most wretched extent." Sometimes, in fact, the sweated laborer himself employed

undersweaters. "And so, in the end," Foster continued, "the at first inadequate payment given for the work is taxed, first by the master-workman for his profits and the support of his splendid shop and his elegant and fashionable family up town; next, for the greedy profit of the remorseless shaver and sharper; and then again, for one or two, and sometimes three, of his underlings." The industrial production of clothing, in other words, had become an interlocking network of mutual dependencies reaching from Broadway clothing palaces down to the lowliest antiquated tailor shop, not to mention to the fresh immigrant working at home with wife and children. All were connected through tiers of subcontractors—veteran artisans, church officials, boardinghouse keepers, or sewing machine agents—who mobilized their own social networks of neighborhood and ethnicity in the atomizing city.[20]

As primitive as his methods and morals appeared to middle-class sensibilities, the sweater proved integral to industrial progress. He promised to meet deadlines, juggled orders, paid deposits on the cloths, delivered the goods on time, hired from a labor pool he knew firsthand, and kept enough hands in employment in anticipation of rush jobs. He assumed, in short, most of the risks of manufacturing. The sweater established his own modest circulation of goods, cash, and credit in order to fill a particular niche in the mass clothing market and avoided most of the fixed costs of business by assembling and disbanding his workforce in accordance to orders. This did not immediately, or necessarily, lower clothiers' labor costs, but it allowed the large firms to pass on produc-

S. Lazarus' Sons & Co. store, Columbus, Ohio, ca. 1877–96. S. Lazarus' Sons was a prominent family-run retail operation in Columbus, Ohio. Established in 1851, this business grew into one of the largest retailers in the United States. Here salesmen pose with their offerings for men's and boys' attire.

Courtesy American Jewish Historical Society.

E. S. Hart, dry goods store, Cotopaxi, Colorado, ca. 1885. The quickly expanding American West offered a wealth of new business opportunities. This Colorado dry goods store provided much-needed clothing and supplies to frontier settlers.

Courtesy American Jewish Historical Society.

tion responsibilities to others while enhancing their capacity to market to the widest range of customers.[21]

By the middle of the century, the "wants of clothiers" had also become a most important factor in the production of textiles. Clothing orders were a permanent fixture in weekly reports on the state of the dry goods market, and woolen and mixed woolen-cotton manufacturers directly catered to the needs of the clothing firms. For instance, the former adapted their production schedules according to the latter's business seasons. Factories no longer made "Spring Goods" on the approach of spring and "Autumn Goods" just before autumn since additional time was necessary to allow the fabrics to first "pass through the [sewer's] hands." In addition, the huge California market that opened up after 1849 gave this seasonal shift an extra push, since it took much longer for garments to make the trip to San Francisco.[22] And so the historical relationship between cloth and clothing was inverted. Ready-made clothing increasingly came to dominate the character of the textile industry. For instance, even as their wool sources moved west, woolen mills remained in the East, because the clothing trade was concentrated in New York and other seaboard cities. And as these mills began to produce specifically for the clothing trade, they adjusted to a multiplicity of smaller orders and learned to sustain a greater number of order cancellations. They diversified their product selection and strained to satisfy the rising standards and expectations of a well-dressed democracy. The efforts of shepherd, carder, spinner, weaver, fuller, and dresser were now dependent on the clothier for success. For the first time in history, the making of cloth was subordinated to the making of clothing. This was, indeed, an industrial revolution in the relations of production.

German Jews in the Early Manufacture of Ready-Made Clothing

PHYLLIS DILLON

In the popular imagination, the involvement of the Jews in the American garment industry is informed by images from Irving Howe's *World of Our Fathers*. It is an image of an industry dominated and driven from the turn of the twentieth century to its middle years by eastern European Jewish garment workers and manufacturers. An examination of the actual history, however, shows that efforts by German Jewish immigrants a half century earlier laid the groundwork for eastern European involvement in the garment centers of American cities.[1]

German Jews were manufacturing men's clothing by the 1840s, and some German Jewish firms remained in the men's formal clothing industry well into the twentieth century. German Jews were also prominent in the women's ready-made industry, which has a separate and distinct history, beginning with the making of mantles and capes in the 1850s. In the women's-wear industry, German Jews first appeared as hoopskirt and corset makers in the 1860s, and then expanded into cloak and suit manufacturing in the 1870s. By the 1880s, they were the primary group supplying clothes to major department stores and specialty stores. They left the industry increasingly after the turn of the century, but not before establishing wholesale distribution of an array of clothing needs in all price ranges to department stores. German Jews also created a system for the mass marketing of French-inspired designs. This chapter introduces the rich early history of Jewish involvement in the American garment industry.

The Historical Context for the Expansion of the Men's Garment Industry

Three important historical factors contributed to the early growth of the ready-made clothing industry: (1) the expansion of the American frontier to the West, (2) American industrialization, and (3) the Civil War.

The production of men's clothing was initially stimulated by population expansion as the frontier moved west during a period of increased industrialization and the creation of new cities. The American textile demand—innovated with drafting systems and production methods in order to make ready-made clothing for a broader consumer base.[2] Even as tailor shops increasingly offered ready-made clothing, they continued to provide traditional custom services since both traveling gentlemen and prospectors needed extra clothing as they moved west. At the same time, New York City developed as the market center for the country, and country merchants traveled to New York to stock their stores. By the late 1850s, the newly invented sewing machine contributed to expanded productivity in the clothing manufacturing industry. The sewing machine was used first in the manufacturing of shirts and furnishing goods before it was practically integrated into the manufacturing of coats and suits in the 1860s.

Fashion also played a role in developing the market for the industry as businessmen, salesmen, and clerks in New York and other cities required affordable business attire.[3] In the antebellum era, somber business attire came to define the American gentleman, and ready-made black suits could be purchased at affordable fixed prices at the new East Coast emporiums. Advice in nineteenth-century American etiquette manuals, written to replace earlier European manuals, defined the honest, dignified, self-made man as the ideal of American gentility. The affordable black suit marked a deliberate distinction from the more ostentatious dress of the class-conscious European gentry, and it accorded with the American ethos of a rapidly growing meritocracy established on democratic principles. Articles in popular magazines also advised the readers that all

Altman & Louchheim, German Jewish clothiers in Philadelphia before 1860.

Courtesy National Museum of American Jewish History.

industry, which dramatically matured from the 1830s to 1860s (with the help of high tariffs), was able to supply manufacturers with suitable woolen goods, thus relieving pressure to import European textiles. Tailoring too, underwent industrialization, and as Michael Zakim, Claudia Kidwell, and Margaret Christman have all described, tailors—stimulated by new business opportunities created by increased

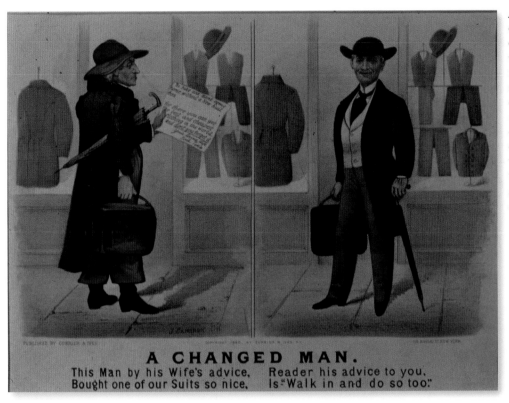

A CHANGED MAN.
This Man by his Wife's advice,
Bought one of our Suits so nice,
Reader his advice to you,
Is "Walk in and do so too."

A Changed Man **by John Cameron, published by Currier & Ives, 1880.** In the print a man reads the note from his wife that says, "Be sure and don't come home without a new suit . . . for there you can get the best and cheapest clothing in the world. And you don't forget it. Your loving wife."

Courtesy Museum of the City of New York.

classes could dress fashionably with ready-made clothing.[4]

The outbreak of the Civil War added further economic opportunities for clothing manufacturers. During the War of 1812, the U.S. government had established a manufactory in Philadelphia to supply military uniforms, and the manufactory had continued to supply clothing after that war ended.[5] The established system—in which tailors cut the fabric in a central shop and then supplied bundles of fabric to be made up by seamstresses working at home—supplied sufficient army clothing for peacetime, but became inadequate during the Civil War.[6] Seizing on the war-generated need, some clothiers switched to the production of military clothing, and several manufacturers created partnerships with former competitors to bid for contracts. While the Civil War hurt some firms that were dependent on selling civilian clothing in the South, it stimulated others to enter military production (for instance, Jewish clothing firms in Cincinnati became especially active in uniform production).[7] In addition, the war gave rise to standardized production methods as the U.S. Army provided guidelines for sizing that became crucial for the expansion of the men's industry after the war.[8] Following the Civil War, increased prosperity and the expansion of the middle class provided further impetus for manufacturing, retailing, and the rise of the mail-order business. Within this context, German Jewish immigrants took advantage of the industry's transformation and laid the foundation for Jewish immigrant success in the decades that followed.

Immigrant Jews Enter the Industry in the 1840s

Ready-made clothing first appeared for sale in large quantities in the 1840s in pioneer emporiums on the East Coast such as George Simmons's Oak Hall in Boston and Lewis & Hanford in New York City. In addition, merchandise was also shipped up and down along the East Coast and to California. Most of the early tailors or storekeepers who initiated the mass manufacturing of men's clothes were Yankee entrepreneurs or Scottish, Irish, and English immigrants, although some small immigrant Jewish firms existed in New York City as is attested by their appearance in contemporary business directories. The Jews who entered the men's clothing business were only a small percentage of the great number of European immigrants who played a significant role in the commercialization and industrialization of the United States during the antebellum period. After 1815, more than

Oak Hall Clothing House, ca. 1854.

Courtesy of the author.

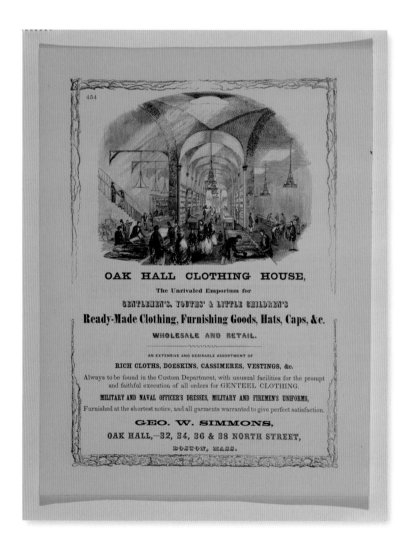

Firms that are members of the National Association of Clothiers in 1911 listed on the back of the association's stationery.

Courtesy L. Adler & Bros. Collection, Department of Rare Books and Special Collections, University of Rochester Library.

five million Europeans immigrated to America after the Napoleonic wars devastated Europe, with German and Irish immigrants comprising the largest percentage. Most Jewish immigrants were from Bavaria and Baden, although smaller groups from Prussia, Silesia, Poland, and Alsace also immigrated, as did Jews from the present areas of central Europe such as Hungary, the Czech Republic, and Slovakia.

In German lands, Jews had lived clustered in small towns where they had worked as peddlers and small merchants.[9] Only a small number were artisan-trained, such as tailors, although the Jewish immi-grants from Alsace, Galicia, and East Prussia included more tailors than those from other areas.[10] These immigrants were primarily young men with few economic prospects who left their homes because restrictions on residence, marriage, and occupation after 1815 disrupted their livelihood. Some German Jews settled in New York City while others passed through New York on their way to new and growing cities, such as Cincinnati, Baltimore, Rochester, St. Louis, and Chicago (others traveled south or followed the discovery of gold to California). In Cincinnati, Rochester, and Baltimore, many immigrant Jews progressed rather quickly from peddling to shop keeping to the new industry of clothing manufacturing—and in some cities, they became pioneer clothing manufacturers as early as the 1840s. New York City retained its position as the center of the men's ready-wear industry and the largest producer of clothing for over one hundred years, but the satellite centers became, and remained, important producers until the eclipse of the industry caused by offshore manufacturing in the 1960s and the decline of formal business-wear. The

distinctive geographical market structure of the men's clothing industry is an important feature. The regional centers and the numerous German Jewish firms listed on the stationery of the National Association of Clothiers in 1911 reflect the early roots of German Jewish emigration to both the East Coast and the new cities of the Midwest, where they established clothing firms. Our story concerns those Jews involved in the industry who settled in New York and other cities that became garment centers.

Occupational Affinity—Tailors and Peddlers

A nuanced understanding of the passage of Jews into the garment industry may be further illuminated by taking into account some traditions of occupational affinity brought from Europe.[11] The background of the Jews in Germany and central Europe as petty merchants, artisans, peddlers, and middlemen, as well as their experience in the clothing and textile trades, most likely provided useful experience to facilitate their entry into garment manufacturing and wholesaling in America. The history of Jews as tailors can be traced to craft activity in early Jewish settlements for the creation of special clothing required by Jewish law.[12] Trade, merchandising, and urban professions (such as medicine) became the most common occupations of Jews in the Middle Ages, although Jews were also a significant presence as long-distance traders.[13] Tailoring and the refurbishing of old clothes, along with the textile trade, became important occupations for European Jews

during the Renaissance and succeeded to such an extent that the guilds viewed them as competition. The first independent Jewish tailoring guilds were established in Poland-Lithuania in the sixteenth and seventeenth centuries, and cap making became an exclusive Jewish craft.[14] By the seventeenth and eighteenth centuries, some Jews in central Europe turned from tailoring and secondhand clothing to the actual manufacturing of uniforms for the military.[15]

In the German lands, selling and trade were more common than tailoring, and many German Jews were small shopkeepers and middlemen who brought agricultural products from peasants to the cities. Others served as horse and cattle dealers who bought flax for textile production. Many of these Jews traveled long distances and formed a network of trade vital to the German economy.[16] And since they were accustomed to such endeavors, peddling

Vot Dosh You Peddles?
by W. M. Carey,
published in *The Aldine*.

The Aldine was an American art journal published from 1868 to 1879. The image depicts a Jewish peddler mistaking a "plein-air" artist for another peddler.

Courtesy National Museum of American Jewish History.

became a logical occupation for German Jewish immigrants. For many Jewish clothiers who started as peddlers, the fact that the United States was an expansive land provided a myriad of opportunities for peddlers prior to the development of free postal delivery in rural areas. In addition, coreligionists aided Jewish peddlers by supplying them with provisions and helping them maintain dietary practices on the road. With small initial profits, these Jewish peddlers could move from carrying packs to buying a horse and wagon and further expand their operation.[17]

From Peddling to Shop Keeping to Manufacturing

Jews were able to become clothiers because the business required relatively small amounts of initial capital. The primary industrial production system of the antebellum era involved tailors (called *cutters*), who cut out the fabric parts, and women seamstresses who worked at home and did the sewing; Jewish clothiers found a ready supply of immigrant and native tailors and seamstresses to hire to make the clothes. At this stage, many clothiers were simultaneously retailers and wholesalers, and New York City business directories indicate a growing number of Jewish clothiers selling ready-made clothing that they manufactured throughout the 1850s. In addition to city directories, Jewish newspapers provide evidence for the identification and description of Jewish firms in New York City. For example, the *Asmonean*, an Anglo-Jewish newspaper published between 1849 and 1858, had a national circulation and included news about coreligionists in other cities, theatre reviews, world news, and classified ads. It also contained advertisements, and the October 21, 1853, issue contained four ads for ready-made clothing dealers: Henry L. Foster, David J. Levy, Jacob L. Bach, and Morrison & Levy. Jacob L. Bach first appeared as a clothier in *Longworth's City Directory* (New York) in 1836 at 46½ Chatham.[18] In 1853, Bach's business was located at 134 William Street (his home was at 107 W. 13th Street) and his ad read:

Wholesale clothing to southern, western and California merchants. The subscriber formerly of the firm Bach and Pander and latterly of the firm of Bach, Burnett and Co., no. 9 Magazine St, New Orleans would respectfully inform his friends and the public that he has opened a sales room in connection with his manufactory at 134 Williams St. where can be found an extensive assortment of ready made clothing suitable for the trade, having had some 18 years experience in manufacturing clothing, he flatters himself that his goods are in taste style and quality equal to any in the city and are offered at prices to suit all who may wish to purchase. Jacob L. Bach.[19]

Henry L. Foster, located at 27 Courtland Street, listed the types of ready-made clothing available in the 1850s: "Black cloth dress and frock coats, black and colored sack and sack frocks, black and colored cashmarette coats, fine linen seersucker coats, business coats of every description, black and colored cassimere pants, fine quality India nankeen pants, bombazine black and colored silk and satin white and fancy Marseilles also linen and muslin shirts, merino and silk undershirts and drawers, gloves, half hose, suspenders, linen, cambric and silk handkerchiefs."[20]

While the earliest small firms were located downtown, they were not on Broadway, the most prestigious commercial address. By 1852, however, the clothiers Bernheimer Brothers were located on fashionable Broadway after having started on Williams Street, and by the 1860s Bernheimer Brothers made Civil War uniforms. In 1861, they had contracts for 1,000 infantry coats, and the following year they won contracts for 10,000 infantry coats, 10,000 infantry trousers, 5,000

WOMEN AND THEIR WORK IN THE METROPOLIS.—Sketched by Stanley Fox.—[See Page 244.]

cavalry jackets, and 20,000 knit shirts with collars.[21]

In the years after the Civil War, New York manufacturing concerns built on their wartime success and consolidated to take advantage of coast-to-coast railroad connections. In the quest for higher profits, merchandising and mail-order business expanded, while national advertising and traveling salesmen, who traveled by railroad carrying suit samples to stores across the country, were introduced throughout the industry. New York, which remained the center for the dry goods market and European-imported fabrics, remained important for high-end ready-made and custom-made clothes, and eventually became the central location for manufacturers to come together to solve industry-wide problems.[22] In New York, David Marks & Sons and Alfred Benjamin & Company were among the most prominent firms, and Marks helped organize a national association in 1884 to deal with retail credit problems.[23] Twelve years later a stronger organization, the National Association of Clothiers, replaced Marks's organization and served as a powerful force in the men's clothing industry for about twenty-five years.[24] It represented the industry in dealing with retail credit, retail, mill and government relations, and while labor

Women and Their Work in the Metropolis, **sketched by Stanley Fox, published in** *Harper's Bazaar*, **April 18, 1868.** The print shows the variety of light industries in New York City that employed women in the 1860s. The woman in the center is a seamstress working at home manufacturing shirts. On the left a woman is working as a hoopskirt maker.

Courtesy Museum of the City of New York.

BROADWAY, N. Y. 1856.
West Side from Fulton to Courtland Street.

problems were practical problems for all
the firms, the association left those problems for the local clothier associations to
address. National delegates from all the
manufacturing cities met annually, and
present at the first convention were many

of the firms founded before the Civil War.
Subsequent conventions met annually, and,
following serious discussions, many toasts,
jokes about the industry, and socializing
took place at black tie affairs at the Sherry
Restaurant in New York City.

A Regional Producer: The Cincinnati Men's Clothing Industry

The history of the Cincinnati clothing
industry is largely the history of Cincinnati's German Jewish community. This
history offers some insights into the
development of the nineteenth-century
industry in a particular locale and illuminates features of the German Jewish
experience that other cities replicated.
Cincinnati, which was a leading western
city by 1830 and became a beacon for
Jewish settlement on the frontier, was

called the "Queen of the West" as a reflection of the richness of its adjacent farmland
and its booming machine trades.[25] It
attracted many immigrants, mostly Germans and Irish, although among the
German immigrants were a small group of
Jews. From a community of 16 in 1820, the
Jewish community grew to 3,000 in 1850
out of a total Cincinnati population of
115,000.[26] Immigrants from the same
European villages followed each other to

Cincinnati, and this chain migration helped ease the way for new arrivals.[27] In addition, these Jewish immigrants initially took advantage of ample peddling opportunities along the Ohio River to Kentucky, Indiana, Illinois, and Missouri, created their own credit system, and stuck to particular aspects of the economy. In particular, they avoided competition with established local trades such as "pork packing, candle and soap making, brewing, iron working, steamboat construction, machine and carriage making."[28] Economic decisions were also made with sensitivity to "local hiring practices, cultural attitudes, perceived potential for success and a desire to work alongside other Jews."[29]

After two or three years of peddling, many German Jewish immigrants in Cincinnati moved into the retail and wholesale clothing business or dry goods selling. Over half of the Jewish immigrants became involved in the clothing trade by 1860, making Cincinnati the leading clothing manufacturing center of the West and South.[30] That year, the city directory listed seventy-five wholesale clothing firms, of which sixty-five were Jewish owned.[31] While the outbreak of the Civil War the following year stopped Cincinnati's sales to neighboring states, Jewish clothing manufacturers became suppliers of Civil War uniforms as an accessible alternative to interstate trade.[32] Bruce S. Bazelon and William F. McGuinn's *Directory of American Military Goods Dealers & Makers 1785–1915* sheds light on the large number of Cincinnati Jews who supplied military clothing—contract clothing suppliers included Jacob Elsas, Marcus Fechheimer, Louis Stix, Mack, Stadler & Glaser, and

many others.[33] Following the war, some of these men passed into other endeavors, although Fechheimer's firm remained active in the men's clothing business, and its history can be reconstructed from evidence in Cincinnati museums and libraries.

In the R. G. Dunn papers in the Baker Library at Harvard University, the Fechheimer firm is noted: "Henderson, Fechheimer, Krause Frankel and Co. had consolidated to manufacture army clothing in large quantities . . . [in] 1861."[34] An exhibit flyer describes the first Fechheimer as Samuel Maier, who lived from 1720 to 1794 and was a clothing peddler in Germany.[35] His son Meyer took the name Fechheimer from a nearby village of Fechheim, where he had a dry goods business. Meyer died in 1832 in Germany leaving fourteen children, and that same year Meyer's children began to immigrate to America, where they founded Fechheimer companies in Wichita, Kansas, New York City, and Cincinnati. Meyer's sons Abraham and Aaron arrived in Cincinnati in 1834, while Max and Marcus immigrated three years later, and peddled in New York, Philadelphia, and Ohio for a time before they joined their brothers in Cincinnati in 1842 when a dry goods firm called Fechheimer and Goldsmith first appeared in the Cincinnati city directory. By the 1850s, they were listed as clothiers. After Abraham's death in 1855, the firm became Marcus Fechheimer; by 1861, his nephews May and Leopold were working for him. During the 1860s, the firm had government contracts for uniforms, and by the time of Marcus Fechheimer's death in 1881, the company was making men's, boys', and children's clothing as well as uniforms.

Photograph of Marcus Fechheimer.

Courtesy Jacob Rader Marcus Center of the American Jewish Archives, Cincinnati, Ohio.

Marcus Fechheimer's life, as summarized in his obituary, illustrates many of the themes shared by other successful German Jewish businessmen in the clothing industry throughout the country. He participated in a variety of religious, philanthropic, and social endeavors, including serving as president of the Reform synagogue B'nai Jeshurun and as a member of the Masons, the Hebrew Benevolent Society, the Jewish Hospital Society, and the Cleveland Orphan Society (he also served on the boards of the Western German Bank and the National Insurance Company).[36] Fechheimer's broad participation in German Jewish life illustrates the variety of institutions built by the German Jewish community in Cincinnati, which were similar to those created by German Jews in other cities. They usually created their own synagogues within a few years of settlement, initially meeting in rented rooms as they fashioned a new kind of synagogue in America. They often worshipped without rabbis, which was a distinct break from the synagogues of Europe that were governed by rabbinic hierarchy and community infrastructure.[37] After these humble beginnings, the congregations built permanent synagogues, which required fundraising, membership fees, and the selling of pews like in Protestant denominations.[38] The new synagogues were free societal aggregates in an open civil society, and the members actively debated a variety of issues, including the order of ritual, music, and temple leadership. Discord sometimes led to internal splits and the founding of new congregations, and the period of initial German Jewish settlement is characterized by a multiplicity of synagogues that included those that retained Orthodox ritual as well as those that became Reform.

German Jews also built new philanthropic, welfare, and social institutions outside of their congregations.[39] In Cincinnati, they established the second branch of B'nai Brith (the Jewish fraternal order) following its founding in New York City in 1843 by German Jewish merchants who sought to provide opportunities for Jews to participate in a fraternal order parallel to the popular Christian groups.[40] Cincinnati families founded the first Jewish hospital in America in 1850 to follow Jewish dietary laws (Mt. Sinai in New York was not established until 1852), and Cincinnati's Jews also founded a men's social club in 1856, the Phoenix Club, which was the first Jewish social club for literary and social pursuits west of the Alleghenies.[41] In 1874, the Jewish community built a larger facility to which women were still only admitted for balls and banquets. It is important to note that the founding constitution was printed in German and described the club as "a German organization for Jewish men."[42]

When assessing the passage of German Jews into American middle-class society, it must be taken into account the degree to which they considered themselves German and their similarity to the large immigrant group of Christian Germans in levels of literacy and interest in culture and literature. In the nineteenth century, both Europeans and Americans regarded high German culture with esteem, and German Jews who achieved financial success led a lifestyle similar to Christians during the Gilded Age. They created their own clubs in Cincinnati, Philadelphia, Baltimore, Rochester, and New York to socialize within their own communities, bought summer homes in Saratoga, and published their own blue books with social listings and statistical compilations (if they were not included in the blue books of their local cities). These features of the affluent German Jewish lifestyle were related to a larger phenomenon in post–Civil War America—the emergence of a self-defined aristocratic culture (most notably in New York City) of private gentlemen's clubs, drawing room entertainments, and balls.[43] In addition, historians Jonathan Sarna and Nancy Klein have illustrated that the success story of the Jews of Cincinnati was important for other reasons, and they cite scholars who claim Jews fared better where they had pioneer status: "The degree in which Jews were involved in the early growth of a city and had achieved a notable and respected place in public and private life directly influenced how later generations of Jews were perceived."[44]

The Growth of the Chicago Garment Business and the Modernization of the Industry

While Cincinnati was prominently involved with Civil War contracts, other garment centers, such as Rochester and Baltimore, developed their surrounding markets through the use of traveling salesmen and national advertising. Chicago, meanwhile, grew to become the second most important clothing manufacturing city in post–Civil War America as railroad transportation transformed Chicago into the major Midwest hub. Chicago developed later than Cincinnati, but grew faster, and while the first Jewish firms were jobbers who sold goods made in the East, the history of Hart, Schaffner & Marx illustrates the growth of Jewish firms within the Chicago economy.

Harry Hart was eight years old when his family arrived in Chicago from Bavaria in 1850.[45] While working for other retailers, he and his brother accumulated $2,700 with which they opened their own store in 1872 called Harry Hart & Brother. They opened a second store in 1875 and began to make suits for their own stores, which they sold wholesale. Their brother-in-law joined in 1879, creating Hart, Abt and Marx, after which they got their first army contracts. Then, their cousin Joseph Schaffner arrived from Cleveland and joined the firm, contributing his idea of national advertising in magazines, which led to becoming a national brand. They continued to cut their clothes in-house and relied on small contract shops to manufacture them until 1905 when they purchased forty-eight contract shops.[46] In 1910, a large strike engulfed the firm, now called Hart, Schaff-

ner & Marx, and spread to other companies in the city. The company was the first to reach agreement with the strikers in 1911, but it took subsequent strikes lasting until 1919 for other Chicago firms to become unionized. Hart, Schaffner & Marx abolished homework and centralized work within the factory.

This centralization was common within the men's clothing industry by the turn of the century as a number of modern companies pursued industrial planning and vertical integration. In Rochester, for example, the firm Adler-Rochester Clothes built a factory designed by the industrial architect Albert Kahn in 1910, complete with a worker's cafeteria, infirmary, and reading room. In Baltimore, Henry and Sigmund Sonneborn built a factory in 1905 that was said to be the largest in the world. The men's industry also exported their expertise in modern factory production and expanded their production to foreign markets. In 1913, E. A. Tishman, formerly of Alfred Benjamin & Co. of New York City, organized a modern coat, pants, and vest factory in Vienna to supply a chain of twenty men's stores in Austria.[47] Tishman supervised a factory of twelve hundred workers with machinery imported from America. American brands such as Alfred Benjamin of New York and Stein-Bloch of Rochester were also sold in the shops throughout Austria. The outbreak of World War I ended this relationship, but during the same period, other ambitious Jewish firms in America competed with English

Photograph of 155 South Market Street shortly after the firm of Hart, Schaffner & Marx was established, 1888. Founded just a year before this photograph was taken, Hart, Schaffner & Marx experienced quick success. Already by 1897, they were advertising nationally. This photograph shows some of the key people in the organization at the time. Left to right: E. T. Winship, salesman; Dave May, salesman; Joseph Schaffner; Henry Schneewind, salesman; Max Hart; Harry Hart; and Sig Frank, who was in charge of shipping.

Courtesy Hartmarx Corporation.

Autumn and winter styles, Wallach Brothers catalog, the home of Hart, Schaffner & Marx, 1920. Hart, Schaffner & Marx promoted an all-wool policy at an early date, before fabric identification was required by law.

Courtesy Special Collections, Fashion Institute of Technology.

wholesalers to supply the English army with uniforms in addition to providing uniforms for the United States.[48] New York firms such as Cohen, Goldman & Co., Heidelberg, Wolff & Co., Bashowitz Bros., and J. Eisner & Co. had extensive contracts to supply the English government with army uniforms for World War I. Such examples demonstrate that the modernization of Harry Hart's business in Chicago was part of a broader expansion and centralization within the garment industry.

German Jews, the Women's Clothing Business, and the Hoopskirt Business

German Jews were also instrumental in the expansion of women's ready-made manufacturing. They entered hoopskirt manufacturing and corset making in the 1860s as well as cloak and suit manufacturing in the 1870s, when the women's apparel industry was in its formative years. Women's clothing was not mass manufactured until later in the nineteenth century because it was more sensitive to yearly fashion changes and remained very complicated in construction for most of the nineteenth century.[49] Women knew how to hand sew and could prepare household linens and make items based on square dimensions such as shirts, but they used dressmakers whenever possible for more complicated gowns, cloaks, and corset stays. Fabric was expensive and fit was important, so dressmakers were expert in the judicious cutting of fabric to create the required fit and silhouette. Even if a woman could not afford a gown totally made by a dressmaker, she would seek someone more expert for the cutting. In addition, until the middle of the nineteenth century, when the American textile industry matured, fabrics were imported and costly. Women could not afford many changes of clothing. Throughout most of the nineteenth century, women were knowledgeable about the vast variety of fabrics and their characteristics, and all classes of women were interested in proper fit and style as well as quality. The transformation in the nineteenth century from the use of custom dressmakers to ready-made clothing required that ready-made clothing have the level of quality expected by consumers.

American women were also interested in fashion. By the 1830s, New York City had become the commercial and fashion capital of the nation, and ladies' magazines filled with fashion advice were distributed nationwide by the 1840s.[50] Broadway was compared to Regent Street in London, and the commercial hustle and bustle of New York City set it apart from other American cities. As a Russian writer said in 1857:

Starting in the morning until late in the evening Broadway and the adjoining streets are crowded with magnificently dressed women and with Americans rushing about on business. Despite the wide sidewalks, the crush is so great that one cannot make a step without poking someone with elbows or body. If you want to excuse yourself or if you wait for apologies, the American has flown by like an arrow.[51]

By the 1850s, New York City emporiums such as A. T. Stewart's and George Brodie's were elegant shopping destinations where ladies could browse for fabrics and try on imported or ready-made mantles and capes. The ready-made mantles and capes were made in New York City as Americanized versions of the original French versions. While women's ready-mades were primarily restricted to capes, umbrellas, and shoes, we have seen that men's ready-made clothing had become a large, diverse, and prominent industry by this time.

By the 1860s hoopskirts were on their way to becoming an early example of mass production in the women's apparel business. A large number of hoopskirt invoices from German Jewish firms dated to that decade (found in the Smithsonian Institution Warsaw Collection of Business Americana) provide important evidence about the earliest Jewish firms in the ladies' apparel industry. This industry seems to predate the cloak and suit firms that proliferated in the 1870s. Making hoopskirts, a fashion that only lasted about ten years, can be compared to later aspects of the women's business built on quick turnaround and niche manufacturing. Empress Eugénie of France set the style for enormous skirts in 1857 as skirts had gradually widened in the 1850s. The French invented hoopskirts made of circles of metal wire suspended by cloth tapes. For women burdened with four or five petticoats, hoopskirts or cage crinolines were a fashion innovation that, because they were much lighter, allowed them greater freedom of movement. The fashion quickly spread through all classes and to all countries, and hoopskirts were mass produced in factory-like settings by women workers without the elaborate tailoring or great expenditures of time in hand sewing that went into petticoats or other items of women's apparel.

The sewing machine could be used to sew the waistband and prepare the tapes that joined the hoops. Wire was used for the hoops, and the tapes were riveted to the hoops. The Smithsonian invoices show that even the preparation of the wire hoops and the woven cloth tapes was specialized. Firms such as M. Cohn and Roeder & Bernstein were located in lower Manhattan on Canal, Dey, Reade, and Warren Streets, as well as the Bowery, and supplied midwestern and southern merchants with requisite supplies through middlemen. The famous retailers, the Bloomingdale brothers, Joseph and Lyman (sons of German Jewish immigrants), made hoopskirts before establishing their first store in 1872, which sold fancy goods, hoopskirts, and corsets.

Further insight into the ways Jewish immigrants entered the early women's-wear business is provided by the story of the Trager and Garfunkel families.[52] Abraham Issac Trager was born in 1809 and immigrated to America in the 1850s, where he met the two Garfunkel brothers, also immigrants at the Beth Hamedrash synagogue on New York's Lower East Side. The rabbi of the synagogue, Abraham Ash, was a successful businessman involved in the hoopskirt industry and introduced the Garfunkels and Trager to the business when he married his eldest daughter to one of the Garfunkel brothers and then brought his son-in-law into the business. Ash also convinced Trager, who had immigrated with some established assets, to enter the hoopskirt business in 1860. Trager's eldest daughter married the other Garfunkel brother so the families became increasingly linked. The Trager and Garfunkel families eventually left New York City and set up branches of the business in Charleston, Louisville, and Chicago. These families became pioneers in this industry in the new cities, while maintaining branches in New York City. The experience of the Tragers and Garfunkels illustrates how family networks provided important sources of labor for new branches of the business as well as loans for the new enterprises.

Besides hoopskirts, corset manufacturing also attracted Jewish immigrants, and especially in the cities of Bridgeport and New Haven entrepreneurs took advantage of sewing machine factories to develop special machines to sew corsets. New Haven German Jews Max Adler and Issac Strouse, who were part of a vibrant German Jewish community in New Haven that dated to before the Civil War, began manufacturing corsets in the 1860s.[53] Following the war, in New Haven and elsewhere, the women's ready-made industry made its most important expansion with the making of loosely fitted mantles, capes, and outerwear by the 1870s and ready-made suits in the 1880s. Towards the end of the nineteenth century, women entered the workforce in mounting numbers and increasingly engaged in active sports like bicycling, skating, and tennis. Women's daytime dress became simpler, and the fashion for simpler washable clothing made popular the shirtwaist blouse and skirt of the 1890s. The tailor-made suit became the uniform for working girls, and coat and suit manufacturers as well as shirtwaist manufacturers multiplied to meet the demand for these items. In addition, department stores and mail-order companies provided a vast array of choices for consumers, and wholesale production for department stores grew quickly. *Wilson's Business Directory* (New York) listed 16 mantilla and cloak makers in 1855, 60 cloak and suit manufacturers in 1878, and the number was 205 by 1890. Over 20 German Jewish wholesale cloak and suit manufacturers made the clothes for Jordan Marsh in 1891, with 7 of them already in business in the 1870s: Danzig Brothers, Benjamin & Caspary, Goldman Brothers, Oppenheim, Collins & Co., Julius Oppenheimer, S. Rothschild & Brother, and Simonson & Weiss.[54] M. D. C. Crawford, long-term editor of *Women's Wear Daily* and historian of the industry, noted that pioneering German Jewish cloak and suit wholesale manufacturers were the backbone of the industry that supplied customers in specialty shops and department stores from the 1880s to World War I.[55] Crawford singled out three individuals who were especially important in the early industry— Edward Mayer, Max M. Schwarcz, and Max Meyer.[56] He credits them with producing Americanized versions of the best that Paris could offer as well as line-by-line copies that set the high quality of style that became available in department stores and specialty shops.

Edward Mayer's family came from Vienna around 1848, and he first worked as a designer in the fabric units of the Chicago department stores Mandel Brothers and Charles A. Stevens before moving to New York City in 1903. By 1916, he was manufacturing his own designs in a large modern factory in Woodside, Queens. Max M. Schwarcz, born in Budapest in 1863, was the son of a wool dealer. He immigrated to America in his teens and became a manu-

MANDEL BROTHERS, CHICAGO

Tailor Made Suits—The designs submitted for this fall and winter are the richest Mandel Brothers have ever created. Even the later productions of Paris, London or New York fail to surpass or equal them. This year the fabrics used are superior in quality and were purchased in such enormous quantities that an exceptionally modest price was secured. For this reason our garments are better values than offered a year ago. Do not fail to give accurate and consistent measurements.

619 Ladies' single-breasted blouse front Norfolk jacket suit, made of wide wale cheviot. Jacket is made with Norfolk plaits running over the shoulders and extending to the waist line in back, finished at bottom of waist with belt and short ripple skirt, lined with a fine quality twilled satin and buttoned down the front as shown in illustration. The skirt is made with the new dip front flaring flounce and lined with percaline. The entire garment is very handsomely stitched and comes in brown, blue or grey; price $10.00.

620 Ladies' single-breasted blouse front suit made of good quality homespun, jacket has new high collar finished with black satin edging, two satin bands down front and around the belt and is lined with mercerized sateen. The skirt is finished with two rows of satin at top of flounce and lined with percaline, colors grey or brown only; price $7.50.

719 Ladies' single-breasted military front eton suit, made of fine quality all wool cheviot. Jacket is finished around the collar, down the fronts, front darts and cuffs with finely stitched black satin, with a double row of small silk buttons and a narrow vest of velvet fastening with hooks and eyes, lined with heavy quality black taffeta. The skirt is made with graduated flounce, finished with several rows of stitching and lined with percaline, a regular $20.00 value; colors blue, brown or black; price $15.00.

894C Ladies' novelty blouse suit, made of good heavy weight homespun. The blouse is covered both back and front with very fine tucks, the fronts, belt, sleeves and novelty collar are finished with a narrow band of black taffeta and ornamented with fancy buttons, fastened in front with hooks and eyes and lined with twilled silk. The skirt is finished at top of flounce with three narrow tucks to match blouse and is lined with percaline. We expect this to be the most popular and best selling number in the catalogue, colors are blue, brown or grey; price $10.00.

540 Ladies' eton suit made of imported all wool serge. Jacket is made with wide sailor collar finished with narrow bands of satin, a band of satin also running down the front, around bottom, two front gores and on the sleeves. It is fastened with one row of buttons to a small vest and finished with loops and olives and lined with black satin. The skirt is finished with two satin bands to match jacket, and is lined with percaline; colors blue, brown or black; price $15.00.

720 Ladies' double-breasted straight front jacket suit, made of medium weight Venetian cloth. Jacket is made with large turn down collar and wide revers and lined with black satin. Skirt is made with flaring flounce finished with stitching and lined with percaline, a good, serviceable, well made suit at very moderate price; colors brown or grey only; price $10.00.

Ready-made "tailor-made suits" in Mandel Brothers catalog, ca. 1904. Mandel Brothers department store was founded in 1855 by Bavarian immigrants Solomon Mandel and his uncle Simon Klein. As the firm expanded, they were joined by Solomon's brothers, Leon and Emanuel. By the 1880s, the store employed approximately eight hundred people, and at the beginning of the twentieth century, the workforce had grown to more than three thousand. The Mandel family was also very active in local philanthropy; many of Chicago's Jewish businessmen helped to rebuild the city after the fire of 1871.

Courtesy Yeshiva University Museum.

facturer of high-quality cloaks and suits for Danzig Brothers, A. Friedlander & Company, and then his own firm. He was considered a great "student of fabrics."[57] Alsatian-born Max Meyer, the final pioneering cloak and suit manufacturer mentioned by Crawford, began work as a teenager for the A. Beller & Co. firm, became a designer and partner in the firm, and was one of the first people to achieve name recognition as a designer of American fashion. From 1897 on, he made two annual trips to Paris to see the collections and prepare ready-to-wear wholesale designs for American specialty and department stores.[58]

Sketch by Max Meyer for A. Beller & Co., ca. 1915.
The sketch is marked for Lord and Taylor. The collection of sketches at the Fashion Institute of Technology provides evidence that A. Beller & Co. was a wholesale manufacturer for Hickson's, Henri Bendel, Marshall Field's, Gimbel's, Lord and Taylor, and Franklin Simon among others.

Courtesy Special Collections, The Fashion Institute of Technology.

Eastern European Jews Enter the Garment Business

While Edward Mayer, Max M. Schwarcz, and Max Meyer were three prominent German Jews involved in the garment business into the 1900s, the mass immigration of eastern European Jews that began in the 1880s led to many changes in the women's-wear business at the time when many German Jews were leaving it. By 1900, the cloak and suit listing in the New York City directory was solidly Jewish, but the fact that many of these manufacturers were eastern European Jewish newcomers indicates the transition from German Jewish to eastern European ownership. The role of Jewish Americans in both the men's and women's garment industries illuminates an important feature of the Jewish American experience and adds to our understanding of American industrial history as well. The industry grew from family capitalism, the model for much of nineteenth-century business, to more modern forms. German Jews had the good fortune to enter this new industry in conditions of open economic opportunity, growing prosperity, and population expansion in the nineteenth century. They were able to use family networks and wholesaling expertise to achieve a prominent role in the development of the American garment industry. The German Jews initially steered clear of industries that had been traditionally closed to Jews or were monopolized by other ethnic groups. The apparel industry required low capital start-up and high flexibility and was attractive to people who valued self-employment. Whereas some German Jews remained in the men's clothing industry well into the twentieth century and left their imprint on that industry, the women's-wear industry would be transformed more substantially by the later emigration of eastern European Jews. After 1880, eastern European Jews were able to enter the clothing industry in large numbers because the women's ready-to-wear industry was expanding. The new immigrants easily obtained work in factories owned by their coreligionists and used those early jobs as stepping-stones to find opportunities to fulfill their own ambitions.

7 The Ready-Made Menswear Industry of Rochester, New York, 1848–1900

BERNARD SMITH

The Origins of Rochester's Menswear Industry and Jewish Community to 1870

A handful of German and Anglo-Jewish immigrants and their families founded the ready-made menswear industry of Rochester in the late 1840s and early 1850s. Meyer Greentree, Joseph Wile, Hirsch Britenstool, Sigmund Stettheimer, and Henry Michaels migrated to America as teenagers and young men, traveled inland from the East Coast, making their living and accumulating capital and commercial connections as peddlers, retail clerks, and tailors, and settled in Rochester. The city was a thriving manufacturing center and a commercial hub of the Erie Canal and the Genesee River Valley of western New York State. It already supported dozens of merchant tailoring establishments and clothing stores that did custom work and marketed men's ready-made wear produced in New York City and Boston. As the wheat belt moved westward and Rochester and its surrounding towns and villages grew more prosperous, Greentree and his fellow immigrants set out to build an industry and a community. Rochester became a center of

ready-made menswear manufacturing and a center of Jewish life.[1]

Adopting practices pioneered in the apparel manufacturing centers of the East Coast, Rochester's immigrant Jews rented factory and warehouse space in their town's center, secured their fabrics and other materials on credit from textile wholesalers, employed basic rules of thumb and standardized designs to make their garment patterns, hired skilled tailors to cut their cloth in bulk, and employed and organized seamstresses in a simple division of labor to do their sewing and finishing work. All their cutting was done in-house, and occasionally they employed tailors and seamstresses on their own premises to do more difficult sewing tasks, such as coat and vest assembly, while subcontracting simpler sewing jobs like pants assembly to homes or other shops in Rochester and its neighboring villages. More often, they subcontracted the entire sewing process to teams of tailors and their families and assistants, supplying them with cut and

bundled cloth, thread, buttons, and other materials. They then gathered the ensemble of coats, pants, and vests, and inspected, finished, pressed, and packaged them for sale and delivery to their own local retail shops, to their wholesale warehouses, or to jobbers and retailers in other towns. By 1870, Rochester's Jewish clothing manufacturers coordinated the production of three million dollars' worth of apparel in over eighty establishments, making Rochester the sixth-largest producer of menswear in the United States.[2]

Typical of many Jewish immigrant merchants and manufacturers in mid-nineteenth-century America, Rochester's German Jewish clothing makers organized their businesses as family partnerships and within ethnically rooted commercial alliances, alternately competing and cooperating for markets and profits. Like other Jewish immigrants to America, they maintained and relied on close ties with their families in Europe, with the larger Jewish communities of the East Coast, and with the tiny but growing number of Jewish enclaves scattered about the expanding western frontier. They used family labor, skills, money, and connections to organize and manage their affairs, to secure shop space, equipment, and trade credit, and to reach peddlers, retailers, and jobbers. A common language, a shared, if not always harmonious or conflict-free understanding of proper, just, or ethical dealing, and a set of multiple familial ties reduced some of the

The Upper Falls of the Genesee at Rochester, N.Y., From the East, **by John T. Young, 1836–37.** Access to major transportation routes, like the Erie Canal and the Genesee River, enabled Rochester to grow and develop as a major industrial center.

Courtesy Library of Congress, lithographer John Henry Bufford.

Man's overcoat, C. E. Furman, 1884–86. The label in this overcoat bears the name C. E. Furman, a firm based in Rochester, New York. From the nineteenth century on, Upstate New York was renowned for garment manufacturing, with certain cities specializing in particular products. Troy ("The Collar City") and Gloversville are well-known examples. Rochester was an important center of men's clothing production and fine tailoring.

Courtesy Rochester Museum and Science Center.

inherent risks and uncertainties of doing business. Their partnerships expanded, contracted, or dissolved in rhythm with the lifecycles of their families as well as in response to fluctuations in industrial and financial conditions.[3]

The early history of Rochester's first ready-made menswear firm, Greentree & Wile, provides a good example of how the industry originated and developed. Meyer Greentree was born in Hamburg in 1818, immigrated to the United States in 1840, and made his living as a peddler in New

England before he arrived in Rochester in 1843. He clerked for three years in a Jewish-owned dry goods firm, married in 1844, and established a merchant tailoring business in his wife's clothing store in 1846. His partner, Joseph Wile, was born in Altenglan, Germany, in 1812, immigrated to the United States in the early 1840s, lived in New York City and Connecticut for a time, and then married Greentree's sister and moved to Rochester in 1847. That year, Wile joined Greentree in a partnership to produce ready-made men's suits, the first

Kirstein family Hanukkah lamp, eastern Europe, nineteenth century. The Kirstein family was prominent in Rochester and in national cultural and civic life. Louis Kirstein was born in Rochester and was renowned for his leadership in Filene's and the Federated Group of department stores. He also served as an industrial mediator and as president of the Federation of Jewish Charities.

Courtesy Rochester Museum and Science Center.

such venture in Rochester. They established their manufacturing facilities along the Genesee River, which flowed through the center of town, and other ready-made clothing firms soon followed them there.

Meyer Greentree's other brother-in-law, Hirsch Britenstool, and Wile's younger brothers, Gabriel, Adam, and Abram, who had arrived from Bavaria a couple of years earlier, joined Greentree and Wile in 1848 and 1849. In 1866, the partners hired Max Brickner, another Bavarian Jew who immigrated to the United States seven years earlier. Brickner spent two years in Talladega, Alabama, and then moved to Rochester with the outbreak of the Civil War. He married Abram Wile's daughter,

Carrie, and took a job with the firm. In addition, Greentree and Wile spun off a number of ventures during its twenty-five-year existence. Britenstool and Julius Wile, Abram's son, opened and operated their own men's coat and suit factory between 1863 and 1866. Britenstool created another partnership with William Guggenheim, which lasted until 1870, while Julius joined his uncle Gabriel in two successive partnerships, G. & J. Wile, Cauffman, and Co. (1866–67) and G. & J. Wile and Co. (1869–77).[4]

The success of Greentree and Wile and a host of other similar partnerships between immigrant Jews laid the foundation for the growth of Rochester's Jewish community. Before 1850, the city's Jews were mostly single young men in their late teens and early twenties, in transit, who peddled their wares in the Genesee Valley region and locales further west. By the mid- to late 1850s, however, Rochester's Jewish population had settled and grown to about 350, a network of about fifty families (over half of them were involved in the clothing business). Joseph Wile and others incorporated Rochester's Congregation B'rith Kodesh, secured a rabbi and a building in which to hold services, and purchased a large plot of land in Rochester's Mt. Hope Cemetery. They founded the Hebrew Benevolent Society to aid poor Jewish peddlers as they came through town and established a parochial school where their children took lessons in Bible, Hebrew, and German, as well as in mathematics, English reading, spelling, and grammar. The economic success that had enabled Rochester's Jews to build these social institutions attracted more of their kin and extended community from else-where in the United States and from Germany. More Jewish immigrants settled in Rochester and became part of both a thriving Jewish community and an expanding Jewish clothing industry.[5]

Despite their early successes, however, Rochester's German Jewish clothing men often faced daunting challenges in plying their trade. They needed to master a new language and learn different commercial laws and business practices. They were a religious minority within a minority immigrant group, Jews within a predominately Christian German diaspora to a predominately Anglo-Protestant town. Yet, they employed a variety of people, including native Rochesterians who had owned or worked in local custom-wear establishments in the 1820s and 1830s, an expanding pool of Gentile German and British immigrant tailors who arrived in Rochester in the 1840s and 1850s, and large numbers of young seamstresses from the city and its surrounding villages and farms. The success of their ventures relied on their ability to craft mutually acceptable employment relations with each of these groups.[6]

Indeed, before the German Jews arrived on the scene, employment relations in Rochester's custom tailoring trade had occasionally been quite stormy. The city had been a center of the Second Great Awakening, a Christian Revivalist movement partly fed by social and political tensions in the city's trades. This tension, which had been caused by Rochester's industrialization, had made Rochester a hotbed of labor and political unrest in the 1830s and 1840s.[7] Rochester's journeymen tailors had struck on a couple of occasions

and had joined the city's other skilled craftsmen in opposing debtor's prison, convict labor (used on the Erie Canal and in the local boot and shoe industry), and the due bill system (payment in script by cash-short firms). In addition, they had championed mechanics lien laws (giving employees first claims to company assets in case of bankruptcy), the ten-hour day, free public education, workers cooperatives, and political clubs.[8]

The birth and expansion of the German Jewish clothing industry in the early 1850s, occurring in the wake of the dramatic events of the 1830s and 1840s and coinciding with a regional and national economic boom, motivated Rochester's growing numbers of young seamstresses to put forth their own claims for just treatment. In April 1853, hundreds of them organized to demand higher wages and to be paid in cash. It was the first time that women in Rochester and its surrounding towns had organized on such a vast scale, and their activism caught the public's attention. Two newspapers came out in support of their demands, noting that "the benevolent, moral and religious people" of Rochester would support them. They quickly won a 25 percent piece rate increase, secured agreement from all but three of their employers that in the future they would receive their wages in cash, and formed the Seamstresses Protective Union, a combination employment and apprenticeship bureau, mutual assistance society, and producer's cooperative.[9]

The economic and political crises of the Civil War decade further challenged Rochester's employer classes, its Jewish clothing manufacturers prominently among them. Wartime price inflation led to dramatic declines in real wages, strikes, and public protests. Rochester's tailors struck and won a 25 percent pay increase in 1865, a rise commensurate with increases granted earlier to tailors in other manufacturing centers. But, local newspapers again highlighted the plight of Rochester's seamstresses, and editorialists argued that the introduction of the sewing machine had reduced piece rates for hand sewers to the miserably low levels earned by Rochester's servant girls. In marked contrast, some of Rochester's German Jewish clothing employers were very prosperous men. Meyer Greentree, Sigmund Stettheimer, Julius Wile, Gabriel Wile, Hirsch Britenstool, and Henry Michaels were among Rochester's wealthiest residents—each earned enough in 1863 to be assessed the Civil War income tax, which hit only the top 1 percent of the northern population. Stettheimer's income of $39,651 made him the third-richest man in town. The newspapers urged these men and their contractors to deal justly with the seamstresses. Stettheimer responded, taking the lead by unilaterally raising his wages, and the local press praised him for doing so.[10]

Did religion play a role in these labor disputes? Did the seamstresses make their claims against the industry's Gentile contractors or against its Jewish manufacturers? Did Rochester's working and poorer classes expect or receive better or worse treatment from Rochester's Jewish clothiers than from other employers in town? We don't know the answers to these questions, but we do know that the confrontations between the clothing industry and its seamstresses affected the livelihood of many Rochesterians, for it was the second-largest employer in town. We also know that Rochester experienced other large and materially consequential strikes during the 1850s and 1860s. And we know that both Rochester's Gentile and Jewish elites funded and supported poverty relief programs and the education of the poor through their voluntary benevolent societies and that they often held interfaith religious services and joint meetings of their respective charitable societies to discuss poverty and other communal concerns. But we do not know the extent to which such paternalist or corporate considerations limited private profit-seeking behavior in Rochester's labor marketplace. Still, at least during the wartime dispute, it is likely that Rochester's Jewish clothing manufacturers believed that they were being held to a higher moral standard and that they could secure their recently won prosperity only by negotiating relationships with their Gentile contractors and employees deemed mutually respectful and just by the wider Rochester community. They must have sensed that maintaining a hard line on wages in the face of rising prices made them vulnerable to charges of profiteering at the expense of men and women whose loved ones were fighting for the survival of the American republic. Indeed, Jewish merchants and clothiers from other towns who did contract work for the Union government during the Civil War were often unjustly tarred with such charges. It is not unreasonable to conclude, therefore, that Sigmund Stettheimer acted boldly and charitably with these facts in mind.[11]

Rochester's Clothing Industry on the Cutting Edge, 1873–1900

Well into the nineteenth century, most of the menswear manufacturers of the United States lacked the means and know-how to design and make apparel that could successfully compete against the style, variety, comfort, and fit of tailored wear, the low prices and availability of second-hand garments, or the low costs of home-made apparel. Ready-made menswear markets were limited to shirts, collars, and cuffs; to work clothing and undergarments; and to less fashionable and lower-priced coats, vests, and pants. Manufacturers simply did not know enough about the average and variation of the male physique to design patterns for more stylish and better-fitting menswear. They used simple labor-intensive methods of production that limited their potential to generate cost-reducing innovation. The costs of distributing their goods to distant places far from navigable waterways—and of accessing timely information on apparel demand from widely scattered markets—were often prohibitive. In terms of sheer numbers, the men's clothing industry of the United States was dominated by small and medium-sized, labor-intensive, single-product, and functionally specialized producers of mid- and low-priced garments. Most apparel firms had little direct access to final consumers, formal credit markets, or textile manufacturers, and regularly succumbed to sharp and dramatic cycles of cutthroat competition.[12]

The Civil War and the material and social development of the United States during the late nineteenth century changed the garment industry, or at least part of it.[13] As aggregate production and per capita consumption of menswear expanded (Tables 1 and 2 on pages 97–98), Rochester's clothing manufacturers, slowly at first but aggressively in time, took full advantage of data developed by the Union Army's quartermaster corps during the Civil War to design coat, vest, and pants patterns that more accurately reflected the sizes and shapes of larger numbers of men. They adopted newly invented coal-, gas-, and electric-powered cutting, sewing, and pressing machinery. With the ever-increasing sophistication, productive efficiency, and ease and specialization of use allowed by these machines, the manufacturers gradually developed and adopted low-cost assembly-line techniques and an extraordinarily detailed division of labor. They took full advantage of the construction of the transcontinental railroad, its feeder lines, and its accompanying telegraph network to gain easy and less costly access to markets and information across the entire expanse of the American continent. Finally, Rochester's menswear manufacturers successfully tapped the nation's rapidly expanding market for ready-made apparel created by the growing size, prosperity, and number of its cities, the expansion of its commercial agricultural frontier, the waves of immigration, and internal migration.[14]

By the mid-1880s, Rochester's dozen plus clothing companies employed two to three thousand workers in their factories

and ten to twelve thousand more in contract shops and tenement houses scattered
throughout the city making coats, vests,
pants, and suits for a national market. By
1899, the city's twenty or so major apparel
firms organized the manufacture and sale
of over eleven million dollars' worth of
men's clothing and employed several hundred
contractors (see Table 3 on page 98).
Rochester's leading menswear companies
relocated their factories from the banks of
the Genesee River to North St. Paul Street
on a succession of properties adjacent to
the Central Railroad depot that came to be
known as "Clothiers Row." From there,
they received materials from New England
and Europe, coal from Pennsylvania, and
wholesale and retail agents from throughout the country. In turn, they sent hundreds
of salesmen and millions of dollars' worth
of clothing every fall and spring season to
their showrooms in New York City,
Chicago, and San Francisco, and to retail
stores, wholesale houses, and jobbers
throughout the country.[15]

But Rochester's clothing makers also
understood early on that the menswear
market was an aggregation of market
segments, distinguishable by product,
price, style, material, and workmanship.
They knew that men had different clothing
needs in different seasons and that their
class, income, age, or occupation influenced
what they wanted or needed, and determined what prices they were willing and
able to pay. Men from the Northeast and
from cities had different needs or tastes
than men from the West or from small
towns or farms. Immigrant men from
different parts of the world, with varying

amounts of resources at their command and
with a desire to fit in with American
clothing norms, also purchased different
kinds of apparel.

Slowly but with great determination,
Rochester's clothing manufacturers began
to distinguish themselves by designing,
making, and selling better-fitting, more
elegant, and more varied ready-made
menswear for the previously untapped
middle- and upper-income market. This
strategy compelled them to dramatically
reorganize the ways they did business.
During the late 1880s and 1890s, they established direct, special, and exclusive ties with
high-end textile houses throughout New
England and Europe, and built large,
capital-intensive and functionally integrated factory-warehouses on "Clothiers
Row." They coordinated design, cutting,
assembly, finishing, and warehousing
operations, which ensured greater control
over their work organization, production
standards and speed, and product quality.
Those who chose to compete for the
high-end market secured the services of
greater numbers of skilled tailors and
employed hand-tailoring techniques more
intensively. Those who reached for the
mid-priced market used more machine-
intensive and rationalized assembly
processes. Some firms continued to rely on
outside contractors for their less expensive
and fashionable lines of garments or during
periods of unexpectedly high demand, but
if they did so they maintained tight control
over their contractors' operations and
access to the industry.[16]

By the turn of the century, Rochester's
menswear makers were displaying and

Interior of the Adler-Rochester Factory, Rochester, ca. 1910. The L. Adler Bros. & Co. factory was designed by Albert Kahn, famed for his designs for Ford automobile plants in Detroit. This factory building was 90 percent glass, providing ample daylight for the twelve hundred workers employed there. The factory also featured a restaurant, first aid facilities, and reading and smoking rooms. Menswear factories developed before women's clothing was mass manufactured. Early on, factories incorporated new working methods, including divided labor, which was specifically designed to enhance efficiency and production output.

Courtesy Department of Rare Books and Special Collections, University of Rochester Library.

Michaels, Stern & Co. employment card, 1916. Employment cards record the wages of the highly skilled cutters and tailors and the various semiskilled and unskilled workers who created the suits and coats that made Rochester's menswear famous. Cards such as this provide a rare glimpse into the generally anonymous and invisible world of factory production.

Courtesy Department of Rare Books and Special Collections, University of Rochester Library.

marketing their wares to thousands of wholesale buyers and retail agents visiting their large showrooms in Rochester, New York City, Chicago, and San Francisco every fall and spring season. They advertised heavily in trade papers and continued to expand and build close relationships with retailers throughout the country. By 1900, Rochester was recognized as the nation's premier center for the manufacture of higher- and medium-grade brand-name ready-made men's apparel.[17] Yet arguably, what made the development of Rochester's men's clothing industry most distinctive and what made its emergence as a center of high-end manufacturing possible, was that it was exclusively owned and tightly controlled by, at most, two dozen family partnerships that had been meticulously built and nurtured over three generations. It thrived on the accumulated experiences, skills, ideas, capital, and commercial interconnections of its German Jewish community.

The most prominent houses in Rochester in 1890 and through the turn of the century could trace their origins to Rochester's first Jewish firms and families. Shared and common histories, as well as interlocking business interests, intimately tied them to one another. Wile, Stern, and Company, an employer of 800 production workers in Rochester, had evolved from Meyer Greentree's and Joseph Wile's original firm into a partnership of Joseph's sons, Julius and Isaac Wile, and his son-in-law, Simon Stern.[18] Michaels, Stern & Company, with seven hundred workers in Rochester, a dozen nationally known traveling salesmen, a New York City showroom, and annual

sales of $1.2 million, was a partnership of Henry Michaels, one of the original founders of the Rochester industry, his sons Joseph and Marcus Michaels, and his sons-in-law, Morley A. Stern and Emanuel Friedlich.[19] Cauffman & Dinkelspiel, one of the town's leading makers of high-end menswear, was a partnership between Marcus Cauffman and brothers Meyer and Abram Dinkelspiel. It had emerged from a series of enterprises built in the 1860s and 1870s, and their leading principals were now members of other Rochester firms.[20] Garson, Kerngood & Company was really a manufacturing hub of a network of family enterprises in Rochester, Buffalo, Syracuse, Oswego, and Denver. It was led by brothers Leopold, Henry, and Moses Garson; Leopold's son-in-law E. Kerngood; Moses Garson's sons, David M. and Joseph M. Garson; and Morris and Theodore Meyer.[21]

Hart, Schaffner & Marx at Wallachs stylebook, spring/summer 1921. Hart, Schaffner & Marx became one of the largest men's clothing manufacturers in the United States in the early twentieth century. The Chicago company was a primary competitor to several Rochester firms. It purchased Hickey Freeman, one of Rochester's last remaining quality menswear companies, in the 1960s.

Courtesy Special Collections, Gladys Marcus Library at the Fashion Institute of Technology.

Finally, Stein-Bloch and L. Adler Brothers, each known nationally for making high-quality men's coats and suits and each employing over eight hundred men and women in their factories on "Clothiers Row," had come out of Stein-Adler, the leading firm in Rochester during the 1870s. Nathan Stein, his three sons, Louis, Abram, and Simon Stein, his son-in-law Samuel Weil, and Leopold Bloch and Abram Katz made up Stein-Bloch. Levi Adler and his brothers Abram, Simon, and Solomon comprised L. Adler Brothers.[22] Material, social, cultural, ideological, and spiritual ties linked these men and their enterprises together. They entertained one another in the Eureka Club, the city's elite Jewish social club; they prayed together at B'rith Kodesh, the city's oldest Jewish synagogue; they read and debated matters of business, culture, religion, and politics in the *Jewish Tidings*, the paper of Rochester's Jewish community; and they discussed, defined, and defended their collective business interests in the Rochester Clothiers' Exchange, the local clothing manufacturers association whose members were mostly, if not entirely, German Jews.

Promotional figurines of Adler-Rochester tailors, ca. 1920. Pride in high-quality tailoring and innovative factory production methods made Rochester an important menswear center in the nineteenth and twentieth centuries.

Courtesy Rochester Museum and Science Center.

The Quest for Growth and the Challenge of Late-Nineteenth-Century Anti-Semitism

The Broad Background

America experienced increasingly turbulent material and ideological conflict in the late nineteenth century. This conflict was the consequence of great shifts in the distribution of income and wealth between its different industrial sectors, geographical regions, and socioeconomic classes and of waves of mass immigration from Asia and southern and eastern Europe, including from the Jewish Pale of Settlement in Poland and Russia. New forms of liberal, republican, populist, and socialist movements and ideologies contended for public favor. These battles for property, power, and ideas collided with the world that the German Jewish clothing manufacturers in Rochester, New York City, and elsewhere were making for themselves. Ominously, for America's Jews generally and for its clothing men in Rochester more specifically, a racialist understanding of religion, ethnicity, and nationality gained some favor in both the popular and elite press and public. America's German Jews, in part because of their history and obvious material success, were seen by some to be a distinctly clever, ambitious, cosmopolitan, and mercantile people. In a nation divided on how to understand and judge such traits of character or biology, these perceptions could be problematic. German Jews, some of whom were occasionally seduced by such race mythologies, found that they could cut both ways. The arrival of masses of impoverished and struggling Russian and

Polish Jews whose blood they shared gave rise to a counter-characterization of "the Jew." In the fractious political, economic, and social environment of nineteenth-century America, proponents of an increasingly popular and virulent form of Anglo-Protestant nativism and nationalism deemed these Jews to be an especially devious, grasping, disloyal, and cutthroat race. Such views had direct, concrete, and material effects on the Jews and their clothing industry, especially in Rochester.[23]

The Challenge of Marketing Jewish Ready-Made Clothing

Creating and supplying a market for medium- and high-grade ready-made apparel required more than the development of innovative designs and ready access to skilled labor and managerial talent. Manufacturers in Rochester seeking to build a national market for their quality menswear also had to overcome ready-made clothing's long-standing reputation for being cheap and inelegant, originating as it did in the slop and secondhand clothing trades and in the manufacture of military uniforms for enlisted men. Its reputation was often inseparable from ethnic, religious, or class prejudices against the Jews who manufactured it, especially among America's Gentile upper classes.[24] In 1883, the ready-made menswear industry's leading trade paper lamented that the menswear industry was the largest employer in New York State and the seventh-largest employer in the country, yet it rarely got the journalistic attention it merited. It stated, "The leading journals of the different cities fail to report its condition, and mention the clothing trade and its members only in alleged humorous details of some Hebrew dealer's transaction with customers."[25]

Competition for middle- and especially upper-income patrons between higher-end ready-made producers, most of whom were Jews, and merchant tailors, most of whom were Gentiles, brought these associations to the surface. In an 1889 editorial debate on the future of the menswear business, the leading newspaper of the merchant tailoring trade chastised the ready-made trade for attempting to reach beyond its limits and beyond the boundaries, "which it can never pass, and over which it glares jealously at its old and successful precursor, . . . the 'art of arts' and those who live by it." It told its gentlemen readers that one must not neglect on account of any "foolish fear" of being "accused of a race prejudice" that "the clothing trade has been absorbed, and is today, as certain speeches of its leading men before their own religious conclaves attest, . . . a wholly and fundamentally Jewish proprietary institution."[26] It praised the "success and worldly prosperity" won by this "poor, miserable and oppressed" people in practicing "the only respectable calling for which they were, by nature and circumstance, fitted to adopt." But it also reminded its fashion literate and Gentile audience how clever Jews were to find a system that gave "a very small percentage of men an almost miraculous perfect fit, just enough to insure the scheme a reputation," and how the majority of their customers

contented themselves with "the cheapness of the article," which made up "for any trifling discrepancy, as an inch or two gone wrong, either way." The review recounted for its readership the fact that the ready-made system originated with the European Jews who had always been "the great contractors of any cheap class of commodities." And finally, it made its most critical and damning observation, that the ready-made trade, the Jew, and the sweatshop were inseparable: "The *writing on the wall* of the Semitic clothier is *We will not be undersold*, and he reasons justly that, if he does not take advantage of the situation some competitor would, and hence drive him to . . . failure. The declaimer against the *sweating* or any other *white slave* system must look to Congress for redress, not to merchants, who see their own ruin in a failure to take every possible advantage of their fellow creatures."[27]

More direct assaults on the character of the Jewish makers and wholesalers of ready-made goods were not uncommon and occasionally quite insidious, or downright vicious. These came from regionally based jobbers who eschewed any and all civic restraint in defense of their turf against outside competition. They posed an especially difficult challenge for Rochester's clothing men who were increasingly reliant during the 1880s on their traveling drummers to reach the country retail trade directly in order to secure more even and steady sales throughout the year.[28] The most outrageous example occurred in 1890 when Ed L. Huntley, a Chicago-based catalogue distributor of menswear, advertised his goods as "Honest Gentile Clothing." He packed his spring 1890 catalogue with dozens of classic degrading and demonizing caricatures of the "plundering," "parasitic," "vulgar," "fraudulent," and "loathsome" race of Jews. He urged retailers to avoid being fooled by Jewish drummers, wholesalers, or manufacturers, "Don't be a Mark," for their deceitful sales methods and their sham assertions about the quality of their goods. Huntley's catalogue bellowed, "There is certainly enough patriotism among the masses of the American merchants to maintain a Gentile clothing firm that is willing to do the square thing; and there is, unquestionably, a widespread desire among the better class of the Gentile store-keepers to check the exorbitant prices charged by the Jews."[29] Another assault was launched in the summer of 1890 by Dickson Brothers Clothiers of Tacoma (Washington) against Gross Brothers, a Jewish firm and a leading regional competitor. Dickson's circular to its retailers that summer read, "To the Thinking Public! Do not waste your time and money trying to get the best of the Jew clothing house, but trade at a White American House, where you will be treated like a friend whether you buy or not."[30]

The Jewish clothing manufacturers in Rochester and elsewhere successfully beat off these attacks on their honor and character and hit back in equal measure through their industry associations and their trade and ethnic newspapers. The *Clothing Gazette* and the *Jewish Tidings* of Rochester ran several editorial and satirical pieces between 1890 and 1892 denouncing Huntley and the Dickson Brothers as con artists and their so-called sales methods as repulsive with titles like "A Wholesale Slander of Jews" and "Despicable Act in Tacoma." The *Tidings* condemned "Jew hatred" and the sordid character of "Jew haters," calling Huntley a "drunkard, debauchee, thief, and swindler" and decrying the "audacity of the Dickson Brothers." It quoted Martin Rosenbaum, traveling salesman for Rothschild, Hays & Co., a Rochester clothing manufacturer doing business in Tacoma: "I forgot for an instance that I was living in the closing quarter of the nineteenth century, and was carried back . . . to the blackest midnight of the middle ages, when ignorance, superstition and crime hung, like a pall, over all Europe." The *Clothing Gazette* investigated and broadly publicized Huntley's checkered career as a Chicago clothing merchant: a partnership gone badly, fraud and other violations of the law, and bouts with alcoholism. It asked rhetorically of one of Huntley's clothing suppliers, W. S. Peck, "a well-known, honorable and respected clothing manufacturer" and "a Christian Gentleman, a trustee of the first Baptist church of Syracuse, and former nominee for that city's mayoralty," how and why he would patronize such a disreputable and dishonest fellow. The trade paper also solicited and printed a public letter from prominent Chicago merchants, including Charles Kellogg and H. N. Higinbotham of Marshall Field & Co., denouncing business methods that are "calculated to provoke race prejudice" as "un-American" and "un-Christian."[31]

Jewish clothing manufacturers sometimes used self-deprecating and self-aggrandizing Yiddish folk humor to deal with the less vicious but still unflattering caricatures of themselves and their trade. The *Clothing Gazette* printed a number of short satirical pieces, often written in the Yiddish vernacular with titles like "Who Sold Dot Coat," "Schnorrers," and "Spring poetry—The Hebrew Clothing Drummer" written by fictional characters like Rube Hoffenstein and Jacob Yokel. They inevitably involved encounters between a stereotypical crafty, but basically honest, Jewish salesman and an equally clichéd country bumpkin or rowdy customer in which only the wit and wiles of the former got him the sale, or out of a nasty fight.[32] In one piece, written in 1888 under the title "Men and Things," the paper offered one such episode:

SPEAKING OF KANSAS, do you know Brunswick & Rosenfeld of Wellington? Well if you don't, you can give a good guess from their names that they are Jews--- THEIR names don't appear on the sign, however, which contains the legend, "GOLDEN EAGLE CLOTHING STORE,"--- NOT long ago a rough and grizzly cowboy, looking about as religious as the unrepentant thief on Calvary, drew rein in front of their place and declared with many oaths that he'd be hornswoggled if he wasn't glad to strike a Christian clothing house, that he'd be dodgasted if he'd trade with Jews etc.--- HE spent about a hundred dollars, and when he got through swore he had never been so well treated in his life, and insisted on 'blowing off' the whole establishment. ----AFTERWARD he sent all his friends there with the hearty recommendation to "trade at the Golden Eagle, boys! They ain't no d--d Jews there."[33]

Indeed, several Rochester manufacturers opened wholesale and retail outlets throughout the nation in the 1880s and 1890s, carrying names that offered no clue of the ethnic origins of their owners. In 1888, for example, Rothschild, Hays & Co. opened stores in Indianapolis and St. Louis and called them both the Model Clothing Company. All of the major Rochester clothing manufacturers sent flowers and congratulations to the firm at their grand openings.[34]

Credit

Amidst the turmoil of an America torn by ethnic and racial conflict, access to trade credit outside of the familial confines of parents, uncles, brothers, and cousins could itself depend on individual and collective self-defense of one's character. This posed a major challenge to Jewish firms who sought to operate on a larger scale, purchase more expensive and higher-quality textiles, and offer more attractive terms to retailers and wholesale houses in distant markets. Rochester's clothing men, in particular, could not pursue their competitive strategies without getting and issuing credit. For this, they needed to establish a reputation for honesty, intelligence, clear-headedness, good judgment, and prudence. During the 1880s, attacks on the creditworthiness of Jewish clothing manufacturers and jobbers or on the allegedly underhanded or usurious practices of Jewish merchant lenders were not uncommon. In November and December 1883, failures among some large Jewish clothing and cloth jobbing houses ignited anti-Semitic tirades from some textile mills and credit men. *Gibson's Monthly Review of the Clothing and Furnishing Trades* came to the defense of the Jewish clothing and textile houses with two editorials entitled "Do Not Injure Your Neighbor's Credit" and "Slander." The pieces supported the *Journal of Commerce*, which called on the "bushwackers of credit" and the "Vampires of Wall Street" to stop their malicious and illegitimate method of competition. It also cited approvingly the *Economist*'s rendering of the episode, blaming the mills themselves for recklessly offering "every sort of inducement to the Israelitish [sic] trade" and then pelting them with mud, allowing "their tongues full sway to speak all sorts of slanderous expressions against their credit" when some failed, "for no other cause but simply because they are Jews." The paper concluded with, "We think it would have been better if some of our Christian friends would only show a little more magnanimity instead of the littleness and narrow-minded spirit of their hearts, the effect in every way would be grander and nobler. Do, gentlemen, stop this ugly back-biting and slanderous gossip about the credit of our Jewish friends."[35]

Clothing manufacturers who sought to build a strong and stable presence in national markets were required to extend their distribution outlets beyond their old family-based retail networks and to begin to grant trade credit to retailers they did not know. This was risky business. They needed to make accurate judgments about the character and creditworthiness of the men who ran the retail shops and keep themselves from granting overly generous payment terms in the heat of a competitive sales season. Retailers, Jew or Gentile, often misrepresented their own financial condition, repeatedly stretched out their outstanding accounts, or extracted zero percent financing during periods of intense competition. Bankrupt retailers sometimes assigned their remaining assets to preferred creditors, typically their closest business associates or their friends and family

members. In January 1885, the *Clothing Gazette* offered the manufacturer's take on these matters in a biting satirical piece entitled "The Latest Declaration of Independence." Six fictional retailers—A. Goniff, John Machullah, Al. Schorem, Leo Kutspur, Ten Per Cent, and T. Wolf—declared their inalienable right "to long credits that would never be paid off, to go bankrupt and have their cases resolved to the benefit of their preferred creditors [i.e., their families] . . . to be left alone by Bradstreet, Dunn and other credit rating agencies, and to extract special favors from drummers and manufacturers."[36]

The first city and national associations of ready-made clothing manufacturers were formed to deal almost exclusively with these retail problems. The Clothiers Association of Rochester, the predecessor of the Rochester Clothiers' Exchange, was founded in 1883 with only this purpose in mind. Its bylaws committed its members to collectively resist late orders and overly generous credit terms and return policies. It obliged them to share reliable and accurate information on the credit standing and trade practices of their distributors, to develop uniform and responsible commercial practices to guide their internal and external relations, and to settle their trade disputes between themselves and others under the auspices of the organization.[37]

Fire Insurance

Finally, obtaining access to competitively priced fire insurance proved another major challenge to those Jewish clothing manufacturers who sought to reach national markets by scaling up and vertically integrating their manufacturing plant. Their businesses were continually plagued by costly and deadly fires due to their location in dense urban neighborhoods, the use of flammable material in concentrated spaces, the employment of equipment, lubricants, and power sources that could set it alight, and stockpiling goods that could be easily damaged by fire, smoke, or water.[38] In the early 1880s, leading clothing manufacturers attempted to reduce these risks and to lower their insurance premiums by moving their facilities to less crowded neighborhoods. In the late 1880s and early 1890s, they built or rented newer buildings whose architecture and construction incorporated the latest fire-retardant materials and firefighting equipment. In November 1888, a large fire at a major metal works in Rochester, which took the lives of thirty-two people, impelled one of Rochester's leading apparel manufacturers to warn his colleagues on Clothiers Row to be on their guard against similar disasters. By then, most of Rochester's major clothing firms had, or were in the process of, building plants that incorporated all of the latest features to prevent and deal with fires.[39]

The most prominent manufacturers in all of the major apparel centers petitioned insurance companies and their industry associations to make finer distinctions between good and bad fire risks in the clothing trades. Elite firms, who designed, cut, and marketed their garments but did not assemble them, asked underwriters to make distinctions between cutting factories and sewing contractors, claiming that their operations were conducted under less crowded conditions and generated less flammable litter and waste than sewing and

"'Mameniu!' Including an Elegy to the Triangle Fire Victims," sheet music, 1911. Rochester's men's clothing industry confronted the challenge of dealing with fire risks long before the Triangle Shirtwaist tragedy. German-Jewish owners fought against popular and official perceptions that Jewish firms were particularly fire prone.

Courtesy YIVO Institute.

pressing shops.[40] Large and well-known firms called on insurers to stop punishing them for the irresponsible behavior and dishonesty of others who the insurers claimed were quick to make false or exaggerated damage claims after fires.[41]

But here again, ethnicity, race, and its contested meanings framed the economic calculations and responses to fire risks. In the late summer of 1890, a report by the fire marshal of the city of Boston that alleged "a mania for arson among Polish Jews" in his city set off a storm of protest and indignation in Rochester and other Jewish clothing centers and a public debate in city newspapers around the country. He claimed that Russian and Polish Jews caused 56 percent of Boston's fires and that 88 percent of these were fully insured. The implications of his claims were clear: at best, Jews were a bad fire risk; at worst, Jews caused their own fires to collect insurance. The responses to these claims varied. An agent for the Boylston Insurance Company announced in a Detroit-based insurance journal that his firm took no "Jew Risk" whatsoever, under any circumstances. He noted, "We wiped the last risk on property owned by Jews off our books a year and a half ago, and wouldn't take another Jew risk if we knew it. When I say that, I refer not alone to the Polish and Russian Jews, but to people of that sect of all nationalities. They resort to all sorts of dodges to get insured. They Americanize their names or adopt a firm name." The *Jewish Tidings* of Rochester jumped into the fray, alleging that several reputable New York City insurance companies had paid a private firm to set up a "Bureau for the Prediction of Fires," one of whose staff members was chiefly responsible for investigating "Hebrew Risks." It revealed that the companies agreed not to take risks on property owned by persons whose names ended with "ski" or "sky."[42]

In a response to the Boston report, the New York City fire marshal offered a different take on fire risks in his town. He preferred to separate German Jews, whom he considered to be as honorable as any other people, from Polish Jews, whom he found to be rather disreputable. The New York official asserted, "the Polish Jews are a different race," that they were responsible for most of the fires on the Lower East Side

of Manhattan, igniting them in order to engage in theft during the ensuing chaos, and that they would never turn one another in for their crimes. The Detroit insurance paper backed up the New York official's distinction between German and Russian-Polish Jews, arguing that the former were good law-abiding citizens, many of them "substantial and trusted businessmen," while the latter were of a lower class, often criminals, having been degraded in their moral sensibilities by Russian tyranny and persecution. The paper argued that the moral hazard involved in insuring the properties of German Jews was quite low. But interestingly, it also noted that the Boston fire marshal's data itself indicated that religion was correlated with, but was not the cause of, high fire risks among Russian and Polish Jews. Instead, it argued, the greater fire risks associated with Russian-Polish Jews was really a function of the kinds of businesses they ran—cheap clothing, secondhand stores, and junk shops—subject to accidental conflagration regardless of who managed them.[43]

But the *Jewish Tidings* of Rochester minced no words in responding to the fire officials of both Boston and New York and to the actions of the fire insurance companies. It called the Boston fire marshal's report a "Vile Slander." It called for the dismissal of the New York City fire marshal, arguing that no evidence existed to support the claim that fires were more prevalent among Polish Jews than any other people in New York or that Polish Jews were any more "addicted to arson" than anyone else. The *Jewish Tidings*' response in defense of its coreligionists revealed its own understanding of the relationship between nationality, religion, and race; it affirmed a close association between the first and the third while denying the existence of a close association between the second and the third. The *Tidings* proclaimed that Polish Jews were as reliable and honest as Polish Catholics or Protestants. It jumped on the insurance companies for the absurd policy of refusing to insure any man whose name ended with "ski" or "sky" or on the "ridiculous means" they went to in using the "scam" services of the "Bureau for the Prediction of Fires." Revealingly, the paper

of Rochester's German Jewish elite responded with, "The standard of intelligence among . . . [Polish Jews] may not be high, but we assert the standard of honor is." And it concluded with, "It is unfair and it is wrong, moreover, to discriminate against nationality. The Poles may not be as advanced a state of civilization as the Americans or the Germans or the French, but they are not a race of criminals or barnburners by any means, and they should not be so branded. . . . Shame upon such pitiful narrow-mindedness!"[44]

Conclusion

Rochester's German Jewish clothing manufacturers faced even more difficult challenges as businessmen and as Jews in Rochester itself during the 1890s. Their commitment to compete in national markets for higher-quality, brand-name menswear required them to invest large sums in new capital equipment and factories, and in hiring, training, organizing, and motivating hundreds of skilled cutters, tailors, and factory supervisors, and thousands of unskilled and semiskilled hand sewers and sewing machine operators. They determined that their new investments would yield them profits only if they also acquired and maintained complete mastery over the organization of production in their shops—over hiring and dismissal, work allocation, production quotas, pay scales, training and apprenticeship rules. In their way stood several local assemblies of the Knights of Labor, led by a cadre of skilled cutters and tailors commit-

ted to maintaining long-standing craft traditions and practices.[45]

Henry Michaels, Joseph Cauffman, Sol Wile, Abram Adler, Max Brickner, Bernard Rothschild, Nathan Stein, and their colleagues, twenty-one German Jewish clothing manufacturers in all, confronted the Knights of Labor in the winter and spring of 1890 and 1891. Proud of their commercial and industrial success, certain of their right to manage their businesses as they saw fit, and confident in their ability to secure the control of their workplace, these Jewish manufacturers organized as the Rochester Clothiers' Exchange and saw opposition from their cutters, their city's labor movement, and the remnants of the national organization of the Knights of Labor. In the ensuing struggle nearly 20,000 Rochesterians, directly or indirectly dependent on them for work and wages, were left idle for weeks, and in some cases, for months. The Knights organized a

Office of the president of Hickey-Freeman Company (Jeremiah G. Hickey seated and Jacob L. Freeman standing), 1912. The city of Rochester stood for high-quality men's clothing; Hickey-Freeman, established in 1899, is a lasting reminder of the city's early dominance in fine menswear. In 1912, the firm adopted a policy of focusing on the manufacture of high-end ready-made clothing.

Courtesy Department of Rare Books and Special Collections, University of Rochester Library.

Man's suit, Hickey-Freeman, ca. 1910.

Courtesy Hickey-Freeman Co., Inc.

national boycott against their goods and secured a statement of condemnation against them by the Farmers' Alliance of the United States. Among those supporting Rochester's clothing manufacturers and their fight against the Knights were the business elite of Rochester, the leading trade paper of the American garment industry, and a newly emergent union of clothing workers, the United Garment Workers of America.[46]

Additional research is needed to uncover the ethnic dimensions of the labor struggle that saw twenty-one German Jewish manufacturers wage a prolonged and bitter battle against a workingman's organization led by German, British, and Irish American cutters and tailors and representing several thousand predominately native-born workers. Enough evidence exits, however, to support the notion that contrasting ideologies of race, nation, and religion, as well as class and material interests, accounted for its character, course, and outcome. The national and local leadership and allies of the Knights of Labor were not shy about proclaiming in public that they were under assault by a particularly clever and ruthless race—by "twenty-one of a thrifty money making class of people," by men whose testimony in legal proceedings could not be trusted for they were not bound by oaths taken on the Christian Bible, and by men who would one day "be driven out of this country" by an outraged citizenry.[47]

In turn, allies of the garment manufacturers were no less gentle in caricaturing the man who led the opposition against them, the Irish American head of the clothing trade assembly of the Knights of

Labor, James Hughes. They described him as a "pestiferous agitator . . . stirring up trouble, drawing a great deal more salary than he ever earned by worthy labor," and they parodied his Irish brogue, picturing him as a brawling brute.[48] They condemned his strike as unjustified and his boycott as an attempt at outright extortion, comparing his tactics with the coercive and criminal activities practiced by foreign anarchists. Indeed, they taunted the few Jewish members of the local Knights for not publicly rejecting the anti-Semitic and un-American rhetoric employed by the leadership of his organization.

Within a year, the German Jewish clothing manufacturers of Rochester triumphed over the Knights, imposing their own labor regime in their own shops. Their commitment to the large-scale manufacture of quality menswear continued. They became the major employers in Rochester and were soon known as the nation's leading makers of premium, high-end men's clothing. In the process, they won the admiration of their colleagues in other apparel centers for their intelligence, tenacity, and unity of purpose in pursuing their collective interests. They elected one of their own, Max Brickner, to head the Rochester Chamber of Commerce, one of the first Jewish Americans to hold such office in a major urban center and a symbol of their ascendance into the elite circles of Rochester and New York State business, politics, and society.[49]

But in the process of climbing the ladder of commercial success and winning acceptance into elite business and political circles, Rochester's German Jewish clothing manufacturers set the stage for a future and arguably more difficult struggle that would one day be waged by their sons and would call into question what it meant to be a Jew in America.

During the 1890s struggle, the Rochester German Jewish community had discussed and debated the respective rights and obligations of employers and employees in American law and in Jewish law. Their views at the time appeared to conform closely to nineteenth-century liberal doctrines on the sanctity of private property.[50] But over the next couple of decades, a set of rival ideologies on property and power—progressivism, socialism, and communism—confronted Rochester's business community as it did businesspeople all over America. Ironically, some of the most vocal and articulate proponents of these oppositional views were part of the growing mass of Jewish immigrants and exiles from the Russian and Polish Pale of Settlement, the overwhelming number of whom were still settling in New York City. But, hints of the character of the oncoming ideological confrontation within the Jewish community of Rochester over employment relations under liberal capitalism were already quite evident in the *Jewish Tidings* during the 1880s and the early 1890s. Rochester's German Jewish clothing manufacturers were drawn into this confrontation as the tide of eastern European Jewish immigration began to crest over Rochester.[51]

Appendix: Tables

Table 1   The U.S. Men's Factory-Made Clothing Industry

Year	Shops	Workers	Output ($)
1849	4,278	96,551	48,312,000
1859	4,014	114,800	80,831,000
1869	7,858	108,128	148,660,000
1879	6,166	160,813	209,548,000
1889	4,867	144,926	251,020,000
1899	5,729	120,927	276,717,000

Source: Department of Commerce, Bureau of Foreign and Domestic Commerce, *The Men's Factory Made Clothing Industry, Report on the Cost of Production of Men's Factory-Made Clothing in the United States* (Washington, DC: Government Printing Office, 1916), 21, adapted from Table 3.

Table 2 U.S. Per Capita Consumption

Year	U.S. Population	Shaw Price Index (1913 = 100)	Output (Real $)	Per Capita Output (Real $)
1849	22,631,000	...	...	...
1859	30,687,000	...	...	...
1869	39,051,000	177.1	83,941,000	2.15
1879	49,208,000	106.7	196,390,000	3.99
1889	61,775,000	101.3	247,799,000	4.01
1899	74,799,000	84.2	328,643,000	4.39

Source: United States Bureau of the Census, *Historical Statistics of the United States, Colonial Times to 1970, Bicentennial Edition, Part 1* (Washington, DC, 1975), Series A 6–8; William Howard Shaw, *Value of Commodity Output Since 1869* (National Bureau of Economic Research, 1947), for the Shaw Price Index. The Shaw index is used to deflate the Output ($) levels from Table 1 to obtain Output (Real $). The Per Capita Output (Real $) is obtained by dividing Output (Real $) by Population.

Table 3 Men's Factory-Made Clothing in Rochester, New York

Year	Shops	Direct Capital Investment ($)	Employees	Direct Output ($)
1879	16	2,000,000	2,738	4,300,000
1889	192	6,200,000	3,123	9,100,000
1899	307	6,000,000	5,293	11,100,000

Source: U.S. Census Office, Tenth Census, *Report on the Manufactures of the United States at the Tenth Census; June 1, 1880* (Washington, DC: Government Printing Office, 1883), 430; U.S. Census Office, Eleventh Census, *Report of the Manufacturing Industries of the United States at the Eleventh Census, 1890* (Washington, DC: Government Printing Office, 1895), 490–92; U.S. Census Office, Twelfth Census, *Twelfth Census of the United States, Taken in the Year 1900; Manufactures* (Washington, DC: Government Printing Office, 1902), 1053–54. The data for 1879 does not count contract shops and home production. The data for 1889 and 1899 does not distinguish between lead shops and their contractors and does not include employment outside of either (of which other primary sources claim totaled 15,000–20,000).

*A sense of fitness is the true key-note to all uses
in the realm of dress.*
Ladies Home Companion, September 1, 1895

Fitting In

Advertising, Clothing, and Social Identity Among Turn-of-the-Century Jewish Immigrants

ROB SCHORMAN

8

To discover the "fit" between advertising, clothing, and social identity, one might well begin by considering the manner in which Americans in the late nineteenth century continually described "fittingness" as an essential component of appropriate dress. In a variety of contexts, fashion commentators stressed the desirability of a good fit, of fitness, of survival of the fittest, and of living according to "the eternal fitness of things." Two aspects of this commentary stand out. First, people considered fit to be crucial in a literal sense, as a matter of comfort, style, and utility in their garments. Second, people also considered fit to be vital in the metaphorical sense, being well aware that clothing helped define an individual's social role in many different ways.

"Nothing but a perfect fit and harmonious combination of color and material are acceptable to the exacting woman of fashion," stated *Godey's Magazine*,[1] while the *Ladies' Home Journal* warned, "Whether it is making you look like a queen in brocade or whether it is just the jaunty pretty cloth, it is nothing unless it fits."[2] No doubt this concern emerged so strongly at this time in part because getting a good fit in clothing had become increasingly complicated as

new manufacturing processes and the onset of the modern fashion cycle rewrote the rules of proper attire. One magazine columnist praised "a willingness to fit and refit," and advised that at least four separate fittings would be required to achieve satisfaction in a tailor-made suit for women.[3] Without question, however, readers were equally aware of clothing's symbolic and sociological importance, which was often conveyed through the concept of fitness as well. Etiquette book author Charles Beezley noted, "The outward garb is usually indicative of the inward personality of the wearer; and our first impressions of those we casually meet are more often formed on the fit of their clothes and their manner of wearing them than upon anything they do or say."[4] According to the etiquette advice of the day, the psychological importance of fitness in dress came not only from its impact on others, but from its effect on the wearer: "It is also a matter of every individual's experience that the knowledge of being fittingly and suitably dressed gives one an ease of manner and an unconsciousness of self that no amount of self-control can command if one is unbecomingly or shabbily attired." Concepts of personal identity and self-presentation are integral to clothing habits under any circumstances, although perhaps these issues gained heightened importance in this period because of the difficulty of finding one's place and knowing one's self during a time when economic, social, and cultural changes were rapidly transforming the material world and the relationships within it.[5]

The last section of this essay will explore more specifically the significance of clothing for Jewish immigrants, but it is worth noting at the outset that the immigrant press expressed similar concerns in similar terms. The *Yiddishes Tageblatt* informed its readers in 1898 that in "the interest of the eternal fitness of things some 'pretties' have to be discarded by the working women, be they factory girls or lady lawyers." The same article offered advice that was strictly utilitarian, in terms of selecting durable fabrics that would not soil easily, and also made suggestions more oriented to impression management, in terms of wearing clothes that would maintain propriety and present a business-like appearance. By implication, a woman ought to know how to balance the utility, comfort, and economy of her clothes while presenting an appropriate gender, occupational, and class identity—all by choosing a fitting wardrobe.[6]

These remarks suggest that dress ought to be considered first as material culture—as garment, physical object, and commodity—but also that it should be considered as something more abstract—as symbol or sign, mode of communication, and cultural indicator. The most common weakness in theories of fashion stems from their efforts to find a single mechanism or pattern to explain changes in clothing habits, whether it be autonomous cycles, business conditions, artistic creativity, class emulation, sexual attraction, or marketing magic. Such approaches tend to oversimplify and generalize because without doubt, the wearers of clothes value them simultaneously as commodities, aesthetic objects, and symbols. To determine the context of any particular fashion trend, it is necessary to triangulate its position using coordinates based on business developments, aesthetic influences, and cultural circumstances. Each plays an important part in establishing the dress codes of an era.

Analysis of clothing styles is further complicated because all symbols are multivalent (containing many possible meanings) and fluid (subject to constant manipulation and reinterpretation by those who employ them). A fashion detail does not necessarily signify just one thing or necessarily mean the same thing in one era as it does in the next. Yet clothing does indeed manifest the categories that define our understanding of the world. Dress depicts the boundaries of gender, class, occupation, and age, as well as group affiliation, concepts of ethnic, regional, and national identity, and the social distinctions between formal and informal, public and private, leisure and work, among many others. Indeed, clothing not only reproduces these categories but also provides some of their key attributes, so that being middle class or feminine or professional by definition involves maintaining certain appearances, wearing certain clothes, and holding certain body ideals.

Advertising messages bear crucially on any assessment of late-nineteenth-century

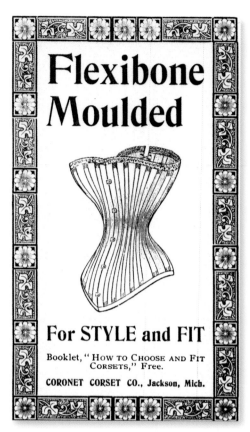

Advertisement in the *Ladies' Home Journal*, **November 1895, page 29.** The Coronet Corset Company underlined the importance of "fit" as a fashion essential by offering customers a free booklet on the subject.

Courtesy of the author.

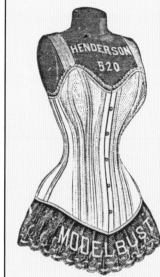

Advertisement in *Chicago Dry Goods Reporter*, **October 12, 1895, page 26.** A stylish woman demands much, according to this advertisement, but above all she demands a "perfect fit."

Courtesy of the author.

dress, because advertising was just assuming recognizably modern form and provided a powerful new medium for conveying the meaning of clothes. Fashion and advertising were separate modes of expression that frequently found common ground, often seeming to fuse into a single channel of cultural discourse. Advertising responded to its own set of economic, aesthetic, and sociological determinants but often reconciled those influences in ways that reinforced the prevailing fashion sense, each side benefiting from the symbolic power and pervasiveness of the other. Not

surprisingly, both the literal and metaphorical concern with proper fit found frequent expression in clothing ads. Advertisers made offers such as "we try on the garment nearest your figure; then alter it to fit your personality"[7] and "we fit your mind as well as your body."[8] An 1895 advertisement summed up the situation: "A Stylish Woman wants a Corset at a popular price, that will give her satisfaction, a Corset that will be comfortable, soft and flexible and not too heavy. *Above all she wants a Corset that will be a perfect fit.*"[9]

A Man Among Men: Business, Aesthetics, Culture

The men's and women's clothing industries developed along distinctly different tracks in the 1800s. By the last decade of the century, probably 90 percent of men's suits were produced ready-made, while perhaps 90 percent of women's dresses were still custom-made. This schism parallels a social phenomenon in which the lines of gender differentiation became more rigid and more insistently expressed during the same era. Looking at men's and women's garments—and advertisements for them—we see the manner in which business interests, aesthetic impulses, and cultural influences achieved a harmony of interests during a particular historical period.[10]

A series of drawings published in an 1895 issue of *Gibson's Clothing Gazette* reveals much about men's clothing, advertising, and American culture. The four drawings show nearly identical-looking men wearing variations of the sack suit, the currently fashionable style. These drawings were the nineteenth-century equivalent of clip art, generic illustrations offered to merchants who wished to use them in their own advertisements. This sales strategy only made sense because men's suits by this time were manufactured in large quantities and sold ready-made in relatively standardized form. During the last half of the nineteenth century, the nation's industrial, transportation, and communications systems grew to unprecedented levels of size and productivity, creating an outpouring of consumer goods, transforming living and working conditions, and generating an atmosphere of whirlwind change.[11] The

style of the sack suit fit this business trend because its boxy shape and long, straight seams were better suited to high-speed, high-volume manufacture than its form-fitting predecessors. Aesthetically, the sack suit emerged from a long line of men's fashion going back to at least the late seventeenth century, when coat, vest, and knee breeches became the costume of choice for fashionable men.[12] Thus, the business and aesthetics of the men's suit had developed in tandem.

Clothing ads also illustrate how advertising developed along its own trajectories of business and aesthetics. In the late 1870s, for example, an ad for men's clothing typically appeared as a simple announcement. Illustrations and brand names were almost entirely absent and even prices were often omitted, as most men's clothing was created individually or generically and then sold locally at a price that was subject to on-the-spot negotiation. Through the end of the century, the explosive growth of magazines and newspapers made advertising more prevalent and valuable as a business tool, while technological improvements in printing and photographic reproduction gave new emphasis to visual communications. As mass production techniques improved, national marketing campaigns and competition for customers increased, as did competition among advertising professionals for clients. All these developments prompted more consideration of advertising content and display, and by the 1890s advertising began to develop many of the

No. 281. $1.00   No. 266. $1.00   No. 294. $1.00   No. 297. $1.00

features that we still associate with it today. Men's clothing ads demonstrated notable progress toward a marketing style that emphasized visual selling, brand names, and price competition.[13]

How does all this fit the cultural moment? Consider that a variety of circumstances threatened middle-class American men with loss of their sense of control at this time. Economic developments—such as the spread of large-scale corporate enterprises—endangered ideals of independence and individuality, and political and workplace challenges from women and immigrants threatened middle-class male power in those realms. In response to these pressures, a new masculine ideal emerged. It stressed virile self-assertion and manifested itself in a variety of ways, ranging from the popularity of boxing matches to

military demonstration of American imperial might. The new masculinity also favored a new male body image, one that was much more muscular and aggressive than previously respectable stereotypes. Teddy Roosevelt's persona and his promotion of what he called the "strenuous life" provided an example and an impetus for these developments. Yet, though men were adapting to changed circumstances, they wanted to keep their sources of power and privilege undisturbed where possible. Therefore, the emerging mode of masculinity, though embracing the future in many ways, also attempted to preserve many older values, including the steadfast dignity and self-mastery that traditionally equated with male privilege.[14]

The ready-made sack suit makes perfect sense in this context. Taking possession of

Advertisement in *Gibson's Clothing Gazette*, **September 1895.** These drawings were sold to clothing merchants at $1 each for use in their own advertisements. They document both the standardization of men's clothing production and the increasing proliferation of advertising in the 1890s.

Courtesy Library of Congress.

Advertisement in the *Chicago Tribune*, May 22, 1897, page 7. By the 1890s, advertisements for men's clothing were more organized, more visual, and more overtly focused on persuasion, although they still represented relatively unsophisticated use of techniques.

Courtesy of the author.

this emblem of modern business know-how implied that the upheaval of industrialization had been mastered, while the relatively unchanging and unadorned styles provided comforting symbols of stability and continuity. In addition, the sack suit's broad shoulders and padded chest created a massive, rectilinear form that roughly corresponded to the new male body ideal. Advertising did its part to put these values into circulation, appearing with headlines such as "Make Him a Gentleman" or "A Man Among Men," and illustrating the new masculine body type. One catalogue promised to deliver a double-breasted sack suit with "athletic shoulders" and a "broad chest." Charlotte Perkins Gilman, the well-known feminist theoretician, perfectly captured the implications of these developments just after the turn of the century when she wrote, "It is masculine to have a broad chest and square shoulders—typically masculine. If the customer chances to lack these distinctions . . . the tailor sees to it that his garments shall symbolize his sex beyond dispute." As these examples indicate, men's dress presented itself forthrightly as an arena for setting the parameters of gender, and advertising presented itself forthrightly as the medium by which these ideals could be expressed. Clothing reflected the current mode in gender identity and in some ways defined it.[15]

As Gilman knew, almost everything

about women's clothing existed in sharp contrast to the men's industry. She once summarized the social norms for women's appearance by saying that they "must so dress as to cry aloud to all beholders, 'I am a female—and don't forget it.'"[16] Whereas men's styles were linear, plain, utilitarian-looking, and ready-made, women's styles were curvaceous, fussy, ornamental-looking, and custom-made. Advertising reflected this gender split. Although brand names, illustrations, and price conscious-ness began to penetrate the women's market by the 1890s, advertisements were more likely to use them to sell sewing accessories rather than whole garments, while still illustrating current social conventions regarding overall female fashion and body ideals. Among ready-made garments for women, some were even advertised as "equal to home made."[17] Observers have sometimes claimed that the elaborateness and volatility of women's fashion styles offered sufficient explanation for the slow transition to ready-made production, but the designation of elabo-rate or rapidly changing fashions as an exclusively female concern was actually a relatively recent historical phenomenon. In the eighteenth century, high fashion for both men and women included vivid colors, elaborate trim, carefully sculpted silhou-ettes, and even corsets.[18] No strong aes-thetic or economic necessity required styles for women to evolve in a manner that rejected ready-mades or maintained an extreme polarity with men's clothing, yet both occurred.

Quite simply, at this time many people found it important—maybe as important as ever in American history—for men and

Advertisement in *Ladies' Home Journal*, March 1895, page 31. Mass media advertisements for women's fashion incorporated some of the signature elements of modern mass marketing—such as brand names—but did so within the context of clothing that was mainly custom-made. This advertisement pictures the full outfit, but only seeks to sell skirt binding.

Courtesy Winterthur Library, Printed Books and Periodical Collection.

women to *look* as different as possible. Victorian America always stressed an ideology of separate spheres for men and women. Now, as changing times threatened this belief system, the cultural pressure to maintain the stereotypes increased and took on new importance. Clothing and advertising expressed, reinforced, and constituted this sense of difference.[19]

Sophie's Hat: Clothing and National Identity

In 1898, a little more than two months after the United States battleship *Maine* exploded in Havana Harbor, the United States declared war against Spain, ostensibly to help Cuban insurgents throw off the shackles of colonialism. Although the cause of Cuban independence meshed nicely with America's own ideals and history, the war matched other trends in American society as well, offering as it did an opportunity for further expansion of U.S. business interests, a demonstration of the Darwinian commitment to a hierarchy of races, and an opportunity to practice the "strenuous life" version of masculinity. The war also produced an upsurge in nationalism that seemed to promise a restoration of consensual values, something that had become increasingly difficult to maintain given the sweeping and sometimes tumultuous changes that were occurring in the country.[20]

Not surprisingly, the concepts of national identity and nationalism figured prominently in advertising and fashions of the day. A wide range of advertisements incorporated war motifs and references, sometimes in the most casual manner. At the same time, garments began to appear "trimmed *à la militaire*," as the fashion writers put it. An advertisement in the *Ladies' Home Journal* declared that military-style capes were "a necessary article in the wardrobe of patriotic American women." Cavalry caps became popular as casual headwear for both women and children, and bunting (the worsted material used to make flags) gained favor as dress material. Fashion and advertising did not merely reflect the popular mood, but offered it substance. The ads proclaimed that to dress patriotically was to be patriotic, and clothing makers developed styles appropriate to the task.[21]

An advertisement from the *Yiddishes Tageblatt* shows how advertising, clothing, and social change converged in the Jewish community of New York City at this precise moment. This document appeared in a periodical that itself signified how the surge of immigration, urbanization, and mass communication was reshaping the

Further News of
Dresses and Jackets

THERE are various grades and kinds of tailor-made Dresses, but we carry only one kind—the very best we can find. That doesn't mean the highest priced sorts only. "Best," although superlative, admits of comparison. There's the best $10 suit, as well as the best at $100. We have tried to get both, as well as all the intermediate bests. We hate trash, and next to trash come "second-bests." You'll find neither here, look as hard as you will.

As to prices, of course good goods cost more than inferior kinds, but not much more, and when you are face to face with such reductions as these, they cost absolutely less.

Here is news of honest and liberal reductions on the very best of garments,—fresh made and correct in every way.

At $8—Value $14
At $10—Values $12 to $18
At $25—Values $30 to $37

At $12.75—Value $18.50
At $22.00—Values $30 to $35
At $30.00—Values $40 to $42

Advertisement in the *New York Times*, May 18, 1898, page 4. This advertisement makes no reference at all to the Spanish-American War beyond the illustration of a woman striking a military pose. It seems to attempt to capture the martial spirit of the day while retaining conventional gender distinctions. Note that the woman is shouldering a parasol rather than a rifle.

Courtesy of the author.

SIX LITTLE TAILORS.

ENLISTING ALWAYS GOING ON.

FOR OUR

$20.00
SUITS TO ORDER

which are honest in every detail of material and construction.

WRITE FOR SAMPLES.
Open evenings till 9 o'clock.

78 Madison-st.   M'Vicker's Theater Bld.

Advertisement in the *Chicago Tribune*, May 8, 1898, page 11. This advertisement for Six Little Tailors is one of many that offered nothing more than strained wordplay as a link between its product and the war effort.

Courtesy of the author.

Advertisement in
***Clothier and Furnisher*,**
May 1898, page 1. The
Manhattan Shirt Company
clearly equates the new,
muscular, aggressive male
body ideal with militarism,
proper attire, and
consumption in this
advertisement.

Courtesy Library of Congress.

Prepared!

A complete line of FULL=
DRESS SHIRTS (compris-
ing NEW and CORRECT
Styles).

A LARGE line of STIFF
BOSOM FANCY SHIRTS
for Autumn wear (all
of them EXCLUSIVE
patterns SPECIALLY
DESIGNED for us).

Patterns which have
CHIC and SNAP, but not
"loud"!

Patterns which are GEN=
TEEL, but not "tame"!

Don't place your order
until you have seen
THE CORRECT STYLES;
always brought out
and introduced by the

MANHATTAN SHIRT CO.

760 BROADWAY =   =   NEW YORK

country. It was for clothing (men only), was headlined with the nationalistic United States slogan of the Spanish-American War (in English), and its sales pitch was clearly aimed at immigrant Jewish consumers (in Yiddish).

Clothing had particular importance to Jewish immigrants in part because they provided so much of the entrepreneurial energy and labor force for the garment industry and its retail outlets. Their close relationship to the clothing industry made it logical for them to attempt to manipulate

the fashion vocabulary to serve their needs. For the newly arrived Jewish immigrants, the acquisition of American clothing was a crucial first step in adopting and asserting one's membership in American society. A Jewish garment worker recalled the importance and urgency of this rite of passage:

My first day in America I went with my aunt to buy some American clothes. She bought me a shirtwaist, you know, a blouse and a skirt, a blue print with red buttons and a hat, such a hat I had never seen. I took my old brown dress and shawl and threw them away! I know it sounds foolish, we being so poor, but I didn't care. I had enough of the old country. When I looked in the mirror, I couldn't get over it. I said, boy, Sophie, look at you now. Just like an American.[22]

Sometimes family members refused to allow recently arrived relatives to leave Ellis Island until they had donned suitably American clothes. One man in 1902 happily greeted his young daughter who had come to join him in the United States. Yet after meeting the girl briefly for the first time in six years, he left her waiting on the island for another hour and a half while he went in search of a new pair of shoes and dress for her. "I want her to look like an American girl," he said.[23] Sometimes immigrants did not even wait until they arrived to make the switch. The disparaging comments of a more experienced traveler prompted one woman to throw her carefully packed clothing overboard during her voyage to America because she believed "it was better to come empty-handed than to arrive improperly dressed."[24] Mary Antin, who emigrated from Russia in the 1890s, recalled proudly the day she and her siblings "exchanged our hateful homemade European costumes . . . for real American machine-made garments, and issued forth glorified in each other's eyes."[25]

This adoption of American dress was not a simple or superficial phenomenon. An unprecedentedly large influx of immigrants—especially those bringing different linguistic, religious, and cultural traditions from southern and eastern Europe—produced uneasiness and backlash among the native-born population. Nativist prejudice was directed at many immigrant groups at this time, and Jews bore the additional

Advertisement in *Yiddishes Tageblatt*, **May 4, 1898, page 2.**

M. Yachnin targeted this ad at an immigrant population. Following the English language headline, the vernacular Yiddish text uses a tongue-in-cheek appeal, combining patriotism and commercialism, to attract customers to a new spring line of clothing.

Courtesy of the author.

burden of anti-Semitic feelings.[26] Nativist zealots saw immigrant dress as an unwelcome effort to erase differences of social class and national background, to encroach on the nativists' own domains of status and self-identification. They complained that "the sewing girl, the shop girl, the chambermaid, and even the cook, must have their elegantly trimmed silk dresses and velvet cloaks for Sunday and holiday wear, [and] the damage done by this state of things to the morals and manners of the poorer classes is incalculable."[27] They warned that "to overdress one's station in the world is always in poor taste."[28] They worried that Jewish immigrant women believed "the essential thing in America is to 'look stylish,'" adding that "in most cases this conviction leads merely to the establishing of false standards."[29]

The *Yiddishes Tageblatt* responded in plain terms: "I think Sarah way down on the East Side has as much right to the daintiness of dress as Ida on Madison Avenue." This statement indicates that donning stylish dress was a form of cultural agency for the otherwise disempowered, as does the comment by a Russian immigrant who recalled her early years in the United States: "I wanted to be an American very much. I saw people who looked better and dressed better and I wanted to be like that kind." Indeed, by the turn of the century, it was a Sunday tradition for young Jewish residents to travel from the Lower East Side to Madison Avenue and promenade in their finery.[30]

Such actions produced conflicted responses within immigrant families as they attempted to find a balance between an ethnic identity and an American one.

Abraham Cahan, who immigrated from Russia in the 1880s, dramatized this tension in his short novel *Yekl*. In this book, the title character comes to the United States in advance of his wife and becomes thoroughly, even comically, committed to American manners. He is crestfallen when his wife, Gitl, arrives to join him, and it is specifically her appearance that triggers his dismay: "His heart had sunk at the sight of his wife's uncouth and un-American appearance. She was slovenly dressed in a brown jacket and a skirt of grotesque cut, and her hair was concealed under a voluminous wig of a pitch-black hue." Gitl is hesitant to abandon her traditional standards of appearance, although later in the story she appears "in her own hair, thatched with a broad-brimmed winter hat of a brown colour and a jacket of black beaver." By this time, however, her marriage to Jake has disintegrated.[31]

Cahan had observed a similar incident while working as a newspaper reporter. In one article, he described a group of "overdressed" young men and women who went to Ellis Island to welcome the arriving family matriarch. After an affectionate greeting, the American progeny presented the woman with "a bonnet of black velvet trimmed with red roses." Her son told her, "this is America, mother, one must be dressed like a lady here," but the woman wanted nothing to do with the hat, even when they told her she could wear it over her wig. The *Tageblatt*, a politically and culturally conservative publication, nonetheless backed up the American relatives on this point, editorializing against the traditional head covering in 1898: "It is this custom of wearing wigs that makes our

Jewish women look so alike and so old." Indeed, at times the paper published fashion advice that could have come straight from the *Ladies' Home Journal* or any other contemporary source of fashion sense:

Some of the dainty hammock dresses and easy gowns worn on sultry days this season are made of dotted and flowered Swiss muslin, pink, blue, or cream batiste, or soft undressed mulls. Many of these dresses have slightly drooping blouse fronts, neatly belted, with little Eton jackets of Swiss embroidery beyond.[32]

The pages of the *Tageblatt* provide a good glimpse at the crosscurrents and paradoxes Jewish immigrants faced in confronting the issue of national identity—and the importance of clothing in their response to this issue. Oldest of the daily papers in the ghetto, it was known as a publication that "fights tooth and nail for whatever is distinctly Jewish in custom." Yet although the bulk of the paper was written in Yiddish, it encouraged and assisted assimilation by providing one page in each eight-page issue in English. It also aggressively solicited advertising from both local merchants and national manufacturers. The ads were almost entirely in Yiddish, although an occasional word or two of English appeared. However, the Yiddish text in the paper often incorporated English words, as speakers of the language were doing as part of their acculturation. Significantly, one historian who has reviewed the advertisements of the *Tageblatt* during this time period has noted that clothing merchants in particular had "spearheaded the drive toward the creation of a dynamic advertising." Once again, we see clothing habits and advertising styles collaborating in the creation of the symbols and images that would define social identity.[33]

After the beginning of the Spanish-American War, advertisements to the immigrant consumer began to incorporate war themes. For a Jewish American seeking acceptance in the United States, it was necessary to demonstrate a commitment to the nationalistic fervor of the day—and what better way than through appropriately American attire? On May 3, 1898, the *Tageblatt* reported that a standing-room only crowd had gathered for a patriotic rally at the Hebrew Institute.[34] The next day M. Yachnin, Gent's Furnisher, first published the advertisement headlined "Remember the Maine," which appeared in the next ninety-one issues of the *Tageblatt* without a miss. It provided readers a way of embedding cultural attitudes into daily life:

Remember and don't forget what the Spaniards have done to you with the ship Maine. And take revenge on them! While the entire public, however, is so busy remembering the Maine, we would like to point out to you that in all your boundless remembrance you should not forget that there are many other important things that one mustn't forget, namely that the famous businessman M. Yachnin, 55 Canal St. . . . has just received a brand-new stack of the finest gents furnishing goods for spring.[35]

Yachnin's strategy is virtually identical to the Boston clothing dealer who at about the same time put a placard in his window reading, "Remember the Maine, boys, and the price of this suit." The Yachnin advertisement made the connection between clothing and citizenship even more explicit, however: "Remember that the United States will surely soon be victorious. Your

**Advertisement in the
*Chicago Dry Goods
Reporter*, November 25,
1899, page 40.** The
Gage-Downs Corset Co.
suggests how prominent
nationalistic feeling—
a product both of the
Spanish-American War
and of nativist fears about
foreign immigration—
became during the 1890s.

Courtesy of the author.

sons and you will need to dress up in honor of this national holiday." Again, proper clothing did not simply reflect and reinforce a standard of personal identity, but helped constitute it.[36]

When the Gage-Downs Corset Company published an advertisement promoting its goods as "American Made for American Maids," it made a claim that relied on a host of assumptions about the relationship of clothing, advertising, national identity, and gender. The slogan was one that could satisfy both nationalistic and nativist sentiments, projecting not only an attitude of "America first," but also one of "America for the Americans." Yet by insisting on an equation between clothing and Americanism, advertisers provided a tool that immigrants could seize for their own purposes. Thus, when the *Tageblatt* proudly announced that "our American women are undoubtedly the best dressed people in the world," it deployed this cultural symbolism on behalf of claims its

immigrant readership was making on American society.[37]

Fashion and advertising do not exist as one-dimensional representations of a single ideal or circumstance, but as a loose assemblage of many influences that coexist at a particular point in time. They clearly depend on market conditions and design traditions, but they also respond to social circumstances. This complexity does not make clothing and advertising less meaningful to consumers (or to the historian who studies them) but more so. Because art, business, and society proceed in ambiguous, complicated, and sometimes paradoxical ways, fashion and advertising track this movement in an appropriately complex manner. The Jewish immigrants who worked in the garment industry, read advertisements in the *Yiddishes Tageblatt*, and bought their clothes at shops like M. Yachnin's demonstrate just how perfect the fit between advertising, clothing, and social identity could be.

From Division Street to Seventh Avenue: The Coming of Age of American Fashion

JOANNE OLIAN

The fundamental strength of American fashion has been the ability of Seventh Avenue to dress a large number of women in attractive clothing that both fits well and is affordable. Due largely to mass production methods developed by Jewish manufacturers since the beginning of the ready-to-wear industry, America is the best-dressed nation in the world. Interestingly, it was Jewish immigrants from eastern Europe who determined the course of American fashion. In much the same spirit that Irving Berlin and George Gershwin defined American music, Seventh Avenue's manufacturers and designers left their imprint on American style.

The women's garment industry had its humble beginnings in lofts on New York's Lower East Side where rents were cheap and labor—consisting chiefly of eastern European Jews—was plentiful. The industry, which was to become the largest employer in New York City and one of the major employers in the nation, began in 1846 with the invention of the sewing machine by Elias Howe, followed in rapid succession by multiple improvements and other manufacturing aids such as cutting and pressing machinery. Initially, many of the entrepreneurs were German Jews who

arrived in the United States before the Civil War, became peddlers, made enough money to open clothing stores on the Lower East Side, and ultimately became garment manufacturers. While men's clothing was machine sewn as a commercial product as early as the 1850s, women's apparel, except for outerwear and hoops, was still sewn by hand, either at home or by dressmakers. Nonetheless, by 1860, the industry had grown to include two hundred women's apparel factories that collectively grossed about $7 million. By 1880 this figure had increased to $30 million, and a decade later it had more than doubled to nearly $70 million.[1]

Between 1880 and 1924, when the passage of the Immigration and Naturalization Act halted the flow of immigration, over two million Jews, largely from Russia and Poland, entered the United States.[2] The majority, many of whom had arrived with tailoring skills acquired in eastern Europe, settled on New York's Lower East Side. In the last two decades of the nineteenth century, coinciding with the influx of Jewish immigration, the garment industry grew at two or three times the rate of other businesses, and by 1890 there were over one thousand women's-wear companies.

Cloaks, suits, shirtwaists, and undergarments accounted for most of the volume, which by 1900 amounted to $159 million in sales nationwide with New York's share at $107 million.[3]

Starting businesses with as little as fifty dollars in capital, eastern European Jews became contractors, picked up workers at the so-called Pig Market around Hester and Division Streets, rented a few machines, and made up cut garments for manufacturers who lacked inside shops. Labor historian John R. Commons described the way it worked:

The Jewish contractor was not a mere middleman; he was necessarily a tailor and an organizer of labor, for his work was done by a system of division of labor calling for various grades and forms of skill. . . .

The man best fitted to be a contractor is the man who is well acquainted with his neighbor, who is able to speak the language of several classes of immigrants . . . and can obtain the cheapest help. . . .

The unlimited hours of work, often seven days in the week, is a feature of the contracting system. The contractor himself works unlimited hours.[4]

The combination of long hours and infinitesimal profit margins drove out the large German Jewish manufacturers. Known as the Giants of Broadway, these German Jews went into other businesses such as department stores and wholesale textiles and left women's clothing manufacturing to eastern European Jews, the so-called moths of Division Street. Many of the eastern European immigrants who founded the most successful apparel firms on Seventh Avenue began working at an early age and learned every facet of the business from production to selling. They

have been described as "a body of gamblers who are engaged in something called the dress business or the coat business or the suit business: each man gambles every season on his new collection—[a] collection that can run into hundreds of thousands of dollars at cost. Those same gamblers, wearing different hats, are astute, cynical, soft-hearted, civic-minded, proud. Most of them are Jewish."[5] Among that number were Fred Pomerantz of Leslie Fay, David Schwartz of Jonathan Logan, Abe Schrader, and Maurice Rentner. First-generation Americans such as Nat and Irving Bader of Originala and David Zelinka of Zelinka-Matlick followed similar career paths. Entrepreneurial spirits, they had strong personalities with little formal education, but having started at the bottom, they understood fit and fabric, as well as the importance of strong personal relationships with retail buyers. All were risk-takers and they had moxie.

These manufacturers resisted the unions as long as possible, and in some instances shut their operations down and moved out of the city. In the mid-1920s, the International Ladies' Garment Workers' Union (ILGWU) picketed Fred Pomerantz's dressmaking factory in Mechanicsville, New York. Pomerantz closed his business and moved to California with $3 million, which he subsequently lost in failed real estate and retail ventures. He eventually returned to New York and the dress industry. During the same period Maurice Rentner, an inveterate poker player, had a factory that employed about one hundred operators. When the union called a strike, Rentner arranged for the non-striking workers to be transported to and from the workplace. His lawyer went before the New York Supreme Court and won the case; Rentner managed to remain nonunion until 1932. On the other hand, Abe Schrader, who was a contractor before opening his own business in the 1950s, got his first job as a cutter in a coat factory after passing the ILGWU exam. He developed a lasting relationship with David Dubinsky, who later would serve as longtime president of the ILGWU, that included helping him in his campaign for president.[6]

Founded by Jews in 1900, the International Ladies' Garment Workers' Union became a powerful apparel industry advocate. At the turn of the century, poor sweatshop conditions were rampant, wages fluctuated with the season, and some workers even had to provide their own machines. Contractors began to subcontract, adding an additional middleman and shaving wages even further. The workday during the busy season might be as long as sixteen hours and sanitary conditions were abysmal. During the Panic of 1907, workers were willing to take any job on any terms and the unions fell apart. In contrast, when the economic climate improved two years later, twenty thousand workers, 80 percent of whom were women, walked off their jobs, paving the way for the Great Revolt of 1910 during which three times as many workers struck. The union successfully negotiated a fifty-hour week, overtime pay, higher wages, and a closed or all-union shop. However, it was the Triangle Shirtwaist Fire of 1911, in which 146 young women lost their lives due to the lack of safety measures, that served as labor's wake-up call. Over time, the ILGWU has come to represent 75 percent of the

industry's workers, and in addition to mandating safety standards in the workplace, it provides generous pension, welfare, and retirement benefits, health facilities, and cooperative housing for its members.

Before the garment district found its home in the Seventh Avenue area, it moved from the Lower East Side to streets in the 20s and low 30s, just east and west of Fifth Avenue. In the early 1920s, the tenant roster at 2 West 33rd Street included Maurice Rentner, J. M. Silverman, and Fred Pomerantz's first employer, M. B. Kaufman. David Levinsky, the Russian Jewish immigrant whose success is chronicled in Abraham Cahan's eponymous novel of the garment industry, described the scene:

That locality had already become the center of the cloak-and-suit trade, being built up with new skyscrapers, full of up-to-date cloak-factories, dress-factories, and ladies' waist-factories. The sight of the celebrated Avenue swarming with Jewish mechanics out for their lunch hour or going home after a day's work was already a daily spectacle.[7]

Concern for preserving the retail character of Fifth Avenue and preventing crowds of factory workers pouring onto the streets at noon led to the formation of the Save New York Committee. This organization was able to convince a group of manufacturers to relocate to a zone bounded by Seventh Avenue on the east and 38th Street on the north, precluding inroads into the Times Square entertainment district.[8] Several successful cloak and suit manufacturers headed by Saul Singer and Mack Kanner formed a cooperative syndicate that erected two sixteen-story buildings, the first major manufacturing and showroom space in the

Man putting pattern on cloth, ca. 1930s.

Courtesy Museum of the City of New York, Federal Arts Project. Photograph by Andrew Herman.

present garment center. Christened "The Garment Center Capitol," 498 and 500 Seventh Avenue were completed in 1921 with total floor space of 1.5 million square feet.[9] These buildings were fully rented as soon as they were finished and were followed three years later by 512, 530, and 550 Seventh Avenue, extending almost to 40th Street.

By 1939, the garment business was easily the largest industry in New York City, with 7,000 factories employing 200,000 workers with a combined volume at wholesale of over one billion dollars a year. While the industry itself and the unions that represented it were "whales; the manufacturers themselves are a school of minnows."[10] Individually, few of them did as much as one million dollars per year and

the failure rate among firms has been estimated to be as high as 25 percent. Yet, as a *Fortune* article stated, "The figure is not to be taken too seriously as a good portion of it involves nothing more than a change in partners or a temporary liquidation to escape unprofitable contracts."[11] The article continued by stating that a strong reason for reorganizing was a contracting system that retained elements of its Lower East Side origins:

A garment industry contractor is a man who rents a loft, owns the sewing machines and equipment, hires the labor, adds a flat percentage (from ten to fifteen percent) to the actual labor cost for his profit, and usually works for one manufacturer who furnishes the cut fabric. A dress house having three contractors can't change one of them without the union's approval, a procedure that is designed to protect

Joseph J. Keyser Company, 1920.

Courtesy Museum of the City of New York, Byron Collection.

Garment Center Capitol stock certificate, ca. 1928.

Private collection.

not the contractor but the contractor's employees. So the changes are few. If shop conditions become too unfavorable a manufacturer can appeal to the impartial chairman via the employers' association he belongs to, but he rarely does because the procedure is slow and the chances are that he will be found wrong anyway.[12]

By the time the garment center had moved uptown and was known as Seventh Avenue, it was, according to *Vogue*'s 1938 Americana issue, larger than the steel industry: "In a year adults, not counting children under fourteen, buy 170,000,000 dresses, 13,000,000 cloth coats, 2,000,000 fur coats, more than a hundred million hats, and God knows how many bags, belts, gloves, girdles, and sundry accessories." Pretty formidable numbers in a year when America remained in the midst of the Great Depression. *Vogue* continued:

Though half the country doesn't know it, most of the ready-made dresses bought in the shops of Fifth Avenue or Main Street come from the West Side of New York City—from that small area colloquially known as "Seventh Avenue" or the "wholesale mawket." Here, in chromium-plated, white-carpeted, thirty story skyscrapers (rabbit-warren sweat-shops have almost disappeared), more than five thousand wholesalers make most of the nation's clothes.

To the women of the country who buy the clothes produced here, it's an unexplored territory. Only a few of the wholesalers have become recognized outside the trade—ambitious ones who have exploited their own names; customarily the dress you buy carries the name of the store in which it is sold, rather than the label of the firm who made it. All in all, there's very little glory in the work—terrific gamble, stiff competition, and money only if you never grow stale. In one large building in the region, only two or three names listed on the lobby address-board six years ago appear there today.[13]

"Push boys" guiding hand trucks through the garment district, ca. 1940s.

Courtesy Museum of the City of New York, gift of the Office of War Information.

Not only were the manufacturers anonymous, but the firms who actually had in-house designers seldom gave them label or advertising credit for their creations. In a letter dated May 15, 1940, to Ethel Kremer, executive director of the Fashion Group, regarding opportunities for designers, the writer states, "the most startling discovery I have made is that 90% and more of American-Manufactured clothes are sold at $10.75 and under, and that the number of houses within those low ranges which employ designers can literally be counted on one's two hands. In a word, 90% of American clothes are adapted, copied or just made somehow—without benefit of designers."[14]

There were several ways to create a dress without the services of a designer. Design studios such as Berley and Edyth Sparag conveniently located themselves near the garment center and supplied their subscribers with color sketches of Paris models, including back views and information about original fabrics. In a speech before the Fashion Group in April 1940, no less a New Yorker than the redoubtable Mayor Fiorello La Guardia called attention to a deplorable practice that failed to give designers the respect they deserved:

The dress industry just now isn't as prosperous or in as wholesome a condition as I would like to see it. There is a great deal to be done there and it is receiving attention from various quarters at this time but I want to say this to dress manufacturers: they have to give more considerate attention to their designers. It is getting to be a habit to hire designers by the hour or sometimes by the day and it is simply disgraceful! You just can't expect creative work to be successful and to be beautiful if the creator is working under the stress of economic problems.

A good designer ought to be employed by the season, at least. Of course, you take a chance. It can't be helped; that is part of the risk of the trade and the only way that can be balanced is to have more than one designer in order to be sure to hit something that is attractive.[15]

Another widespread practice was for manufacturers and their wives to window shop at night when the stores were closed. The next morning the wife would purchase the dress, and after her husband had copied the design she would return it to the store. According to a *Fortune* article devoted to Seventh Avenue, if wives began to look too

familiar, manufacturers used sisters and daughters.[16]

Even if the firm did employ a designer, it was not commonplace for retailer, advertiser, or fashion magazine to give credit. In a *Life* magazine article about Nettie Rosenstein, the caption accompanying a photograph of one of her designs reads, "Nettie Rosenstein's fertile mind conceived this crinkle satin dress, her workshop made it, her models paraded it, and from her salon it was sold to Bergdorf Goodman. But when the lady who buys it for $195 takes it to Florida or California this winter she will find in it not the Rosenstein label, but Bergdorf Goodman's and unless she is a supersmart customer its origin will be unknown to her."[17]

Another difficulty for the American designer was the popular belief in the superiority of French fashion. Paris lent instant cachet to even the most prosaic frock. The glamour of French couture had long been familiar in even the most remote farmhouses of America through mail-order catalogues that proclaimed styles direct from Paris. Attempts to combat French dominance began as early as the 1890s in periodicals such as the *Illustrated American*, which urged its readers to purchase clothes by American dressmakers instead of the models imported by New York modistes. Fashionable women, however, never wavered in their devotion.

World War I inspired ladies' magazines to new heights of patriotic prose. In 1916, the *Ladies' Home Journal* offered to publish any sketch or idea sent to them that refuted the Paris mystique, stating, "We Are Told This: That the Only Women in the World who can trim a hat, make a new jabot,

Sketch of imported ensemble available to subscribers of Berley Studios design service, ca. 1935.

Courtesy of the author, collection of Joanne Olian.

Chanel design for copying by Seventh Avenue dress manufacturers, ca. 1935.

Courtesy of the author, collection of Joanne Olian.

design a new frock, or create a new shirt-waist are in Paris—that American women, clever as they are in other lines, cannot create their own pretty things."[18] Further attempts were made to promote American fashion, but these efforts fell largely on deaf ears. The Paris couture never closed its doors during the war, and imports continued virtually uninterrupted. Once the Armistice was signed, fashion lemmings lost no time in resuming their semiannual transatlantic peregrinations in search of *la mode*.

In the 1920s and 1930s, Seventh Avenue's anonymous designers were turning out between 200 and 450 samples apiece each year. Considered mere technicians whose primary function was to make salable French dresses at a reasonable price for the American consumer, most American designers found themselves hidden from view somewhere behind a Seventh Avenue showroom. Their employers, meanwhile, were manufacturing garments in quantities undreamed of by Paris and proudly announced that these dresses were copies of—or inspired by—French designs. In 1935, R. H. Macy & Co., one of the first to import and copy French clothes, staged fashion shows featuring models wearing

Nettie Rosenstein dress and photograph, 1948.

Installation photograph of exhibition at Bruce Museum, Greenwich, CT. Dress from collection of the Museum of the City of New York.

identical dresses—the Paris original and the Macy's copy—and invited the audience to guess which was which.[19] The only Americans acknowledged by the fashion press were custom designers such as Valentina, Sophie Gimbel, Jessie Franklin Turner, and Arthur Falkenstein. A few forward-thinking retailers such as B. Altman, Best & Company, Russeks, and most prominently Lord & Taylor began to lay the groundwork for the recognition of American fashion and featured designers' names in their advertising. Dorothy Shaver, Lord & Taylor's vice president and director of style bureau and the first woman to serve as president of a major retail store, believed "in clothes that are intrinsically American, and that only the American designer can create them," and commended "the spirit and enterprise of these New York women who are working so successfully to create an American style."[20] Still, Seventh Avenue had a collective inferiority complex when it came to fashion, and most retailers continued to imply that their apparel was Paris-inspired.

While American designers were acclaimed by a foresighted few, it was the vacuum created by the fall of France in 1940 and the subsequent closing of the Paris couture that resulted in their discovery by the public and the media. Yet, skepticism continued to abound and Stanley Marcus, vice president of Neiman-Marcus, wrote, "The American garment industry is now in a position to prove whether it can make a silk dress, or whether it will be a sow's ear."[21] The means of mass production of American fashion had long been in place, but it took a war and the complete dependence on native talent to bring about its coming of age. In 1941, in the mistaken fear that war would dampen feminine interest in fashion, the newly formed New York Dress Institute mounted an advertising campaign, "Don't be a One-Dress Beulah." The organization, a brainchild of publicist Eleanor Lambert, was comprised of better dress manufacturers whose garments bore the label "A New York Creation/N.Y. Dress Institute/Made under the standards of the ILGWU."[22] The following year, the American Fashion Critics' Awards were established as a further encouragement to business and were to be given annually to a Seventh Avenue designer for outstanding work during the previous year. The single most prestigious honor in American fashion, it was the Oscar of the ready-to-wear industry and marked a turning point in the status of American designers. In 1943, the first award, a bronze statuette by Malvina Hoffman and a one-thousand-dollar war bond, was presented to Norman Norell by Mayor La Guardia, who remarked, "the position we've acquired as a fashion center we intend to hold, and not even a peace treaty can take it away from us."[23]

For the first time, the industry celebrated native talent for its uniqueness, creativity, and originality. Over the next few years, the awards reflected the diverse talents of designers who were meeting the varied needs of the American consumer with taste and style. Between 1943 and 1960, Jewish recipients included Gilbert Adrian (Adrian Greenburg), Hattie Carnegie (Henrietta Kanengeiser), Jo Copeland, Jack Horwitz, Anne Klein (Hannah Golofski), Leslie Morris, Norman Norell (Norman Levinson), Nettie Rosenstein, Arnold Scaasi (Arnold Isaacs), Adele Simpson, Pauline Trigère, and Ben Zuckerman. Honorees received treatment previously reserved for the Paris couture, and the Americanization of fashion had finally been acknowledged formally by an industry that had largely ignored its existence until World War II. The American Fashion Critics' Award, which transformed American designers into celebrities of the caliber of their Parisian counterparts, gave them the status to make the clothing they believed in. They developed new kinds of apparel, including a versatile sportswear wardrobe consisting of separate pieces to mix and match, as well as a distinct style for the customer whose figure and pocketbook were smaller than those of her more mature counterpart. This look was exemplified by the clothing of Junior Sophisticates' designer Anne Klein, who believed "junior" referred to a size rather than an age. These areas, largely ignored by Paris, helped to

Adrian tailored ensemble, 1940s.

Courtesy Joseph Simms.

broaden the base of the largest manufacturing industry in New York City, and designers such as Copeland, Rosenstein, and Simpson, who had been in business over the preceding decade or two, began to see their names featured in both editorial and advertising copy.

Sportswear, an American innovation, gained immediate acceptance and has continued to grow in popularity; today, it accounts for the bulk of the ready-to-wear business. Designers turned to such indigenous notions as denim, gingham, South America, and the American West for inspiration. Early exponents were Claire McCardell, Carolyn Schnurer, Bonnie Cashin, Stella Sloat, and Anne Klein. College clothing was a way of dressing that somehow managed to reconcile "conservative" and "fashion." Based on classics such as sweaters, grey flannel, and camel hair coats derived from male campus attire, none of which had the remotest French antecedents, it consisted primarily of separates. Women welcomed this sportswear concept partly as a thrift measure, and the possibility of freshening up one's wardrobe without having to buy a complete outfit was a boon to consumers. The industry also embraced sportswear for economic reasons as it was easier to fit the customer in separates than in dresses or coats, since the length of the torso was not a factor. Therefore, less precision is required, and production costs are lower.

Another Seventh Avenue innovation was apparel for small and short women— junior and petite sizes. Jack Horwitz, whose firm Horwitz & Duberman manufactured dresses under the labels Judy 'n Jill, Dani, Jr., and Deanna Durbin, received

We **know**

what you want

and

we **have** it

in the College Shop

On every Eastern campus,

you said

this neat, classic look.

Here, our own suede jerkin
imported from England,
a marvel of brilliant colors,
29.95—our own black
turtleneck jersey, 11.95—
our own all-round pleated
grey flannel skirt, 17.95

AUGUST 15, 1951

Advertisement for Lord & Taylor College Shop suede jerkin and grey flannel skirt in *Vogue College Issue*, August 15, 1951.

Courtesy of the author.

his award for design in that area. Several manufacturers established "petite" or "diminutive" dress divisions. These solutions addressed problems of fit that astute manufacturers were able to turn into profit.

Wartime shortages and limitations imposed by the War Production Board presented a challenge to American ingenuity that was met with resourcefulness and originality. Nylon, rubber, and metal were allocated for war purposes while the law limited dyestuffs and wool. Then in 1942 the War Production Board passed the L-85

ruling restricting the yardage in a garment, which stated that a jacket could be no longer than twenty-five inches and the depth of a hem was not to exceed two inches. Superfluous details such as hoods, scarves, capes, and pleats were eliminated. The New York Dress Institute debunked the idea that the new regulations had "frozen" fashion, claiming, "The slim silhouette appeared as a fashion fact as early as 1941," and that "Chemistry and Fashion agree it's the 'Very Hot' that freezes!"[24] Neither Adrian nor Norell found L-85 a hardship, since they were already designing apparel that used

Spring

at first sight of our Judy 'n Jill prints
with wonderful new soft-blown skirts.
Of Mallinson's pebbly rayon crepe
in green, blue or brown on white.

Sizes 7-15. 19.95

Young New Yorker Shop

Lord & Taylor

less than the minimum yardage decreed by law. In reality, the war did not dampen women's ardor for new clothes. By 1946, the wholesale value of the dress industry's output had reached $750 million while the coat and suit industry's volume in 1947 was $645 million. In 1948, dresses alone amounted to over $1.5 billion.[25]

After the war, the editors of *Vogue* and *Harper's Bazaar*, both of whom had staunchly championed Seventh Avenue talent, took one look at Christian Dior's revolutionary full-skirted, tiny-waisted, curvy silhouette, defected to Paris and declared, "fashion has moved decisively." Even popular-priced stores were quick to applaud the New Look, the antithesis of spare, slim, and tailored wartime apparel. Ohrbach's, not an establishment ordinarily frequented by New York society women, staged fashion shows featuring its "line-for-line" copies. Since the store had a no-frills policy toward such niceties as delivery, some of these very same women could be seen carrying home their purchases on the spot. The speed with which so-called knockoffs became available increased so rapidly that by autumn 1959 "Dior's hobble skirts were hanging on Macy's racks before a single one had been delivered to a private Dior customer in Paris."[26] Still, American fashion held its ground. While society women were photographed scooping up exact copies of Balenciaga and Monsieur X (Dior), Norman Norell commanded equal prestige in the realm of high fashion. And as far as casual and moderate-priced garb was concerned, America won hands down. Seventh Avenue continued to grow by leaps and bounds while a new generation of retailers and fashion writers discovered designers who owed nothing to Paris and whose influence was being felt abroad. Many American designers, such as Karen Stark (Harvey Berin's designer), Mollie Parnis, and Adele Simpson, were Jewish; their beautiful day, cocktail, and evening clothes were acceptable to all but the most extreme fashion avant-garde; and their names appeared in editorial and paid advertising copy. Sportswear continued to gain in popularity and volume in a society that had both money and leisure time and was rapidly adopting an informal, suburban lifestyle.

Until the 1950s, women's apparel was manufactured by relatively small, privately owned businesses that specialized in a single type of product, and few large or publicly owned firms existed in the industry. By 1959, however, there were twenty-two publicly owned companies in the garment field—two of the giants that went public were Bobbie Brooks under the aegis of Maury Saltzman, and Jonathan Logan,

Advertisement for Harvey Berin dress at Bergdorf Goodman, *Vogue*, **February 15, 1947.**

Courtesy of the author.

Dress, Mollie Parnis, ca. 1954. Mollie Parnis grew up on the Lower East Side, the eldest child of Austrian immigrants. She started her career in fashion as a blouse saleswoman in 1923, and in 1933 she and her husband, Leon Livingston, opened the wholesale firm Parnis Livingston, Incorporated. They were immediately successful, focusing on comfortable yet feminine dresses, quality fabrics, and fashionable, but not trendy, designs. With customers ranging from First Ladies to suburban mothers, Mollie Parnis adapted fashion to fit the needs of American women. Less well-known, however, is that involvement in the garment trade was endemic to her immediate family: her sister Jerry ran a moderately priced wholesale house, and her sister Peggy was the head designer for the lingerie company Chevette.

Courtesy Yeshiva University Museum.

whose founder was David Schwartz. Their volume was in moderately priced sports-wear—everyday apparel and casual clothing for women, misses, and juniors. According to the authors of an important study of the fashion industry, "In the late 1950's, and throughout the 1960's, however, the situation changed and huge, publicly owned, multiproduct corporations made their appearance in the apparel field, usually by means of mergers with and acquisitions of existing companies. Many influences contributed to this phenomenon. Among them was the increase in consumer apparel spending resulting from an expanding economy. Another factor was the need to become large enough to deal successfully with ever-larger textile suppliers, on the one hand, and enormously large retail distributors, on the other."[27]

In less than fifty years, Seventh Avenue had attained heights undreamed of in 1917 when David Levinsky observed, "Foreigners ourselves, and mostly unable to speak English, we had Americanized the system of providing clothes for the American woman of moderate or humble means.... The average American woman is the best-dressed woman in the world, and the Russian Jew has had a good deal to do with making her one."[28]

THE EXHIBITION: *A Perfect Fit*

"Levi Strauss & Co. Section," *A Perfect Fit.*
At Center, Men's 501® Jeans: This pair of
nineteenth-century "waist overalls" was
made of 9-oz. denim from the Amoskeag
Mill in Manchester, New Hampshire.
Discovered in a barn in northeastern
California in the 1990s, these pants are
remarkably similar to the jeans we know
today.

Installation photograph by Jeremy Bales.
Courtesy Yeshiva University Museum.

"Dressing Men," *A Perfect Fit.* This section conveyed how the nineteenth-century men's industry reflected an American trend toward democratization of style. Working-class and middle-class, immigrant and native-born—everyone aspired to a kind of gentility typified by fashionable clothing. By mid-century, it was within reach. The dark suit became the uniform of respect-ability. It was available to every American man who wanted one, and was especially sought out by the growing middle class. Branches of the men's industry quickly evolved to make waterproof clothing, sports attire, work clothes, and underwear. The new field of advertising devel-oped in tandem, stressing the simple requirements of acceptable taste, and encouraging mass-market consumption.

Installation photograph by Jeremy Bales. Courtesy Yeshiva University Museum.

"Dressing Women," *A Perfect Fit.* For most of the nineteenth century, women's clothing was custom-made. When mass production finally entered the women's garment industry, its transformation was slow and gradual. Women's clothing was sensitive to sudden changes in style, and, until late in the century, its construction was very complicated. In addition, fabrics were imported and costly, and most women could not afford many changes of clothing. Skilled dressmakers could be found almost anywhere, and they generally worked inexpensively and efficiently.

Installation photograph by Jeremy Bales. Courtesy Yeshiva University Museum.

Day dress, ca. 1859. Women's wear, such as this taffeta dress, largely continued to be made individually, by dressmakers or at home, even while mass manufacturing took over the production of men's clothing. But the hoopskirt used to support this dress's wide skirt was mass-produced.

Photograph by Ben Cohen. Courtesy Western Reserve Historical Society.

Hoopskirt invoice, Roeder & Bernstien, February 14, 1865.

Courtesy Warshaw Collection of Business Americana, National Museum of American History, Smithsonian Institution.

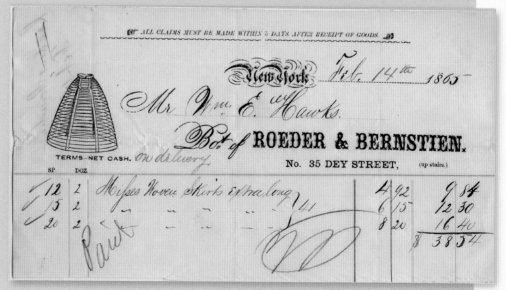

"A Tale of Six Cities: Rochester," *A Perfect Fit*. German Jews came to dominate the menswear industry in the wake of the Civil War. Although New York City remained the center of production, the westward migration of Jews and other Americans established a widening network of Jewish manufacturing centers in smaller cities, such as Rochester and Cincinnati. Urban hubs of the garment industry were not simply places of manufacture; they were communities where families and individuals socialized, maintained traditions, established places of worship and philanthropic support structures, and fostered community networks to build and expand business.

Installation photograph by Jeremy Bales. Courtesy Yeshiva University Museum.

Cutter's shears used by Kalman Haas, ca. 1932. Kalman Haas was born in Galicia, and came to America at the age of eleven. He used these shears for twenty-five years as a cutter for a New York City menswear manufacturer. Tools of the trade defined divisions of labor. The cutter was a highly skilled position, responsible for laying out patterns efficiently to avoid wasting costly fabric. Work done with scissors was improved in the 1880s with cutting swords, and later with electric cutting machines.

Photograph by Ben Cohen. Courtesy Yeshiva University Museum.

"Eastern European Immigrants: The Lower East Side," *A Perfect Fit*.
Writing in 1917, Abraham Cahan credited eastern European immigrants with the creation of American style: "Foreigners ourselves, and mostly unable to speak English, we had Americanized the system of providing clothes for the American woman of moderate or humble means. . . . The average American woman is the best-dressed woman in the world, and the Russian Jew has had a good deal to do with making her one."

Installation photograph by Jeremy Bales. Courtesy Yeshiva University Museum.

"Surging Forward: Manufacturing American Style," *A Perfect Fit.*
By 1900, the average working family could be completely outfitted in ready-made clothing. Distribution was handled through a network of department stores and shops across the country. Department stores offered a huge range of goods to a broad spectrum of shoppers. Special sales, giveaways, newspaper advertisements, and window displays helped entice customers to urban stores. Mail-order catalogues offered an array of products to consumers in smaller towns and rural areas. American designers worked for manufacturers, and remained largely anonymous until the 1930s. The wholesale industry, however, did produce a number of outstanding designers who set the standards for the highest-quality ready-to-wear clothing.

Installation photograph by Ben Cohen. Courtesy Yeshiva University Museum.

Evening coat, Beller, New York/Neiman-Marcus Co., Dallas, 1921. Founded in the late nineteenth century, A. Beller & Co. became well known in the first decades of the twentieth century for its tailored, yet feminine, suits and for sumptuous evening coats. While most department stores did not give credit to wholesale manufacturers, instead placing their own labels in the garments they sold, Beller was considered significant enough to receive top billing.

Max Meyer was only fourteen when he started to work for the Beller firm in 1890, sweeping sidewalks in front of 65 Greene Street and carrying bundles of cut garments to Lower East Side sweatshops. In 1897, he took his first trip to Paris to buy couture models for Beller to copy, and later became a partner at the firm, remaining there until his retirement in 1929.

Photograph by Ben Cohen. Courtesy Texas Fashion Collection, University of North Texas.

Yiddish ILGWU Constitution and Membership Book, Allied Printing, New York, 1913.

Courtesy YIVO Institute.

"Sally, Hattie, Nettie," *A Perfect Fit.* From the blossoming of American readywear in the 1920s to the 1960s and beyond, the names Nettie Rosenstein, Hattie Carnegie, and Sally Milgrim became synonymous with high style. These three matriarchs of the industry crafted and operated definitive fashion empires, leaving a legacy of elegance and entrepreneurship.

Installation photograph by Jeremy Bales, Courtesy Yeshiva University Museum.

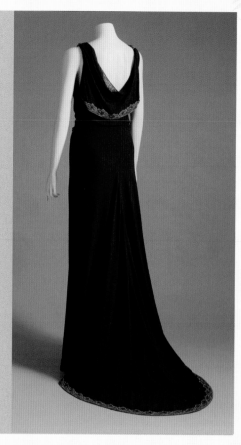

Evening dress, Nettie Rosenstein, ca. 1936. Rosenstein was known for the superb quality of her dresses, as well as her elegant and innovative designs, created by draping directly on a live model. Easily mistaken for a custom-made garment, this dress is one of two nearly identical examples known to exist; the other is trimmed with pink beads rather than coral.

Photograph by Ben Cohen. Courtesy Yeshiva University Museum, Gift of Sandy Schreier.

Nettie Rosenstein, *Look*, October 20, 1953. Nettie Rosenstein preferred to drape directly on the figure, and was known for her use of high-quality fabrics. "Good material regardless of cost is my extravagance," explained Rosenstein.

Photograph by James Hansen. Courtesy Library of Congress.

"West Coast Sportswear and Lifestyle," *A Perfect Fit.* As the California garment industry expanded, it increasingly promoted a California lifestyle based on the car, the beach, and outdoor recreational activity. This lifestyle, along with the sunny climate, had a lasting influence on American casual fashion and culture. At once youthful and inexpensive, sportswear became emblematic of the emerging "American Style," which was a mainstay of the ready-to-wear industry in the twentieth century.

Installation photograph by Jeremy Bales. Courtesy Yeshiva University Museum.

Western ensemble, Nudie's Rodeo Tailors, ca. 1950. Later dubbed the King of Cowboy Couturiers, Nudie Cohn (Nutya Kotlyrenko) first became a tailor's apprentice at the age of eight in Kiev. After immigrating to New York City, he made burlesque costumes and then went west and opened a shop in Hollywood in 1923. Nudie's tailoring business was similar to the shops run by his fellow eastern European Jewish immigrant entrepreneurs and cowboy outfitters, Nathan Turk and Rodeo Ben. These western-style clothing businesses made flashy outfits for rodeo stars and western performers. Nudie's designs combined traditional Ukrainian folk embroidery with Mexican motifs, later adding rhinestones and baubles. This suit was worn by Roy Rogers and depicts his beloved German shepherd Bullet.

Photograph by Ben Cohen. Courtesy Autry National Center, Museum of the American West. Gift of Roy Rogers and Dale Evans.

Western shirt and jeans, Levi Strauss & Co., ca. 1950. Levi Strauss & Co. initially manufactured functional work wear, but their clothing styles also became popular for casual wear. Lady Levi's®, introduced in 1934, were the first women's jeans produced by the company. They were made of a lighter-weight denim, and were designed with a more feminine fit. Sold as dude ranch wear in the 1930s, by the 1950s they were increasingly worn by women around the country.

Photograph by Ben Cohen. Courtesy Levi Strauss & Co.

Winnick Gallery, the Seventh Avenue section, *A Perfect Fit*. During the first decades of the twentieth century, Jewish immigrants from eastern Europe built the New York–based garment business into a billion-dollar-a-year industry. By the 1930s, Seventh Avenue was a teeming conglomeration of small factories based in modern skyscrapers. Most of these concerns turned out ready-made copies of Parisian couture, and American designers toiled in anonymity. But when World War II suspended the influence of Paris, the designers and manufacturers of Seventh Avenue closed the gap by demonstrating that Americans could successfully design and mass-produce a range of stylish clothing on their own.

Installation photograph by Jeremy Bales. Courtesy Yeshiva University Museum.

Clockwise from silver shoe:

Shoe, Delman for Saks Fifth Avenue, ca. 1932–1937. Originally from California, where his family owned a shoe business, Herman Delman came to New York City with the goal of designing shoes for stars of the stage and screen. He established his first store at 588 Madison Avenue in 1919. In 1932, he partnered with Saks Fifth Avenue, but like many designers of the time, he faced difficulties in getting his name on the label. In 1937, he severed his ties with Saks and opened an eponymous shop in Bergdorf Goodman. Herman Delman retired in 1954, but the brand remains successful to this day.

Courtesy Nina Shoes.

Shoe, I. Miller, 1935. Israel Miller emigrated from Germany as a boy, and entered the shoe industry in the late nineteenth century as a designer and maker of theatrical footwear in New York City. He quickly expanded beyond this world, becoming one of the leading shoe manufacturers in the United States. I. Miller shoes were known for both their style and quality of workmanship. At the time of his death in 1929, the company operated 228 branches around the country, producing and importing fine women's footwear. Israel Miller was a noted philanthropist, giving liberally to numerous charities, including Beth Israel Hospital, the Federation for the Support of Jewish Philanthropic Societies, and the Jewish Educational Alliance. He also established the "Millerite" system for the insurance, protection, and welfare of his workers. His sons continued to operate the company after his death.

Courtesy Nina Shoes.

Shoe, I. Miller, 1920s. Women's shoes came into focus as hemlines rose in the 1910s. By the 1920s, an emphasis on detailed decoration matched the shortened skirt styles, while the popularity of t-straps and bar shoes highlighted the importance of activities such as dancing.

Courtesy Yeshiva University Museum.

Shoe, Delman, ca. 1945. Delman shoes were loved by celebrities and "well-heeled" customers alike. Finely crafted (and pricey), they were an enduring investment. After World War II, the firm launched Delmanettes, less expensive and directed at younger career women. These shoes were manufactured under a new, groundbreaking industrial system.

Courtesy Nina Shoes.

Shoe, Nina, 1962. Nina Footwear was founded by brothers Mike and Stanley Silverstein in 1955. The family came from Poland by way of Cuba, where their father had been a designer of clogs in the 1930s. By 1967, the firm was one of the largest makers of better-quality women's shoes in the East, producing more than 5,000 pairs of shoes a day. Nina's 1962 shoe collection became extremely successful. The design of this shoe, made from scraps of suede that were seamed inside out, resonated with the emerging bohemian youth culture of the 1960s. The outside seaming stemmed from a practical matter: it was designed to prevent uncomfortable rubbing against the foot.

Courtesy Nina Shoes.

Shoe, Nina, ca. 1957. Nina Shoes has always been a family affair. The firm was named Nina after Stanley Silverstein's first-born daughter.

Courtesy Nina Shoes.

Photograph by Ben Cohen.

CLOTHING A NATION AT WAR

"Clothing a Nation at War," *A Perfect Fit.* World War II influenced the American fashion industry in fundamental ways. With limited access to Parisian tastemakers, American designers and manufacturers could no longer look to Europe for inspiration, and American designers came to the fore. It was then that the American fashion industry truly came of age. Another stimulus to the industry was regulation #L-85, issued by the War Production Board in 1942. This regulation controlled every aspect of clothing production in an effort to preserve scarce resources. Shorter hemlines, slimmer silhouettes, and trousers without pleats or cuffs transformed American style, while reflecting patriotic support of American troops abroad. The industry embraced these wartime restrictions, coming up with ingenious solutions such as fastening with tabs and hooks instead of metal zippers, or self-ties instead of belts. This photo features Cole of California's "Swoon Suit" that was made without any elastic.

Installation photograph by Jeremy Bales. Courtesy Yeshiva University Museum.

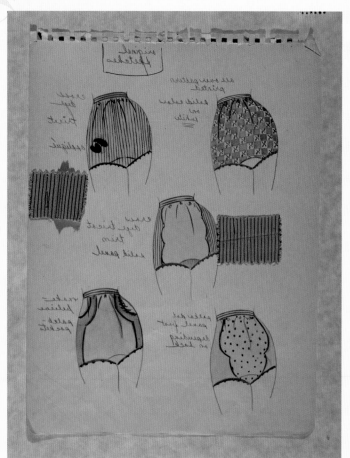

Sketch with swatches, ca. 1955. Brothers Marco and Solomon Mitrani, Sephardic immigrants from Turkey, started Milco (Mitrani+Lingerie+Company) Undergarment Co. in 1921 in New York City. The private label company originally made low-cost panties and slips, and expanded into sleepwear in the 1930s. Around this time they received their first contract from Montgomery Ward and moved to Bloomsburg, Pennsylvania, to avoid the rising labor costs associated with union shops. They became an "integrated" company in the late 1940s when they added textile production to their operation, a move that has allowed them to ride out fluctuations in the market to this day. The development of nylon and synthetics had a major effect on the underwear industry in the mid-twentieth century, and the swatches attached to these printed panty designs offer examples of these new fabrics.

Courtesy MILCO Industries, Inc.

Making parachutes at Milco Lingerie, ca. 1942. During World War II, the lingerie company Milco transformed its production. Factory workers, skilled in the cutting, sewing, and packaging of delicate undergarments, quickly learned the skills of parachute construction. In addition to making parachutes for supplies and bombs, Milco also made "bloomers" for the WAACs (Women's Army Auxiliary Corps).

Courtesy MILCO Industries, Inc.

"Priced to Fit," *A Perfect Fit.* After World War II, American prosperity resulted in an abundance of affordable consumer goods, from clothing to household appliances. Every sector of the garment industry expanded, with particular postwar booms in bridal, maternity, and infant wear. The ready-to-wear industry offered the American mass market a tremendous variety of products at all price points. In this period, blends and synthetic fabrics were embraced. New styles included clothing for college girls and women active in their communities. The industry also achieved a high level of quality in fit and fabrics. Lady-like clothes typified the era, but casual clothes had found a permanent market. Magazines beamed fashion news to all levels of the market.

Installation photograph by Jeremy Bales. Courtesy Yeshiva University Museum

Dress, Adele Simpson, 1955. Born in New York in 1903, Simpson studied at Pratt and worked for Ben Gershel. She then moved to Mary Lee, another Seventh Avenue firm, and in 1949 she bought the company, which then functioned under her name. Simpson adapted French couture to an American ready-to-wear market, giving high style at a mid-range price. She was noted for her color-coordinated dresses and jackets, and was a pioneer in using cotton as a serious fabric.

Photograph by Ben Cohen. Courtesy Texas Fashion Collection, University of North Texas.

Time clock, Broadway Time Clock Company, 1940s. Used for decades in Pauline Trigère's New York workrooms, this time clock regulated the structured work environment that typified Seventh Avenue production. While Pauline Trigère was acclaimed for her designs, the company's early business success was achieved through the good business sense and salesmanship of her partner and brother, Robert. Although she was the creative genius behind the label, it was Robert who handled the finances. In the early years, he would travel around the country with suitcases packed with her innovative designs, developing lasting relationships with buyers and department stores across the United States.

Photograph by Enrique Cubillo. Courtesy Jane Trigère and Ken Schoen.

Workers at Abraham and Vlock Dress Factory observe two minutes of silence in memory of the first anniversary of the Warsaw Ghetto Uprising, Acme Newspictures, New York, April 19, 1944.

Courtesy National Museum of American Jewish History, Philadelphia.

10 Labor Relations and the Protocol of Peace in Progressive Era New York[1]

RICHARD A. GREENWALD

In the history of labor-management relations in the United States, the New Deal framework looms large. When pre-1930s systems of industrial relations are studied, if at all, it is often, to borrow historian Steve Fraser's apt term, as "dress rehearsal(s) for the New Deal."[2] While the New Deal is obviously a significant watershed in twentieth-century labor relations, preceding events are not simply introductions to the main event. Labor relations were not invented in the 1930s, nor, unfortunately, were they solved. In addition, industrial relations had a distinctly ethnic flavor prior to the New Deal that has been missed by industrial relations scholars. One pre–New Deal labor-management agreement, the Protocol of Peace, stands out above the rest. A revolutionary industrial agreement designed by Jews specifically to solve the problems of the predominantly Jewish New York City ladies' garment industry, the Protocol of Peace deserves special attention. Historian Stanley Vittoz states, ironically in a book on the New Deal, "this arrangement [the Protocol] became *the* basic framework for the most durable system of union-management cooperation in the history of modern American capitalism."[3] How did a

labor system designed for New York's garment industry become a model for the nation? What was it about this industry and those involved in it that made it so special? And, was there a special *Jewishness* to the industry that helps explain the Protocol?

Before we can properly understand the Protocol, we must understand both the ladies' garment industry and the nature of reform in New York City.[4] While substantial, employing tens of thousands of workers, it was one of the most unrationalized and primitive industries in the United States at the time. In many ways, it had not changed since the mid-1850s. Its very nature led to a kind of fluidity, where small shops—the so-called moths of Division Street—could enter at will with little investment. The ease of entry and the low level of technological investment needed made labor costs the most significant economic factor for the success of a business. In an ongoing effort to remain profitable, small shop owners repeatedly cut wages—sweating labor—to remain competitive. This forced larger shops to follow suit to remain competitive. And since it was predatory small shops that drove industry standards in the garment industry, it led to what we would now call a

Rose Schneiderman sewing her day's assignment.

Courtesy Kheel Center for Labor-Management Documentation and Archives (5780 P box 30 ff 24a).

race to the bottom, where lower labor costs equals profits.

This primitiveness led observers to point out that this industry was unlike others in industrializing America. It was not an industry of modern factories, but one of small shops in immigrant neighborhoods. It was overwhelmingly Jewish in its makeup, perception, and demeanor—at various times, nearly 80 percent of the workforce and the vast majority of the owners were Jewish. In addition, Jews made up the majority labor until World War I, which led the garment trades to take on a distinctly Jewish character in the United States and be seen as a foreign trade. This was not lost on those involved in the industry or those who watched closely from a distance. There was a firm belief from many established (read assimilated German) Jews that the chaos and foreignness of the rag trade, as it was commonly known, reinforced pernicious anti-Semitic stereotypes of Jews in America. Simply said, it harmed the community. How could Jews become American if Jewish workers were forever

seen as foreign? Historian Daniel Bender, in his book on the image and perception of sweatshop workers, reminds us that Jewish garment workers represented "weak bodies," diseased souls, feeble workers, and un-American ways.[5] This was a powerful cultural image and led reform-minded Jews (social workers, educators, and Progressives) to pay close attention to the garment industry because, in many ways, it affected them through reflection.

Assimilated middle-class German Jews, especially those with professional educations, were active in the settlement house movement, public health reform efforts, educational efforts, aid to immigrants, and labor reform. Education and professionalism became important social markers throughout the period, opening opportunities for Jews who possessed these skill sets. As wealthy German Jews established ethnic aid programs for recently arrived eastern European Jewish immigrants, Jewish social workers found greater professional employment. Jews were thus prominently involved in reform organizations in New York City during the Progressive Era, and historian Daniel Walkowitz has recently argued that

Typical cramped Lower East Side sweatshop in the early twentieth century.

Courtesy Kheel Center for Labor-Management Documentation and Archives (5743 P box 50 ff 6a).

Cluttered shop interior, floor covered with scraps.

Courtesy Kheel Center for Labor-Management Documentation and Archives (5783 P box 1 ff 3a).

Sweatshop with workers crowded next to windows.

Courtesy Kheel Center for Labor-Management Documentation and Archives (5783 P box 1 ff 3).

Jewish welfare agencies and social workers played a dominant role in New York City's reform efforts for the period.[6]

Within this context, the labor agreement—the Protocol of Peace—signed in 1910 ended decades of labor unrest in the ladies' garment industry and pointed toward a new era of cooperation. Industrial relations in the United States had been a bloody and violent affair, and labor history is filled with stories of violence: Homestead, Ludlow, and the like. In fact, it was the violence of the 1892 Homestead strike at Carnegie Steel that brought Louis Brandeis to the labor question. Brandeis, then teaching business ethics at MIT, was appalled at the level of violence and the destruction of Homestead. It was wasteful, and, more to the point, it demonstrated the power of monopolies and the weakness of workers in the American economy. From this point on, he became a dedicated industrial reformer in search of a laboratory for reform. In 1910, Brandeis received his chance when he was invited to New York City to help settle the largest garment strike in that city's history.[7]

That agreement, the Protocol of Peace, was unique for a number of important reasons. Primarily, it went beyond typical bread-and-butter matters in an effort to transform the industry as a whole. It was fashioned in 1910 in the heat of what we now call the Progressive Era and was therefore a product of this reform impulse. At its heart, Progressivism was an effort to square capitalism and individualism with democracy and social justice—an effort to limit the excesses of the late nineteenth century. In this way, the Protocol was a perfect example of Progressivism in action.

It represented a concrete effort to improve life. Academics, journalists, politicians, social workers, and trade unionists alike imbibed the spirit of reform and sought to right economic wrongs, to aid the poor, improve the cities, and modernize America. Garment workers were naturally in the gaze of such reformers because they seemed to cry out for paternal care. They were mostly young, immigrant women, and poor. Progressive Era reformers, in New York as elsewhere, as Robert Wiebe told us, were driven by "the search for order."[8] Their belief in notions of efficiency, professionalism, and objective social science drove their attempts to reconcile the excesses of free-market capitalism with the promise of American democracy, placing them at the forefront of labor reform efforts. In the chaotic garment industry, they found a perfect laboratory for experimentation. If, somehow, they could transform this industry in this city, they could provide a model for the rest of America. In the process, they could improve the image of Jews in America. The reformers involved in the Protocols, therefore, were interested in more than just the production of ladies' garments.[9]

The Protocols[10] established a tripartite labor relations system in the United States: labor, management, and the public were all equal players. These agreements also introduced a generation of reformers, unionists, politicians, and industrial workers to a style of labor relations that set the pattern for the rest of the twentieth century. The Protocols were no mere dress rehearsal for the New Deal. Rather, I would argue that the Protocols should be seen as a profound experiment in industrial relations that influenced the New Deal.

Women hand finishing garments along right side of room.

Courtesy Kheel Center for Labor-Management Documentation and Archives (5783 P box 1 ff 3).

I

The spark that set off the change in industrial relations came from an unlikely source, the predominately Jewish garment workers in New York City. Two great strikes in 1909 and 1910 set the stage of the Protocol. The Cloakmakers' Strike of 1910, the Great Revolt as it has been called, followed on the heels of the Uprising of Twenty-Thousand of 1909, the largest strike of women workers in America. The 1910 strike was, to use Samuel Gompers' apt phrase, "more than a strike . . . [it was] an industrial revolution" because it created a new system of industrial relations.[11] In 1909, the industry awoke to a spontaneous strike of women shirtwaist makers. As the

largest strike by women workers in the country, the Uprising was no doubt significant in countless ways. It had a profound impact on both the industry and the union for five principal reasons. First, it involved to a large degree middle-class reformers who were critical in settling the strike, setting a pattern for all future garment strikes. Second, the strike was settled by shop agreements with individual manufacturers rather than with an industry-wide agreement, which proved to be a major weakness. Third, this strike was essential in rebuilding the International Ladies' Garment Workers' Union (ILGWU), which prior to this had been a

Women raise hands pledging to walk the picket lines, voting for strike.

Courtesy Kheel Center for Labor-Management Documentation and Archives (5780 P box 32 ff 26d).

weak, moribund organization with only a few dollars in its treasury. In the aftermath of the strike, the ILGWU became a more centralized, bureaucratic trade union. Fourth, it brought a heightened worker consciousness to garment workers, radicalizing them in the process. And finally, it brought to light the larger, critical issue of sweated work to the public's attention.[12]

In June 1910, in preparation for a general strike in the industry's cloak sector, the union's leadership created a General Strike Committee and several subcommittees to coordinate the effort. From its inception, this strike was different from that of 1909 in that it was controlled from the top. The Strike Committee consisted of five representatives from each of the nine locals affiliated with the Joint Board (a coalition of locals), with leaders of the ILGWU playing decisive roles. By contrast, the 1909 strike was controlled mainly from the locals. At the center of these new subcommittees stood the Settlement Committee, which was responsible for negotiating and drafting model contracts. This group was dedicated to seeing that this strike would be different in that manufacturers would have to come to labor. Similarly, every aspect of the strike was to be controlled and regimented. Before a striker received strike benefits, they would have to meet the approval of the shop committee chair (the union representative at the shop level), the hall chair (district level), and the local relief chair (local union level). Only then would their claims go to the Relief Committee (international union level).[13]

At 7:00 a.m. on the morning of July 7, the Press Committee began the distribution of the strike edition of the *New Post* in Yiddish, Italian, and English. With the "Red

Post," as the *New York Times* called it, the Great Revolt began. At 2:30 that afternoon, tens of thousands of idle workers clogged the district—and by the end of the afternoon, 75,000 workers were on strike.[14] Large manufacturers, usually a fiercely independent lot, responded to the strike with a unique call for the formation of a manufacturers' association. On July 8, a select group of manufacturers met at the Broadway Hotel to draw up plans for a cloak makers' association. Three days later, a few hundred manufacturers met to form the Cloak, Suit, and Skirt Protective Association. There they elected their leaders, all of whom were major manufac-

turers, including A. E. Lefcourt as chair, Max M. Schwarcz as treasurer, and Max Meyer as secretary. But the major force behind the association was industry lawyer Julius Henry Cohen, who served as legal counsel.

As the strike began, a legion of reformers watching from the sidelines offered their advice and services. They saw this strike as a unique opportunity to begin an experiment in industrial relations. These reformers and their experiment, the Protocol of Peace, would have enormous consequences for more than just the garment workers.

II

Soon after the strike began, Meyer Bloomfield, a prominent Boston social worker and industrial reformer, began efforts to end the strike on behalf of A. Lincoln Filene, owner of the Boston department store. Filene was active in labor reform circles and, as the owner of one of the nation's largest department stores and retailers of clothing, had a keen interest in the garment industry. More to the point, Filene believed he was performing a public service through retail. In this new consumer society, citizen consumers became interested parties in labor disputes involving consumer goods. It was from this involvement that the Protocol would spring.[15]

Filene brought in Louis Brandeis, the famed Boston attorney, to mediate a settlement between leaders of both sides. Brandeis, the model progressive, represented how far Jews could come in America.

A Harvard Law graduate, well-respected corporate lawyer, and nationally recognized reformer, Brandeis would soon be appointed to the U.S. Supreme Court. In meeting with the union, Brandeis urged that they put aside the demand for a closed (union) shop and focus on what he believed to be more realistic and obtainable demands, bread-and-butter issues such as hours and wages. Together they drew up a revised list of grievances.

Brandeis set the mood for the conference. He told the twenty men assembled that they were witnessing an important moment in history, the birth of a new system of industrial relations. They would help shape the future. "Gentleman," Brandeis stated,

we have come together in a matter which we must all recognize is very serious, and an important business, not only to settle this strike, but to create a relation which will prevent similar strikes in the future. That work is one which it seems to me is approached in a spirit which makes the situation a very hopeful one and I am sure from my conferences with council of both parties, and with individual members whom they represent, that those who are here are all here with that desire.[16]

Talks stalled over the union's continued demand for the closed shop. To restart the talks, Filene brought in noted Jewish leader Louis Marshall. Marshall met with Brandeis to work out the details on what would become the preferential shop, which recognized union standards and gave a preference to union members, but was not a closed union shop. Marshall in turn brought in Jacob Schiff and Joseph S. Marcus, prominent Jewish bankers on the Lower East Side. The presence of Marshall and the prestigious representatives of the New York City Jewish banking system was enough pressure for the manufacturers to return to the bargaining tables. On August 25, Cohen, representing manage-ment, had agreed to meet with Meyer London, the union's lawyer, and Marshall to resume talks.[17] When the meeting adjourned, Marshall, Brandeis, Filene, and Benjamin Schlesinger, of the union's Strike Committee, continued to work out language acceptable to both sides. The crux of the matter was that both sides wanted to claim victory. Finally, after several drafts, a revised Marshall Compromise was sent to London and Cohen. Marshall's central role in this process has gone almost unnoticed. As a Jewish leader, Marshall had enormous respect on both sides, and his central role signaled that this was a Jewish community matter that needed to be solved through consensus and compromise, not conflict.

At the same time, an injunction that barred picketing forced the ILGWU's General Executive Board to rethink the strike. The union finally dropped its demand for the closed shop and moved closer to the Marshall Compromise. On September 2, the two lawyers, Cohen and

Strikers arrested and taken to Jefferson Marked Prison.

Courtesy Kheel Center for Labor-Management Documentation and Archives (5780 P box 32 ff 27).

London, met with Marshall to draw up a settlement.[18] In a decision that would foreshadow the increasing bureaucratization of a top-down labor movement removed from the rank and file, the ILGWU took control of the strike away from the Strike Committee. Ratification would not come through a massive rank-and-file voting campaign. Instead, only the shop chairmen (two hundred in all) would vote to accept what would become known as the Protocol of Peace.[19]

As word of the settlement spread, both sides quickly called it a victory. Cohen told the *New York Times* that the Protocol provided "a great opportunity to build up a strong working relation between the unions and the manufacturers." All sides thanked Marshall, Filene, Henry Moskowitz, and Bloomfield, but Marshall offered special thanks to Brandeis, whom he saw as a true hero. Many respected Brandeis because he seemed to remain above the fray.[20] The union and the strikers declared victory and, what is more, a new day in labor relations. The celebrations lasted for well over a week.[21]

One measure of the Protocol's success is the unionization that followed, as well as the new role played by union leaders and outside arbitrators. Union leaders, cheered by swelling membership rolls, were vested with increased authority and respectability by the Protocol. In 1910, the New York City cloak makers represented three-fourths of the entire ILGWU membership. The agreement covered 1,796 out of a possible 1,829 shops. By 1912, 90 percent of all cloak makers were in the union. Manufacturers could take a measure of hope that the anarchy and chaos of the seasonal wildcat strikes were over as all garment workers

were being brought into a disciplined and maturing labor union.[22] The signing of the Protocol of Peace finally institutionalized for the cloak makers, and then for the whole industry, some of the major features that the shirtwaist workers had struggled for in 1909.

The Protocol created "a kind of industrial self-government," which Brandeis had been trying to establish for some time. There were three major parts to the Protocol. First were the normal labor contract issues of hours, minimum wages, and paid holidays. In this regard, the Protocol was better than most contracts of the day. Under the Protocol, wages (the piece rates) would be set through an elaborate system involving workers and managers. The second aspect of the Protocol involved features unique to the garment industry: abolition of charges for electricity and supplies, the establishment of shop committees to set piece rates, and, most revolutionary, creation of a Joint Board of Sanitary Control, a committee made up of representatives of both the union and the association who would oversee working conditions. The third and most important feature was Brandeis's conceptions of efficiency and industrial democracy. In short, the higher wages and better conditions would be paid for through increased productivity and efficiency.

The Protocol had been designed to rationalize and modernize the industry and to improve the plight of workers. In doing this, the Protocol favored the large shops that could modernize production through efficiencies of scale. By leveling the wage structure—placing a floor on labor costs that would be universal industry-wide—smaller shops, now stripped of their ability to sweat labor, were no longer competitive. The Protocols were designed to propel the industry into the mainstream of the American factory system. Julius Henry Cohen, chief counsel for the employers throughout the life of the Protocol (1910–1916), recognized the substantial benefit management had reaped. Writing in 1916, he explained how the ILGWU helped make the ladies' garment industry a modern industry:

Into this industry came a union. Another nuisance to add to the plagues of the manufac-turer: Is it any wonder that at first it was ignored, then fought, and only with reluctance accepted as a factor. Then, if, through the union, some order could be brought out of this chaos, hailed with hope! If all paid the same price for the same labor, as all paid for merchandise, efficiency as manufacturers would count for something against unscrupulous competitors.[23]

By standardizing labor costs and control-ling its own members, the union became the policing agency for the industry, doing what manufacturers could not: bring stability and rationality.[24]

III

Even before the ink dried on the cloak makers' Protocol, reformers were heralding it as *the* solution to industrial war. Noted journals such as the *North American Review, Forum, Atlantic Monthly,* and *Outlook,* as well as the scholarly *Annals of the American Academy,* published feature articles on the historic settlement. These essays, taken as a whole, were fawning in their praise. They proclaimed the Proto-col—the *idea* of the Protocol—as the savior for American democracy in an age of excessive industrialism. They also gave full credit to Louis Brandeis, whom they called the father of the idea. What they neglected to discuss was the role of the workers. Read carefully, the press coverage of the Protocol depicts the distrust most affluent Ameri-cans had for labor. What made the Protocol unique was that it placed an organizational structure above the shop floor. It was principally designed to control workers. The Protocol set up a paternalistic top-down bureaucracy, more interested in rationalizing industry and controlling work-ers than with true democracy.

Brandeis insisted that this new approach would transform the American industrial landscape, fulfilling America's democratic promise. He wrote to the leading journal and newspaper editors of the day urging their support. "This seems to be the time," he wrote to journalist Ray Stannard Baker in 1912, "to commence the campaign of education."[25] Brandeis firmly believed that the root causes of "the present [industrial] difficulty" belonged to the rise of big business and cutthroat competition.[26] "Is there not a causal connection between the development of the huge, indomitable trusts and the horrible crimes now under investigation," he wrote to editor Paul Kellogg in 1911. Because of their sheer size, Brandeis saw large corporations' potential to exert undue influence on the market and society, creating an economic jungle. The nature of the economy, and the newly arrived immigrant groups, jointly threatened American society. The Protocol, therefore, could be a tool of corrective "civilizing" action by bringing industry and labor into line with the forces of democracy.[27] Brandeis did not favor unionism per se; it was a useful means to an end. The Protocol, he proposed to journalist Lawrence Fraser Abbott, "seems to offer a solution consistent with American spirit and traditions as well as with justice."[28] Through it, he believed he could preserve democracy.

At the top of this system established by the Protocol stood the Board of Arbitra-tion, which consisted of three members—one from management, one from labor, and Brandeis, who represented the public. All decisions of the board were binding. Below the board was the Committee on Grievances, which consisted of four members: two from labor and two from management. This committee heard all grievances filed by either side, and a majority vote brought settlement—meaning that at least one member from the other side had to switch to the other. Only if a deadlock occurred—which happened all too often—would it go to the Board of Arbitration.[29]

Another remarkable feature of the Protocol was the Joint Board of Sanitary

Mass march to City Hall.

Courtesy Kheel Center for Labor-Management Documentation and Archives (5780 P box 32 ff 27).

Control. This was a prototypical Progressive Era reform effort. This board consisted of seven members: two from the union, two from management, and the remainder chosen by those four members to represent the public. Its first order of business was a systematic investigation into the sanitary conditions (i.e., health) of the cloak, suit, and skirt industry. This was one of the first full-scale public health surveys of an industry. The Sanitary Board did not, at first, have enforcement powers; instead, its power lay in its ability to marshal public outrage against unsanitary conditions. Members of this board had great faith in the public at large, believing that if they only knew the true conditions, they would become outraged and demand action. The board members saw themselves as illuminating the dark spaces of industrialism, bringing them to the light of justice.

While the machinery of the Protocol was being put into place, Protocolists began to spread the agreement beyond the cloak trades to all sectors of the ladies' garment industry in New York City. Soon all trades had their own Protocol. It was clear to many from the beginning that the founding fathers of the Protocol, as Brandeis and company were known, did not become involved in the strike just to settle the unrest in one branch of one industry. To prove their thesis about the Protocol's revolutionary potential, they needed to demonstrate its potential to bring peace to an entire industry. Thus, even before the bugs were worked out of the initial settlement, Brandeis and company were seeking to implement the Protocol in new sectors of the ladies' garment industry.

IV

The Protocol's most unique feature was the complex grievance process it established. If a problem arose in a given shop, the worker was to inform the shop steward, who then informed management's representative in the shop to try to settle the issue immediately. If no settlement could be reached, the shop steward presented the grievance to the union's Joint Board, the federation of the various cloak, suit, and dressmakers' locals. At this level, a formal complaint was issued and sent to the Committee on Grievances (later renamed the Board of Grievances) for investigation and a hearing. All the while, the worker(s) was to remain on the job producing garments. Failure to do so could result in management replacing the offending worker with another union worker and rendering the grievance moot. If the complaint made it to the board, two clerks (one from each side) were dispatched to investigate. Once both were satisfied with their findings, they attempted to settle the matter themselves. If they failed to do so, the grievance went to the two Chief Clerks—*the* main labor and management representatives. If they failed to solve it, a formal hearing of the entire board was called.[30]

The Board of Grievances was charged with the seemingly impossible task of settling all disputes through consensus. Yet, for a time, the new board functioned smoothly and quickly. From April 1911 until October 1913, 7,956 grievances were filed with the board. Of these, 7,477 were handled or settled by the clerks. Only 179 went to the Board of Grievances, and only 20 continued on to the Board of Arbitration—the high court of the Protocol. The pace of grievance filing, however, escalated with each passing month as it proved a highly successful feature. From early in 1911 to April 1912, there were an average of 150 petitions filed per month. But, by spring 1913, the number mushroomed to 384. Because of this pattern, as early as 1912, the real power of the Protocol machinery seemed to rest in the offices of the Chief Clerks.[31]

The grievances that were filed and eventually went to the full board reveal a pattern. Of the initial 179 cases brought forward, 122 came from the union. Many of these, 48 in all, involved some form of discrimination against union members by shop owners. Of the petitions brought by the Cloak, Suit, and Skirt Manufacturers' Protective Association, the vast majority dealt with wildcat strikes, often resulting from perceived discrimination of union members by owners. As early as 1912, it appears that workers, perceiving discrimination, increasingly took matters into their own hands rather than wait for what was beginning to slow the Protocol machinery of justice. This shop-floor militancy, which was so much of a tradition among the ladies' garment workers, was increasingly problematic for the proper functioning of the Protocol.[32]

In an effort to win back rank-and-file workers and renew interest in the structure of the contract, Brandeis conducted a successful one-man public relations blitz. The troubles of the Board of Grievances

centered on the key element of the Protocol: the meaning of the preferential shop. Trying to convince America that this element would "be a way out of our current difficulty," he tried to revive interest in his idea, contacting over a dozen major magazines and writers. In his correspondence with muckraking journalist Ray Stannard Baker in February 1912, Brandeis argued that "this could be made into a great human story. Would it not be possible for you to take it up?"[33] Brandeis's efforts paid off, and almost all the major journals and reform magazines of the era produced feature articles on the Protocol that served to reinvest public confidence in it that it did not possess of its own accord.

One unique aspect of the Protocol was that in recognizing the union as an industrial partner, the ILGWU now had responsibilities. For one thing, it had to police its members and force nonunion shops under the Protocol umbrella. The structure of the agreement was such that all strikes for Protocol-member shops were forbidden, unless authorized by the Joint Board of Sanitary Control. The union received the benefits of the preferential shop only if it could assure both a steady supply of union workers and could assume continuous efficient production. Every time workers wildcatted, the entire agreement was in jeopardy. Over the course of the agreement, the ILGWU became increasingly centralized and bureaucratic. It placed troublesome locals into receivership and fought with the Joint Board over who represented the union at the Protocol table. Ironically, what made the Protocol so promising and potentially effective also sowed the seeds of its ruin. By recognizing that labor—responsible labor, that is—had an interest in the management of industry, the Protocol unleashed a discourse of industrial democracy within the union.[34] Industrial democracy held out a promise to workers of a truly democratic industrial system. There was, however, a built-in contradiction. The democracy reformers envisioned was more limited and constrained than that envisioned by the workers. As workers became more invested in the Protocol, the more democracy they demanded and the more unruly the system became, eventually collapsing under its own weight. Thus, ironically, the driving force behind the Protocol—industrial democracy—was also the source of its eventual demise. Indeed, many of the designers of the Protocol feared this problem from the start and sought to create institutional safeguards that were profoundly antidemocratic. For instance, the "peacemakers," as the creators of the Protocol were called, established a rigid top-down bureaucratic system. When this proved ineffective, as the agreement was a voluntary contract, some advocated that the state should be called in to enforce a systemization of industrial relations.[35]

The Protocol put in place a system of establishing minimum wages and maximum hours that would be mirrored nationally in the New Deal's Fair Labor Standards Act and a system of setting industry standards that influenced the National Industrial Recovery Act codes. It created a definition for what constituted a legitimate shop and tried to outlaw sweatshops. It established, through the framework, a system of employee health care as the ILGWU quickly established the Union Health Center modeled after the Joint Board of Sanitary Control. In addition, the Protocol introduced into labor relations the notion that the public had an important role to play within industrial relations. Binding arbitration, industrial partnership, and the notion of consumer interest and economic stability were at the core of the Protocol.

Historians have long compared and rightfully connected Progressive Era reforms to the New Deal. Recently, historian Alan Brinkley has reminded us that the New Deal was not a coherent whole; rather, he argues, it was made up of parts. What we think of as "New Deal liberalism," or modern liberalism and the modern administrative state, he argues, are policies that found form after 1936 and most importantly during World War II. The modern liberal state, as Brinkley attests, was born after "the end of reform." The first half of this reform impulse, he asserts—ending in 1936—stretches back to Progressive Era reforms. The experience of the Protocol seems to reinforce Brinkley's claim and suggests that a reexamination of the connections between Progressive Era reform and the New Deal is needed. What is missing from Brinkley's treatment, however, is the centrality of ethnicity to the early reform efforts. The Protocols influenced a generation of industrial reformers, many of whom went on to important careers in the federal government. Yet, one reason why the Protocol worked, even if briefly, was that the main actors on both sides (the majority of the owners and workers) shared a similar ethnic identity, that of being Jews in America. Louis Brandeis, Louis Marshall, Meyer London, and Julius Henry Cohen used culture to bind the sides together even as economics tore them apart. This is an important part of the story, worth pondering and remembering.[36]

11 Acclimatizing Fashion: Jewish Inventiveness on the Other (Pacific) Coast, 1850–1940

WILLIAM TOLL

Introduction

The clothing industry of the Pacific Coast, like the region's general economy, grew at first to meet local needs. Though eastern manufacturers filled the initial demand for men's ready-made clothing, the remoteness of the region and the distinctive features of its terrain and climate provided manufacturers in San Francisco and other cities with opportunities to satisfy local demands.[1] From the work pants of Levi Strauss and the overalls of Cohn-Goldwater to the fabrics of the Oregon City Woolen Mills and the canvas rain gear of Hirsch-Weis, early West Coast mill owners and apparel makers focused on the demands of work and climate rather than a more refined sense of fashion. Their efforts to have form and raw materials follow function would, by 1915, lead to a regional sense of style.[2] The production process, in conjunction with the mercantile network that brought it into existence, would also transform provincial young men into regional civic as well as commercial leaders.[3]

In the 1920s and 1930s, the aesthetic isolation of the Pacific Coast from the rest of the country—and the world—would dramatically end. The motion picture studio system, with its international distribution network, brought high fashion to the West from Paris and projected Hollywood's adaptations to movie audiences everywhere. By the late 1930s, studio designers combined Parisian couture and French fabrics with a Southern California emphasis on bright colors and casual attire to create a new sense of style.[4] Just as Los Angeles surpassed other Pacific Coast cities in size and wealth, the glamour of the new mass media enabled Southern California clothing styles to become a fashion symbol for the region. As one Los Angeles journalist noted in 1935, "the movie stars—to a greater degree every year, are setting the fashions for the world."[5] And it was good for the Jews.

Origins in Merchandising

The Jewish role in the regional clothing industry grew from the activities of Jewish pioneer merchants in satisfying local tastes.

Present at the founding of towns and cities all along the Pacific Coast, Jews from central Europe utilized a supply chain created by family and friends to bring consumer goods to the most remote mining camps and ranches. Jewish merchants soon became the mainstays of Main Street, from Sacramento to Virginia City, as well as Portland, Los Angeles, and smaller towns in the interior. They sold supplies on credit to miners, farmers, and ranchers, and took their produce in exchange.[6] For example, wool received from ranchers was routed through a Jewish mercantile network to mills owned by Jews in San Francisco and Oregon City. By 1880, San Francisco's merchants handled 99 percent of the region's imports, and its manufacturers, who were becoming equally important to the city's economy, produced 60 percent of the region's goods, including clothing.[7]

In the fluid economy of Gold Rush California, the early Jewish entrepreneurs moved easily between merchandising and manufacturing, and occasionally into banking. They had little initial expertise in any of these undertakings, but branched out as opportunities appeared. The Bavarian immigrants Lewis Gerstle and Louis Sloss, who met in San Francisco, made their initial profits by importing merchandise, which they sold through a general store in Sacramento and through a string of young Jewish peddlers. Sloss and Gerstle relocated to San Francisco in the late 1850s, and within ten years they were importing leather goods, furs, and hides, had gained a franchise to hunt seals in Alaska, and even branched into the manufacture of leather soles for shoes. Sensing yet another consumer need, they opened the Pioneer

Woolen Mills, which was managed by William Steinhardt, who like themselves would become one of the city's leading philanthropists.[8] In the 1850s, Levi Strauss also imported dry goods, which he sold to retailers and to small manufacturers of work clothes, like Jacob Davis of Reno. When Davis needed capital to patent and manufacture large quantities of heavy cotton work pants with a unique system for reinforcing the seams, he went into partnership with his more affluent supplier, Strauss. Davis moved to San Francisco to supervise the cutting-out procedures. When their conventional putting-out process of production could not meet demands, they recapitalized their factory and hired women to sew up the garments.[9]

Virtually none of the early Jewish clothing manufacturers built their businesses on the skill of hand tailoring. Historian Hasia Diner has noted that Jewish boys growing up in the towns of Prussia were more likely to be apprenticed to craft skills like tailoring than were boys growing up in the villages of Bavaria.[10] And indeed most of the Jewish tailors in an 1880 sample of eight Pacific Coast cities, including Portland and Los Angeles, had been born in Prussia, Prussian Poland, or Russia. Yet with a few conspicuous exceptions, all of the men starting major woolen mills or ready-made clothing factories were from Bavaria, not Prussia. They had earned their initial capital as merchants, not as artisans. Ready-made clothing manufacturing seems to have been a form of vertical integration, extending back from the wholesale distribution node of the merchandising chain. It was an outgrowth of innovative merchandising in a region with special climatic demands rather than a modernization of an artisan craft.

Non-Jews as well as Jewish entrepreneurs built new manufacturing plants into established chains of commerce. After the discovery of gold in Idaho in the early 1860s, several Portland merchants led by William S. Ladd started a small factory in Portland to make miners clothing; the grand enterprise employed fourteen men and four women working at ten sewing machines.[11] In the mid-1880s, Ben Selling, a Jewish merchant in Portland, followed a more modest pattern. Selling owned a large men's clothing store and supplied dry goods, crockery, and shoes, which he acquired from Jewish importers, to general stores managed primarily by relatives in small Oregon towns. When he believed that the prices charged by the San Francisco manufacturers of underwear were too high, he financed his own factory. Selling first supplied a local man experienced in the production of garments with the capital to acquire the necessary machinery and then distributed the product through his chain of rural retailers. Selling soon boasted to a relative in San Francisco, "We are now perfectly independent of your city and can tell Mr. H. K. & Company what we will do and what we won't."[12]

Two Jewish brothers from Prussia who did venture into production were Ralph and Isaac Jacobs, who became managing partners of the Oregon City Woolen Mills. Despite their Prussian origins, they became part of the enterprise because of their marketing interests, not because of tailoring skills. By 1860, merchants and bankers in Portland knew that gold miners in Idaho needed clothing and blankets. Encouraged by the success of a small woolen mill in Salem, Oregon, they conceived of a new mill where the Willamette River plunges

Oregon City Woolen Mills, ca. 1905. The mill utilized the power of the Willamette River flowing north over the falls to Portland.

Courtesy Oregon Historical Society.

Cutting room, Oregon City Woolen Mills, ca. 1918. Tables spread with bundles of cloth, bolts, and patterns.

Courtesy Oregon Historical Society.

Interior of garment factory, Oregon City Woolen Mills, ca. 1918. Long room, sewing machines, garments in piles.

Courtesy Oregon Historical Society.

White Stag catalogue cover, for two generations a Portland icon, ca. 1939.

Courtesy Hirsch-Weis Manufacturing Company, Business Collection, Mss 1510, Oregon Historical Society and Research Library.

**John Zehntbauer
(Jantzen), Clarence
Bishop (Pendleton), and
Max Hirsch (White Stag)
at White Stag factory,
Portland, Oregon, 1957.**

*Courtesy Oregon Historical
Society, Jantzen, Inc. Collection.*

over the falls at nearby Oregon City. With the help of William S. Ladd, they raised the initial capital and hired a superintendent. The Jacobs brothers, who had made money in the Gold Rush and opened a general store in Oregon City, had been among the initial investors and gained control of the mill in 1866. They acquired modern machinery and survived a fire that destroyed the initial building in 1873 and rebuilt on an even larger scale the following year. They marketed much of their merchandise, which included shirts and blankets as well as cloth, through Jewish wholesale supply firms like Fleischner-Mayer & Co. in Portland and also in local dry goods stores.[13] In San Francisco, Levi Strauss similarly undertook woolen manufacturing to augment his commercial operations, when he and two partners acquired the Pacific Woolen Mills from the estate of the banker William Ralston. The mill's higher grades of woolen cloth, which had been cut into blankets, were then used to line Levi's more expensive pants and coats.[14] A generation later, the Miller family of Seattle expanded from wholesale dry goods to manufacture quilted sleeping bags for the Alaska gold rush.[15]

Merchandising could also lead ambitious young men anticipating a market to manufacture specialized clothing. Morris Cohn, who emigrated as a young boy from Germany, arrived in Los Angeles from New York in 1889 in the wake of a great land boom. He expected to create a product that had nothing to do with fashion, but which would meet a growing local demand—

Workers cut stacks of fabric to patterns in cutting room at White Stag, well-known sportswear manufacturers, Portland, Oregon, 1954.

Courtesy Oregon Historical Society, #006824.

Brownstein, members of pioneer Los Angeles mercantile families, borrowed money from Brownstein's uncle, banker Kaspar Cohn, and in 1897 started a plant to manufacture overalls. By 1912, they too appealed to fashion by expanding to manufacture shirts.[17]

In Portland, the Meier merchandising family provided the expertise and capital to launch another manufacturing firm that for many years produced unique items for regional consumption. As Aaron Meier and Sigmund Frank's original general store grew, Meier's wife, Jeannette, followed a common practice by bringing her younger brothers, Max and Leopold Hirsch, from Hesse, Germany, to apprentice in the business. As Meier & Frank grew into a large department store and as the sons of the principal partners came to manage the business, the Hirsch brothers wished to run their own firm. They sold their stock to their sister and shifted to manufacturing by buying a local company that produced water-resistant sailcloth. The Hirsch brothers knew very little about the production process, so they took the manager of the sailcloth company, Harry Weis, as a partner and called their new firm Hirsch-Weis. As the business prospered by developing new uses for sailcloth, Max sent his son Harold to Dartmouth College, where the western boy learned the eastern sport of skiing. Harold graduated during the Depression and wished to contribute to the family business, so he suggested that the company adapt its unique cloth to manufacture a product still unknown to the Portland area, skiwear. Since another local company, Jantzen, had already adapted heavy knitwear to make rowing trunks and

men's work clothes. His innovation with electric-powered sewing machines apparently led to high profit margins and an expanding business. By 1899, Lemuel Goldwater, son of Arizona's mercantile pioneer, Michael Goldwater, became Cohn's partner. He linked the production process in Los Angeles to his family's network of general stores throughout the Southwest, and Cohn-Goldwater grew rapidly. As the regional standard of living increased, the firm expanded its line from work to sports clothing like shirts, slacks, and jackets.[16] By 1930, Fred Cole had joined the firm, and it marketed the line of sports clothing under a new name, Cole of California. Perhaps inspired by Cohn's initial success, Henry Louis and D. J.

White Stag sign, signature of the Portland waterfront.

Courtesy Oregon Historical Society, Daily Journal of Commerce.

swimwear, the adaptation of a cloth unique to the area toward new clothing conformed to local practice. And just as Jantzen learned to advertise by developing a logo, the diving girl, Harold Hirsch advertised by translating and inverting his firm's name and by creating a huge neon "White Stag" as an illuminated logo for the Portland waterfront.[18]

Because their stores and factories were integral to urban growth, many Jewish pioneers, like their Gentile counterparts, fortified their entrepreneurial success with civic activism. As permanent residents, Jews joined volunteer fire companies, and were subsequently elected to school boards and city councils, and served as mayors and sheriffs. In the early twentieth century, Jewish department store owners, because they controlled large parcels of real estate at the heart of the city, were particularly influential in rudimentary ventures in city planning. As the wealthy elite to which they belonged retreated from electoral politics, they were often appointed to various commissions overseeing waterfronts, parks, and law enforcement. Indeed, successful pioneers who combined merchandising and light industry like Bernard Goldsmith, Ben Selling, Bailey Gatzert, Levi Strauss, and the Goldwaters created a Jewish regional tradition of governmental leadership.[19]

Hollywood Fashions, Ladies' Ready-to-Wear, and a New Pacific Jewry

When Russian Jews arrived in the early twentieth century, they too usually started with small business ventures but in a far more specialized business environment than their central European colleagues had faced forty or fifty years before. Rather than serving the general public of small towns and mining camps, they created a niche by opening pawnshops and second-hand clothing and furniture stores to serve a large, drifting, and racially diverse working class in the region's commercial hubs.[20] As the population of Pacific Coast cities grew between 1900 and 1930, Jewish newcomers also opened small and more specialized retail stores and became identified with a new garment industry. The most successful families, like the Shemanskis of Portland and Seattle, the Sierotys of Los Angeles and San Francisco, and the Gottsteins of Seattle, opened large low-priced stores and supplied inexpensive ready-made clothing in order to shift the emerging lower-middle class away from secondhand merchandise and toward their business.

In Seattle and Portland during the 1920s, Jewish newcomers with some tailoring skills began to expand into more modern forms of ready-made production for women. As Jenna Joselit has noted, the expansion of the women's ready-made clothing industry brought inexpensive copies of dresses and suits designed originally for the elite to a mass audience. Women could now use clothing to express personal taste rather than to designate class allegiance.[21] Designers on the Pacific Coast, with its more flexible sense of proper clothing for specific occasions, and with the essential help of that most democratizing of media—the motion pictures—would further free fashion from its elite European origins and give sartorial identity more flexible American styles.[22]

The small size of the new firms, their dependence on communal contacts, and the positioning of manufacturing in the regional economy are well illustrated in the oral history of Hyman Kirshner, who opened a two-man coat and suit factory in Portland in 1924. Born in Russia in 1904 and brought to Portland as a child, Kirshner stumbled into the business after high school when he took a temporary job sweeping floors in a small women's cloak and suit factory. When he expressed an interest in learning to cut fabrics, his employers allowed him to learn the skill. Within two years, his ambition led him to raise minimal capital from his family and form a partnership with Ben Vogel, a determined young pattern maker, whose cousins would play a large role in the women's clothing industry in Los Angeles. Though Kirshner's "Modish Cloak and Suit" copied more expensive styles, its products were unique because they used only local woolen cloth, some of which came from the Oregon City Woolen Mills, which the Jacobs family still managed. Kirshner also used local retail stores to carry samples of his cloaks and suits, which were designed to meet local tastes.[23]

While Portland's garment factories were scattered throughout the downtown, Jews—and some Lebanese and Italians—created an authentic clothing district between Chinatown and Market Street in San Francisco. Over two dozen tiny factories were concentrated between Sutter and Post, Montgomery and Grant Streets, with over a dozen more west of Grant

Street and south of Geary, and two dozen just south of Market between First and Fourth Streets. Some owners, like the Malouf family and Joseph Zukin, operated a branch in San Francisco of main operations in Los Angeles, while owners of smaller plants like Matthew DiGesu and Harry Breitstein would soon move to Los Angeles. Jewish involvement in the garment industry extended to union organizing as well. Rose Pessota tried to organize the women's clothing factories for the International Ladies' Garment Workers' Union (ILGWU) in 1934, but found that most of the employees were Chinese women and that unions could make no headway without Chinese-speaking organizers.[24]

While Jews were involved in the garment industry in Portland and San Francisco, Los Angeles's rapid expansion in the 1920s induced over two hundred small manufacturers to create the largest clothing district west of Chicago.[25] As in San Francisco, it was concentrated in loft buildings, which stretched along Los Angeles Street and Broadway between Second and Tenth Streets.[26] Many of the early workers in men's clothing in Los Angeles were Jewish, and a local of the Amalgamated Clothing Workers' union had been organized before 1920.[27] But the great majority of the factory operatives in women's clothing were Mexican women already residing in the area.[28] An article in *Fortune* in 1939 estimated that one needed perhaps $10,000 to acquire the equipment, the supplies, and space to start a factory in New York, while in Los Angeles lower rents and labor costs would have lowered operating expenses substantially.[29]

The residential patterns of clothing

manufacturers highlighted the general migration and clustering of the Jewish population in new middle-class neighborhoods. In San Francisco, Jewish clothing manufacturers moved directly west of their small factories, following the car lines to the Western Addition and into newer homes in the Richmond District, north of Golden Gate Park. Temple Emanu-El and Congregation Sherith Israel soon relocated there, in what became the center of the city's Jewish community. In Portland, clothing manufacturers followed a car line on East Glisan Street, with the most affluent settling farthest out in the Laurelhurst neighborhood. In Los Angeles, larger numbers led to a wider dispersal, albeit with a re-clustering on particular blocks in specific neighborhoods. The residences of the 115 manufacturers who could be located in the Los Angeles city directory for 1927 followed clear patterns. The most concentrated contingent of 21 manufacturers had settled in pleasant, multiracial Boyle Heights, where streetcars on Brooklyn Avenue could take them easily to the garment lofts downtown.[30] Though an immigrant area, undeveloped hilly land to the north and east permitted the journalist Harry Carr to note that "the clean wide streets, the lawns and flowers—most of all the splendor of the mountain panorama, make considerable contrast to the pushcarts, tenements, and dirty streets from which they came."[31]

The residential trajectory of the majority of garment manufacturers illustrates how the industry promoted social assimilation rather than cultural conservatism. Like the general (white) population of Los Angeles, most Jewish clothing manufacturers were moving to the west side or to suburban cities like Pasadena and Alhambra. A group of thirty-two men, for example, moved to an area flanking Wilshire Boulevard, between Vermont on the east, and Crenshaw and Rossmore on the west. This district held not only the offices of smaller motion picture producers, as well as Paramount Studios and 20th Century Fox, but new Orthodox, Conservative, and Reform synagogues. Another group of thirteen clothing manufacturers settled farther south in the West Adams Boulevard area, the site of the new West Adams Hebrew Congregation.[32]

During the Depression, most observers attributed the growth of the local women's clothing industry to the undiminished popularity of motion pictures. The promotion by the studios of glamorous film stars meant that even as family incomes declined millions of women could still attend a fashion show each week on the silver screen. The movies, which adapted financially and thematically to the Depression by reducing budgets and dramatizing the travails of daily life, also promoted clothing designed in Hollywood and produced for broader consumption by Los Angeles firms.[33] In the 1920s, movie studios employed wardrobe designers, whom they sent to Paris to consult with leaders of the fashion industry. But by 1927, twelve cloak and suit manufacturers formed the Hollywood Fashion Associates, while the larger (Los Angeles) Associated Apparel Manufacturers coordinated national promotion of locally based fashion lines.[34] Hollywood legend has it, however, that in late 1929, as hemlines suddenly dropped in Paris, producers believed that movies scheduled

"Filmland Fashion Flash,"
The California Stylist,
April 1939.

*Courtesy Los Angeles County
Museum of Art, The Doris Stein
Research Center for Costume
and Textiles.*

APRIL, 1939   **Thirteen**

Sylva Weaver, *Los Angeles Times* **Fashion Editor, Sees All and Tells All About the Hollywood
Fashion World in This Open Letter to One of Her Buyer Pals**

*Black and white
organza is this
lovely gypsy dress.*

Blues and greens are Sonya Henie's newest colors in a costume with a
full skating skirt of Parisian blue, a blouse of green, blue, and white challis,
and a brief blue bolero lined with printed challis. Sonya likes colored prints
so much she even has a pair of paisley silk sandals which wrap and tie
around her ankles, a matching bag and gloves—all in orange, yellow, char-
treuse, white, and green—and she wears these with all-white dresses.

Green and gray is Wendie Barrie's choice in a print dress with a quilted
bolero jacket and a vivid Irish-green taffeta ruffled petticoat peering from
the full hemline. A leghorn poke bonnet finishes her outfit while Alice
Faye wears a large white hat with green grosgrain twisted in a bandeau
effect to complete her newest print costume which includes a plain black
dress and a black and white tie silk print redingote fastened with a wide
Kelly green patent leather belt. White polka dots on navy make Priscilla
Lane's newest costume which has a very full skirt worn over an equally
full white petticoat with a hand-embroidered lace hemline ruffle.

But half your customers are still wondering what kind of suits to buy
for their spring daytimes, their after-Lent parties, and their coming vaca-
tions and trips, aren't they, Dora? I know everyone of them would love
to look like Claudette Colbert, for instance, so here's how. Claudette's newest
spring suit is her most lavish in seasons, designed by Irene. In sap green
lightweight wool, it has a straight short skirt and a loose hip-length jumper.
Under the jumper is a soft white crepe blouse which shines with strands of
bugle beads strung back and forth from the side seams. Her green pillbox
hat has a starched, matched veiling tying under the chin but not over the

face and she carries a large muff of blue fox matched by suede shoes and
gloves. Her color contrast comes in her antique gold jewelry studded in
cabochon ruby stones.

Edith Head's even coloring up the proverbial black and navy blue by
giving exotic Dorothy Lamour dark red to wear for street. One outfit is a
cape suit with a dark red sweater striped in Mexican green, red and white
over a straight skirt while the swashbuckling full-length cape looks Spanish
too. One street dress in dark red has three gold strands at the neckline
repeated at the waistline while another chic dark red dress has three series of
white wings embroidered down the shirtwaist front. With this last dress,
Dorothy wears white gloves and hat, dark red shoes and bag. Incidentally
with many smart Hollywood stars, it's white hats and gloves this spring as
accents to black and dark shades.

Bette Davis loves blue so her newest azure blue daytime dress is simply
cut with long sleeves and high neck and back fullness suggesting a bustle.
Her flower-laden hat is blue, too, while she has still another French blue
boucle afternoon dress with a deep purple belt. Shirley Ross' newest suit
has a powder blue tucked chiffon blouse under a royal blue bolero with a
full blue skirt while her wide blue hat has a violet band and she wears
violet antelope accessories. Ellen Drew accented her mauve kasha outfit with
violet and cyclamen while Barbara Stanwyck's beige dressmaker suit has a
coral pink chiffon blouse, a coral pink hat trimmed in feather flowers, and
deep beige accessories.

Well, I must buzz off to tea, now, and I'm wearing my new California
wildflower print which has bright azure lupins, yellow suncups and white
desert lilies against a deep blue background. I look quite as colorful as the
California countryside when I get on my sun yellow boxcoat with its round
pockets and its collarless neckline, and when my auburn curls fall under a
deep blue straw hat, and I pull on my azure blue suede gloves. So long,
Dora, how about coming out to see the wildflowers yourself?

*Bernard Newman made
Irene Dunne this print
dress with only one seam!*

Devotedly, your super-snooper-scooper,

Sylva Weaver

P. S. See page 19.

RKO RADIO PICTURES, INC.

GALAXY OF FEATURE MOTION PICTURE PLAYERS WEARING "THE PERFECT-FIT TAILLEUR FOR 1939"

A Glorious Parade of Smartness   *DESIGNED BY REINGLASS OF HOLLYWOOD*

Eleanor Hansen wearing our "Success of Successes" No. 405   Kay Sutton in the new "Tishma" creation No. 406   Frances Gifford in our foremost three piece outfit, Coat Style No. 702, Suit Style, No. 408   Eleanor Hansen, displaying the 1939 "Fashion Trend"—the "Gunga Din" Norfolk No. 411   Dorothy Lovett, the beautiful, in the fine pin stripe No. 408

PERMANENT SAN FRANCISCO OFFICE IN CHARGE OF MR. W. R. COHEN PLAZA HOTEL, UNION SQUARE   ## PERFECT GARMENT COMPANY   SEATTLE   DALLAS ST. LOUIS   DENVER CHICAGO

PHONE VANDYKE 8607   127 EAST NINTH STREET   LOS ANGELES, CALIFORNIA

IN OUR SHOWROOMS DURING MARKET WEEK TILL 9 P. M. EVENINGS

Advertisement for Perfect Garment Company, *The California Stylist*, January 1939.

Courtesy Los Angeles County Museum of Art, The Doris Stein Research Center for Costume and Textiles.

for release in 1930 would seem out of date. To avoid such problems in the future, studio heads were determined to make Hollywood a rival to Paris as a fashion center.[35] From a sociological perspective, as motion picture costume design turned to fashion promotion, the two wings of the eastern European immigration to Los Angeles—motion pictures and sportswear—came to reinforce each other.

During the 1930s, fashion magazines recognized that Hollywood was developing its own style, which Los Angeles clothing manufacturers would reproduce at cheaper prices for a mass market. In effect, costume designers had the stars model a shift in acceptable occasions for wearing sleek but informal clothing and expanded the frequency with which such clothing could be worn.[36] The California climate, of course, enabled women to wear shorts or slacks outdoors most of the year and made a shift from dresses for afternoon or even evening occasions much more acceptable.[37] Edith Head (lead designer at Paramount Studios) and others signed contracts with manufacturers, who would reproduce cheaper versions of what were in effect film costumes for middle-class consumers. Miss Head shrewdly noted that when Adrian at

MGM gave Joan Crawford a "broad shouldered look," copies appeared in department stores all over the country.[38] In 1930, Bernard Waldman in New York had organized the Modern Merchandising Bureau to link studio designs to department store sales, and established in-store departments. Beginning with Macy's, these departments were called variously Cinema Fashions, Screen Star Styles, or Cinema Modes, and sold tens of thousands of copies of individual dresses that women saw modeled by their favorite stars.[39] Milo Anderson, the head designer at Warner Brothers, clearly understood his real market when he noted, "the fact that 60,000,000 people go to the movies every week in the United States is the Hollywood designer's advantage over Paris."[40]

Due to the unique nature of the Los Angeles garment industry, which in general saw that Los Angeles designers remained in charge of production, factories remained small and entry to the business relatively easy.[41] Therefore, despite the national depression, the number of dress manufacturers in Los Angeles greatly expanded, the density of the downtown garment district increased, and the residential mobility of the families of factory owners accelerated.[42] In 1927, approximately 133 owners and managers of men's and women's garment factories could be identified in the Los Angeles city directory; in 1938, that number had grown to 344.[43] While most manufacturers in 1927 were no longer in business by 1938, over a dozen had survived to provide a nucleus for the more cosmopolitan industry. Financed in part by Benjamin Meyer at Union Bank and Trust Company, men's firms like Brownstein-Louis, Bell Cloak and Suit, Mayer Michaelson, and Moses Jackson were doing business around the corner from their previous locations, as were even larger numbers of women's clothing manufacturers like Isidore Teitelbaum, Joseph Zukin, Louis Lipson, Jacob Schwartz, Louis Karpf, and Sigmund Eck.[44]

Owners of Cohn-Goldwater, *The California Stylist,* **May 1939.**

Courtesy Los Angeles County Museum of Art, The Doris Stein Research Center for Costume and Textiles.

THEY WEAR THE SAME LABEL

Stamped on the canopy of a parachute for the Army Air Forces or sewed
in the seam of a swim suit ... the name COLE OF CALIFORNIA stands
for perfection. Today we give precedence to parachutes, make only a
limited number of Cole swim and play fashions. If you now buy less ...
because you invest in the best and give it the best of care ... you will
want a swim suit bearing this label of perfection ... COLE OF CALIFORNIA.

Awarded to
PARACHUTE DIVISION
COLE OF CALIFORNIA
Los Angeles 11, California

Advertisement for Cole of California, "They Wear the Same Label," 1943.
World War II offers a poignant moment of intersection between manufacturing, patriotism, and American-made apparel. In compliance with wartime rationing regulations, Cole of California's "Swoon Suit" was made without any elastic. Cole also turned over the majority of their manufacturing to the production of parachutes. As the company's wartime ad campaign patriotically boasts, "Stamped on the canopy of a parachute for the Army Air Forces or sewed in the seam of a swimsuit ... the name COLE OF CALIFORNIA stands for perfection. Today we give precedence to parachutes, make only a limited number of Cole swim and play fashions."

Courtesy Yeshiva University Museum.

As the number of firms grew, they concentrated more tightly in several large downtown loft buildings, on South Los Angeles and East Eighth and East Ninth Streets.[45]

If we take a sample of eight buildings in the Los Angeles garment district in 1938, we can see how patterns that began in the 1920s, persisted through World War II. The buildings held 176 manufacturers, and included 4 in the eight hundred block of South Broadway that held 51 shops with 74 principal owners or managers; a building at 315 East Eighth that held 19 factories with 28 owners; and the largest building in the group at 127 East Ninth, that held 27 factories, with 42 owners or managers.[46] The largest manufacturers, like the Maloufs (who operated Mode O'Day) and Joseph Zukin, had their own large operations at 939 South Broadway, while Catalina, which specialized in swimwear, had its production facilities a few blocks away on South San Pedro Street.[47] In addition, the culture of women's garment production intensified as factories clustered three, four, or even five to a floor on almost every floor of each of the buildings, some of which were thirteen stories tall.[48]

Residential clustering by the manufacturers to some degree reinforced the intensive work style. The streets on which garment manufacturers lived had changed since the mid-1920s, which illustrates their propensity to migrate close to one another. A small contingent of manufacturers, including several widows, remained in the Boyle Heights area. The great majority, however, clustered about two miles farther west from the population focus of the mid-1920s. Jewish clothing manufacturers now bought homes between Olympic

Boulevard on the south, Melrose Avenue on the north, Highland Avenue on the east, and Fairfax on the west. While none lived next door to each other, they did cluster on specific streets. Seventeen families, most of whom had factories in the eight buildings mentioned above, resided on three consecutive streets, Sierra Bonita, Curson, and Stanley, in the heart of the district. Dozens more lived within five streets to the east or west. Their migration, in effect, redefined the center of Jewish settlement. A study of Jewish population distribution in 1941 estimated that what was called the West Pico–Wilshire district (which included these blocks) held twenty thousand more Jews than did Boyle Heights and contiguous City Terrace.[49]

By the late 1930s, the tight-knit circle of Los Angeles clothing manufacturers began to entertain the notion that they, and the casual styles they promoted, might define world fashion. After Paris fell to the Nazis, Stanley Marcus, vice president of Nieman Marcus, wrote in *Fortune* that designers in New York, Chicago, St. Louis, and especially California had already demonstrated the ability to use native fabrics to meet local tastes. "The California manufacturers," he wrote, "had a freer range of color, and they derived inspiration from native sources."[50] But Marcus ignored what had been for over a decade the primary source of fashion inspiration on the Pacific Coast—the Hollywood studios. In 1938, a writer for the Los Angeles garment industry's trade monthly, the *California Stylist*, had already boasted that "Hollywood has superseded Paris and New York as style arbiter of the world."[51]

This attitude permeated the community

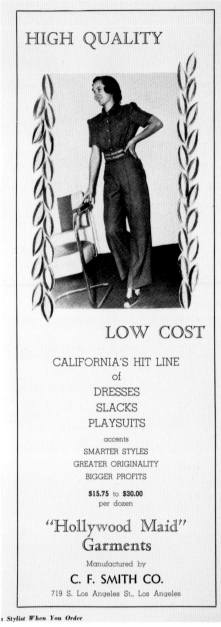

HIGH QUALITY

LOW COST

CALIFORNIA'S HIT LINE
of
DRESSES
SLACKS
PLAYSUITS

accents
SMARTER STYLES
GREATER ORIGINALITY
BIGGER PROFITS

$15.75 to $30.00
per dozen

"Hollywood Maid"
Garments

Manufactured by

C. F. SMITH CO.
719 S. Los Angeles St., Los Angeles

Stylist When You Order

of movie costume designers and downtown manufacturers. From July 30 to August 4, 1934, more than four hundred Los Angeles manufacturers of apparel, dry goods, furniture, housewares, and other lines held their first trade fair, which was highlighted by cheaper versions of clothing worn by female movie stars. By 1936, the fair attracted over ten thousand buyers.[52] By the late 1930s, fashion designers at Warner Brothers, Paramount, and MGM had "showings" at the Biltmore Bowl and Bullocks Wilshire, while movie stars modeled their latest sport suits and accessories in advertisements in trade monthlies. Local manufacturers then displayed their designs at Los Angeles's semiannual "Market Week" and took them to shows in St. Louis, Chicago, and elsewhere. In 1940, *Business Week* ran an illustrated article with models wearing casual clothing from Levi Strauss & Company that noted that buyers from New York now flew to the coast to attend style shows in San Francisco and Los Angeles. But, most important, over five hundred department stores across the country were sending buyers to Los Angeles for sportswear.[53] By 1945, *Fortune* noted that resident buyers in Los Angeles worked on commission for eight hundred retail outlets, that 85 percent of the local factories shipped their product east of the Rockies, and that Filene's, Snellenburg's, Marshall Field's, and Saks had opened "California Wear" sections in their stores.[54] Isidore Teitelbaum, whose Paramount Dress Company advertised "costumes, dresses and suits size 16 to 46," knew that while not every woman had a figure like Betty Grable or Lana Turner, the perfect fit came in all sizes, and that "fitting in" allowed the more casual styles of the Pacific Coast to become national fashion.[55]

Teitelbaum demonstrated the ability that Jews along the Pacific Coast have always shown in meeting, and even defining, the region's consumer tastes. In the nineteenth century, Jews with mercantile experience manufactured woolen cloth and durable men's work clothes. These, along with all manner of consumer goods, were sold through Jewish family networks branching out from San Francisco, and to a lesser degree from Portland and Los Angeles. Like their Gentile counterparts, Jewish pioneer merchants, mill owners, and manufacturers also augmented their commercial success by participating in local government and contributing heavily to city-wide philanthropic institutions. The large buildings that housed Levi Strauss, Cohn-Goldwater, and the Oregon City Woolen Mills, and the even larger high-rise structures for major department stores not only signified individual achievement, but also gave the broader Jewish community immense civic prestige.

In the 1920s and 1930s, as urban economies and social structures on the Pacific Coast grew larger, new Jewish clothing manufacturers, most of whom had eastern European origins, expanded production primarily by focusing on the tastes of middle-class women. In Southern California especially, Jewish manufacturers derived designs from the distinctive outdoor lifestyles and coordinated promotion with the predominantly Jewish movie industry to project regional styles into national fashions. But the role of Jewish newcomers in an expanded and bureaucratized public life became far less conspicuous. Movie moguls like Louis B. Mayer and Harry Warner may have had influence with national Republican Party luminaries such as Herbert Hoover, but the lesser wealth of clothing manufacturers could not be translated into civic recognition.[56] The status of Jews had not been diminished as woolen mills, clothing factories, and movie studios made notable contributions to local economies. Rather, as Jewish populations grew and Jewish districts became a feature of regional cities, Jews focused more on their own communal interests. In San Francisco, to a lesser extent in Portland and Seattle, and especially in the new regional center of Los Angeles, clothing manufacturers worked in close proximity to one another and spent their leisure time clustered in new districts that had a conspicuous Jewish presence. Jewish philanthropy became largely directed inward to support a new federation of Jewish institutions. In effect, the Jewish image had been transformed from a cluster of elite pioneer mercantile families into large ethnic communities, with a new clothing industry providing much of its economic support.

Appendix: Tables

Table 1   Clothing Production, Selected Cities, 1919, 1929, 1939

	1919			1929			1939		
	No. of Estab.	No. of Propr.	Wage Earners	No. of Estab.	No. of Propr.	Wage Earners	No. of Estab.	No. of Propr.	Wage Earners
New York									
Men's wear	2,273	4,759	47,311	1,809	3,935	33,634	1,598	2,691	47,263
Women's wear	5,089	11,750	95,842	5,781	19,205	104,202	2,901	4,848	88,348
Apparel							608	983	12,473
Chicago									
Men's wear	464	1,554	30,822	283	3,040	17,706	265	407	14,093
Women's wear	374	816	9,147	373	1,261	11,590	180	302	9,160
Apparel							62	99	2,424
Los Angeles									
Men's wear	25	48	822	44	165	1,555	104	168	3,462
Women's wear	80	178	1,938	205	686	5,376	96	142	3,202
Apparel							169	229	3,707
San Francisco									
Men's wear	32	59	1,511	40	52	683	49	67	547
Women's wear	68	116	1,074	82	192	1,459	47	55	609
Apparel							65	112	1,065
Portland and Seattle									
Men's wear	9	36	783	...	...	...	...	...	...
Women's wear	23	32	245	55	162	1,539	15	22	382
Apparel							61	101	1,742

Sources: *Fourteenth Census of the United States Taken in the Year 1920, Manufactures, 1919,* vol. 9 (Washington, DC: Government Printing Office, 1923); *Fifteenth Census of the United States, Manufactures, 1929,* vol. 3, *Reports by States* (Washington, DC: Government Printing Office, 1933); *Sixteenth Census of the United States, 1940, Manufactures, 1939,* vol. 3, *Reports for States and Outlying Areas* (Washington, DC: Government Printing Office, 1942), table 9.

Note: Apparel signifies a new category of "Apparel" manufacturers added to the U.S. Census for 1939; Estab. signifies establishments, or individual businesses; Propr. signifies owners and officers of businesses.

Table 2   Los Angeles Clothing Manufacturers, Persistence, 1927 to 1938

Type	Total, 1927	Still in Business, 1938	Total, 1938
Men's wear	71	13	35
Women's wear	62	14	270

Source: Lists of men's and women's garment manufacturers, *Los Angeles City Directory,* 1927, 1938.

Kansas City's Garment Industry

12

LAUREL WILSON

The garment industry in Kansas City and Jewish involvement in the industry occupies an important chapter in the city's manufacturing sector that contributed to its growth as an urban center. In 1908, Joseph Chick, Kansas City's first banker, said, "The Jews could have no higher compliment than to say that they were the first to realize Kansas City's future possibilities."[1] Beginning about 1844, Jewish settlers established a store to provide goods to nearby residents as well as to those traveling the Santa Fe Trail. The apparel manufacturing industry started with custom tailoring and dress-making in the second half of the nineteenth century, advanced to mass manufacturing during the 1880s, and experienced steady growth throughout the first three decades of the twentieth century. By the mid-1940s Kansas City's apparel industry was characterized by a mixture of Jewish and Gentile companies that employed workers representing a variety of ethnicities, races, and religions. Most of the midsized companies were owned by Jews who sent non-Jewish factory representatives to small western retailers in small towns that stretched from Canada to Mexico. In addition, many companies sold their goods to catalogue companies including Montgomery Ward, Sears and Roebuck, and National Bellas Hess. The garment manufacturing industry thrived until economic changes forced the closure of most of the businesses during the 1970s.

Jewish Settlement

Kansas City's location on a geographic boundary where the Kansas River meets the Missouri River's turn to the north was the reason for its growth in the 1840s and 1850s as traders settled in the area to serve the thousands emigrating on the Oregon Trail and to goldfields in California and Colorado. In 1853 it became the City of Kansas, which it was called for the next sixteen years as it grew from a town to a city of over five thousand residents.[2] The story of Jewish involvement in Kansas City began when Louis Cahn and E. Block opened a store in about 1844 on the bend where the Missouri River shifts direction from south to east. One of the most important Jewish residents was Louis Hammerslough, who, in 1858, opened a retail store that sold men's clothing manufactured in the family's factory in Baltimore, Maryland. According to Frank Adler, author of *Roots in a Moving Stream*, Hammerslough "shared in his family's war-time business success," including outfitting the Illinois militia.[3] After the Civil War, Hammerslough promoted Kansas City's location in the center of the country as a railroad hub, a designation realized through the completion of the Hannibal Bridge, which spanned the Missouri River in 1869, linking Kansas City goods to population centers in the East and carrying people emigrating to the West.[4] His influence was so strong that the first train to reach Kansas City was pulled by a locomotive called "The Louis Hammerslough."[5] Hammerslough, A. B. Feineman, who was in the wholesale liquor business, and Joseph Cahn, another clothier, were among the organizers of the Kansas City Board of Trade, an indication that the Jewish population was an integral part of Kansas City's business life in 1869.[6]

Among Jewish people who populated Kansas City during the 1870s were those from Germany or regions under German

influence. Of the thirty-five people who were part of the Jewish congregation of B'nai Jehudah in 1871, thirteen were proprietors of men's clothing stores, a large proportion of an ethnic group employed in a single occupation.[7] The number suggests the importance of Jewish involvement in trade. This was not unusual even though the common occupation of many Jewish immigrants in the eastern United States was as tailors or other forms of garment manufacturing.[8]

Jewish refugees from Russia began arriving in Kansas City in large numbers during the 1880s and 1890s. The B'nai Jehudah aid committee helped the newcomers find work and, in some cases, helped them set up businesses, including a shoe shop. In 1890, the temple opened an Industrial School for Girls where 174 girls learned needlework skills. A reporter for the *American Israelite* wrote that the Jews of New York could profit greatly by following the example of the Kansas City community.[9] By 1910 the Jewish population numbered 3,431 in a total population of 18,287, a sizable minority that made an important contribution to Kansas City's garment industry, especially between 1920 and 1980.[10]

Garment Manufacturing in the Nineteenth Century

There was little growth in the Kansas City garment industry between 1860 and 1880 when there were nine or ten tailors and a number of dressmakers plying their trade at any one time during that period.[11] This was changing by 1879 when brothers Samuel Woolf and Alfred Woolf, a member of the

Board of Directors of B'nai Jehudah, moved their shirt manufacturing operation from Leavenworth, Kansas, to Kansas City, taking advantage of a growing population and better transportation.[12] This also marks the time when Kansas City's wholesale trade area was "exactly one-half the land surface of the United States" because of the twelve railroads that converged in the city.[13] Two of the largest dry goods retailers, Burnham, Hanna, Munger & Co. and the W. B. Grimes Dry Goods Company, manufactured duck and denim work clothing during the 1880s, which they distributed throughout Kansas, Missouri, Colorado, Texas, and New Mexico. Although there had already been a trading system in place in Kansas City before the railroads were built, the fact that Kansas City was a railroad hub made it even more important as a distribution center, a critical factor in the growth of the garment industry. Historians Jeannette Terrell and Patricia Zimmer reported that the wholesale trade jumped from over $4,125,000 in 1884 to $6,000,000 in 1885. A major factor in this increase was distribution of rough cotton goods manufactured in the South.[14] The growing garment industry in Kansas City benefited from those distribution networks that continued to build until the economic slowdown that occurred during the early 1890s.

The experience of the Hipsh family was typical of those who settled in Kansas City during the late nineteenth century—the family began business selling dry goods, moved to manufacturing, and finally to businesses in financial services. Harry Hipsh left Russia to start a new life in New York but immigrated to Kansas City in 1898, where he established a dry goods store. Hoping to get rich quick, in 1903 he joined the California Gold Rush, leaving

his wife and three (soon to be four) sons in Kansas City. He didn't do well at the Gold Rush and returned to Kansas City and the dry goods store. One day during a typical lull in business Harry picked up a discarded vest. Using skills honed during an apprenticeship in an English cap factory before he immigrated to America, he made a cap. Kansas City Cap Manufacturing Company was born and became the largest cap manufacturing company west of the Mississippi River. Harry saved enough money to pay for two brothers and three sisters to come to the United States. Years later, and in business with his sons, he predicted cap sales would slow because of the closed automobile and the resulting bare-headed fad. At this point Hipsh and his son Charles branched out into men's neckwear, shirts, and handwoven fabrics, and they changed the name of the business to Textile Distributors, Inc. In 1931, they started making their own cloth on looms. After establishing a successful hand-weaving department, they made their own looms. Hipsh's company grew to five factories, most of which were located in small communities surrounding Kansas City. All four of the sons, Carl, Martin, Charles, and Sam, were involved in the business, which was one of the few vertically integrated apparel manufacturing businesses in the area. In 1963 the family gave up manufacturing to establish Empire State Bank to serve the needs of the Kansas City garment industry.[15]

Garment Manufacturing in the Early Twentieth Century

A comparative summary of industries, appearing in the *Thirteenth Census of the United States* of 1910, shows that in 1899 there were ten businesses employing 1,485 people in the men's clothing category.[16] This marks a significant shift from custom sewing for a small customer base to mass manufacturing clothing for a broad market, thus indicating growth of Kansas City's garment industry, which continued through the 1910s.[17] By 1919 there were 1,090 employees manufacturing men's clothing and 422 manufacturing women's clothing, much of it work clothing, a very slow growth rate in the apparel industry.[18] Companies established during this time included a mixture of Jewish and non-Jewish owners that hired local employees representing a variety of ethnicities and races. African Americans were employed as pressers and packers whereas those who did the cutting and sewing were of European descent.

Work Clothing

Kansas City was surrounded by rural communities for which farming was the principal means of making a living. Therefore it is not surprising that the target market for many of the garments made in Kansas City were working men and women who owned small family farms that produced most of the food for family consumption as well as cash crops that furnished income to purchase manufactured goods, including clothing. Kansas City garment manufacturing firms sent representatives to solicit orders from rural retailers and mail-order companies serving this market, which spanned all forty-eight states but especially the western states and those adjacent to Missouri.[19]

One large manufacturer of work clothing was a non-Jewish company established during the 1910s, the H. D. Lee Mercantile Company of Salina, Kansas. They began manufacturing work wear in 1911 because the company's founder, Henry David Lee, was unhappy with the quality of work clothing manufactured in the East. In 1915 he opened manufacturing plants at a number of locations including Kansas City and in 1917 moved the company headquarters to that city.[20] The H. D. Lee Company may have been the designer of coveralls, a combination of trousers and jacket usually worn over trousers and shirt. According to the company history, Lee Union-alls, as they were called at the time, originated with Lee's chauffeur/mechanic who often had to repair the automobile, soiling his clothes. He suggested that the company make a garment that could be easily worn over regular clothing—a suggestion that Lee took to the design department, resulting in a garment that is still being sold.[21] The H. D. Lee Company was among the largest of Kansas City's garment manufacturers and one of the longest-running businesses in the area. It is now owned by the VF Corporation, which still maintains a corporate presence in Shawnee Mission, Kansas, a suburb of Kansas City.[22] The company does not manufacture anything there, however.

The Donnelly Garment Company was established in 1916 by Nell Donnelly, an American woman of Irish descent. It focused on another form of work garment, the housedress. The Nelly Don housedress was more attractive than the Mother Hubbard that had previously been the most common everyday work clothing of housewives.[23] The pink, gingham frock that Nelly Don manufactured was loose, like its Mother Hubbard counterpart, but included ruffles at the neck, at the side-front closure, on the opening of the pocket, on the bottom of the above-the-elbow-length sleeves, and on all the edges of the belt. The garment was not only functional but more attractive than other housedresses.[24] It sold well enough to launch a company that became known for well-designed, moderately priced women's clothing. At its zenith, the company had over fifteen hundred workers. Nell Donnelly ran the company from 1916 until she sold it in 1956. The new owners renamed the company Nelly Don, the same as the company's brand, and operated a profitable business until the 1970s when changes in the industry began to negatively impact sales to such a degree that they were forced to file for bankruptcy in 1978.[25]

Other smaller garment manufacturing companies that made work clothing included the Liberty Garment Company,

which made "wash dresses" that it distributed through warehouses in New York, Cleveland, Chicago, and Los Angeles.[26] Owner A. B. Passman attributed the company's success to lower rents for space and the abundance of women workers.[27] The Carroll Dorn Company also made wash dresses, aprons, and smocks that were shipped throughout Missouri, Kansas, Texas, Oklahoma, Nebraska, and Iowa.[28] The Dean Jones Manufacturing Company was yet another firm making wash dresses that it sold in the Southwest and central West.[29] The Missouri Garment Company, owned by Benjamin Feinberg, began when Feinberg's wife began making dresses to sell in their dry goods store, but by 1921 the dresses were selling so well that they sold the store and opened a manufacturing operation. They reported that theirs was a "southern consuming market, Alabama, Mississippi, Louisiana, Arkansas, Texas and Oklahoma being the manufacturer's 'big' states."[30]

The apparel industry in Missouri was important enough to be included in the 1922 Missouri Bureau of Labor Statistics report on the number of women employed in manufacturing.[31] There were 494 Kansas City women making men's shirts and overalls and earning an average of $17.75 per week, the highest earnings for women reported in any manufacturing category.[32] Kansas City women in clothing manufacture earned $4.65 more each week than their counterparts in St. Louis, Missouri, where there was a higher cost of living.[33]

Expansion of the Garment Industry

By 1921 the garment industry in Kansas City had grown to forty companies that were manufacturing a variety of products including hats, caps, work wear, men's and ladies' suits and coats, men's shirts, and ladies' dresses. All these companies prided themselves on making high-quality garments at reasonable prices. Bob Slegman, owner of Stern, Slegman, and Prins, said that Kansas City companies were able to maintain high quality because they maintained their own manufacturing plants rather than contracting the work out to other factories, which he believed was a practice in other regions.[34]

The Gernes Garment Company began in 1928 after DeSaux Gernes's mother, Sarah, made a tutu with a circle skirt over it. Soon neighborhood children were asking her to make skirts for them, and the company was born with the help of thirteen seamstresses. The company did not order fabric until they had orders. In 1931 Gernes went to a bank to get a loan so she could meet her orders. The bank refused, so she went to Milton Gordon, the Jewish owner of Frances Gee Manufacturing, who agreed to loan the money if he were made a silent partner and could approve the samples. Gernes agreed and the company went on to thrive. The Gernes Garment Company label, Gay Gibson, became familiar far beyond the borders of Missouri, its youthful styles modeled in the fashion pages by Twiggy and worn by fashionable young women throughout the country. Even so, the company eventually could not compete with companies whose garments were sewn outside the United States, and Gernes Garment Company closed in 1978.[35]

Suits and Coats

It was during the 1920s that ladies' coat and suit manufacturers began making Kansas City home. Frances Gaw, a researcher for the Kansas City Research and Information Department, wrote that "mail-order houses wanted factories nearer to their points of distribution . . . [and] practically subsidized some of the garment companies in coming to Kansas City. The National Coat and Suit Company, in particular, brought garment manufacturers here."[36] Meyer Present was the first to bring ladies' coat and suit manufacturing to Kansas City in 1924 with his Fashionbilt brand, a segment of the apparel industry that flourished there until the 1980s.[37] Soon after, Brand and Puritz relocated their ladies' coat and suit manufacturing operation from New York to Kansas City "through the influence of mail-order houses," probably J.C. Penney, Sears and Roebuck, Montgomery Ward, and National Bellas Hess (a New Jersey Company with a Kansas City presence), all of which had distribution centers there.[38] Brand and Puritz brands included Curtsy Coats for children, Dee Dee Deb for juniors, and Mary Lane for women's coats. Another apparel manufacturer described

This two-piece dress was the work of the Mende'l Company, which was owned by Owen Mendel Silverman, ca. 1958. It displays the quality of design and workmanship for which Kansas City companies were known.

Photograph by Howard Wilson. Courtesy of the author.

Hyman Brand, one of the owners, as the "godfather" of Kansas City's garment business.[39]

The Stern, Slegman, and Prins Company began as a jobbing house in 1923 then shifted to manufacturing ladies' coats and suits in 1926. By 1927, according to the *Kansas City Star*, Stern, Slegman, and Prins produced six hundred coats each week. The article went on to say that a selling territory that stretched from Texas to Minnesota helped eliminate the seasonal shutdowns that were inherent in the coat market.[40] The company made mid-priced coats that sold for $6.75 wholesale and for a retail price of about $10. Fur trim brought the price for each coat to $16.75 wholesale, retailing at about $30. According to Slegman, manufacturers carefully monitored the Kansas City coat and suit manufacturing business to control quality since the reputation of all the coat and suit companies was at stake. During the 1930s and 1940s, most of the company's cutters were Serbians and Yugoslavians, the sewers were Italians, and packers, pressers, and custodians were African Americans. The company employed fifteen to twenty salesmen who sold coats to retailers in large and small towns in nearby states and went to the big markets in New York and Los Angeles. The company's best years were the 1950s and 1960s and at its peak made over $12,000,000 in profit.[41]

Leon and Julius Karosen's Youthcraft brand was known, along with Fashionbilt, for high-quality coats. Leon Karosen understood the importance of good design but did not necessarily recognize it. He told Gene (Eugene) Lebovitz, one of the designers he recruited from New York in

the 1960s, "if it sells, I like it."[42] Karosen made sure that the company made money by having pattern makers trim a bit or use less expensive buttons. According to Lebovitz, Karosen was "a difficult man to work with, but paid the bills, no question." Youthcraft and Fashionbilt led the standard for quality ladies' coats and suits, but Kansas City suit and coat companies that made even more moderately priced clothing were also known for consistent quality and good value, and their goods were sold all over the country. Lebovitz said that sales associates at Bullock's, a California retailer, loved to see him since he often bought $3,000 or $4,000 worth of coats that he took back to Kansas City as inspiration for his designs.[43]

Sol Stolowy, known for quality men's suits, was born in Poland in 1906 and immigrated to America with his mother and four siblings in 1926. He found a job at the Kansas City Garment Company almost immediately with the help of the friends of his father, who was already living in Kansas City. Stolowy's experience in Poland making uniforms was very valuable to Mr. Goldberger, who owned the company until 1952 when Stolowy was able to buy the company from Goldberger when he retired. One of Stolowy's friends and clients was Harry Truman, a friendship that began when Truman and Eddie Jacobson opened a haberdashery in Kansas City.[44] In the words of Rose Stolowy, her husband showed Truman how to "measure a man" and then they became friends. Truman's business failed, but his relationship with Sol Stolowy proved to last for the rest of Truman's life as attested by a *Kansas City Star* article headlined "Truman and His

Tailor Cut from the Same Cloth."[45] After Harry Truman's death, Mrs. Truman wrote a note to Stolowy thanking him for a beautiful suit. Stolowy maintained the Kansas City Garment Company until 1980 when he opened a much smaller custom tailor business to serve a smaller clientele in line with his preference for personal service. According to his wife, Stolowy did what he enjoyed and he enjoyed the people for whom he made clothing and who remember him with affection.

The Vic-Gene Company, named for founder Hyman Dreiseszun's sons, Jerome Victor and Herbert Eugene, opened in 1946. One of the Vic-Gene Company's most successful designs was a women's plaid jacket patterned after the "49er" jacket, which was a shirt-style jacket with large patch pockets made by the Pendleton Company. Both Sears and Roebuck and Montgomery Ward catalogue companies bought over two million dollars' worth of jackets in that design from Vic-Gene.[46]

The Depression

Terrel and Zimmer reported that Kansas City "suffered extensively" from the Depression; however, the exceptions included companies making necessities.[47] Since the basic work garments that were among the principal products manufactured in Kansas City during this time were among the necessities, apparel companies suffered very little if at all. In 1930, the Kansas City Chamber of Commerce began promoting Kansas City and its potential trade territory to convince companies to relocate there, citing, "twice a year, between 1500 and 2000 buyers of textile goods come into the Kansas City market to attend Fashion Shows and advertised Market Weeks."[48] This strategy of promoting Kansas City goods to retailers seems to have worked since the Brand and Puritz Company that made women's coats and suits moved to larger quarters in 1932, showing that they were able to increase their business in spite of adverse condi-

tions.[49] Pioneer Cap, owned by Jacob Yeddis and his brothers, moved to Kansas City in the 1930s. The Fried–Siegel Company was founded in 1930 by Joseph Fried and Isidore Siegel as a women's outerwear and sportswear wholesaler; Fried handled administration and sales in Kansas City, and Siegel ran the New York office. The company eventually also moved into manufacturing and continues today as a small-scale operation. The Styline Company, a separate company founded in 1939 by Fried, Siegel, and Isidore Epstein (Epstein was the designer/head of production), was a manufacturer of Juniors until 1957.[50] The Rice Coat Company, one of the smallest of the Kansas City coat companies, opened in the early 1930s and managed to hang on until 1993, long after most companies had closed their doors.[51] These examples disprove Terrel's and Zimmer's assertions that Kansas City suffered an economic downturn.

Garment Workers Unions

According to records in the Western Historical Manuscript Collection at the University of Missouri–Kansas City, there was a union presence in Kansas City by the end of the nineteenth century. Collection WHMC0458 includes minutes and other documents of the United Garment Workers of America beginning in 1898 but ending in 1915, indicating that the union was no longer active after that time. The union represented workers who made men's ready-made clothing, one of the main products of the Kansas City garment industry during that period.[52] By the 1930s no garment workers union existed in Kansas City when International Ladies' Garment Workers' Union (ILGWU) organizer Abraham Plotkin came to the city to organize a union. In 1933, he began with the coat and suit industry, which was considered the aristocracy of the garment trades in Kansas City. Seven employers, represented by Frank Prins of Stern, Slegman, and Prins, negotiated with Plotkin, who represented the garment workers. By August, many of the garment industry shops were organizing unions, but union

records indicate that some companies were resisting by firing union workers. It was not until 1938 that the coat and suit industry was fully unionized under the leadership of the new union organizer, Meyer Perlstein.

The Donnelly Garment Company owned by Nell Donnelly Reed resisted union efforts in 1938 by organizing a company union and "inculcating anti-Semitism" in her workers, which caused them to distrust the ILGWU leadership. Because the Donnelly Garment Company was so powerful, it undercut the unions in the other dress companies.[53] The National Labor Relations Board ordered Reed to cut all ties with the independent union formed by her workers and to engage in fair labor practices. Reed took the matter to federal court, where it was in litigation for seven years before the 8th Circuit U.S. Court of Appeals sustained the right of the company to have its own union.[54] It wasn't until 1968, twelve years after the company changed hands and thirty-one years after the first attempt, that the Donnelly Garment Company was finally unionized.[55]

World War II

When World War II began, some manufacturers produced clothing for the military. During the war, Hipsh, Inc. shifted from making neckwear to manufacturing army fatigues and jackets for enlisted men, including a type that had special devices.[56] The Fried–Siegel Company also made uniforms for the military.[57] The Donnelly

Garment Company made military underwear instead of ladies' dresses. When one of the male workers was drafted into the army, women in the plant made a pair of boxer underwear that they embroidered with their names. Their coworker returned safely along with the never-worn boxers that are now part of the collection of the

Kansas City Garment District Museum.[58]
The Gernes Garment Company made
WAC uniforms to keep the company alive
during the fabric shortages that apparel
manufacturers faced during the war. H. D.
Lee Company manufactured fatigue suits,
flight suits, and field jackets for the U.S.
Army. Because much of their production
was going to the military, they had a
difficult time meeting the needs of their
domestic customers. One of the advertisements that appeared in *Life* magazine
stated,

War conditions make it impossible to meet the
growing demand for Lee Work Clothes. Your
Lee Dealer is receiving his fair share of all we are
able to make after the needs of our men in the
armed forces have been supplied. If your Dealer
is out of the Lee you want, please ask him to
reserve one for you out of his next shipment.[59]

The war also affected the output of
other companies that were continuing to
manufacture garments for the home front.
Quotas based on sales before the war were
put into place and carefully monitored by

Detail of dress in figure on page 169. The detail shows the workmanship of the Mende'l Company.

Photograph by Howard Wilson. Courtesy of the author.

the government and by retailers that wanted
merchandise. Bob Slegman of Stern,
Slegman, and Prins coat company said that
companies could not produce more than the
quota allowed even though retailers were
unhappy when they could not get all the
goods that they wanted.[60]

The Golden Age

Many of the people who owned garment
manufacturing companies consider the
1950s and 1960s the golden period of the
Kansas City garment industry since that is
when sales volume reached its peak. Once
the war was over, demand for all kinds of
manufactured products exploded and the
Kansas City garment industry flourished.
Gaw reported that by 1945 there were "over
80 busy garment factories doing an annual
business estimated at between 75 and 100
million dollars."[61] Gaw also wrote that "the
foreign-born or Eastern manufacturers

[predominantly Jews] who helped establish
the garment industry here in the early days
have stayed in Kansas City and become
permanent and respected citizens."[62] A
survey conducted by Fairchild Publications
in 1945 found that Kansas City ranked
seventh in the United States in the amount
of clothing made for men, women, and
children.[63] At that time, New York was still
producing 90 percent of the garments sold
in the United States; even so the garment
industry was very important to the health
of the Kansas City economy.[64] The garment

Kansas City Board of Trade advertised Kansas City labels, ca. 1960.

Photo courtesy Kansas City Garment Industry Museum.

industry ranked third in dollar value at $100 million compared to the livestock industry at $375 million and grains at $284 million.[65] In 1949, there were ninety-nine garment industries that represented some large firms but a considerable number of small firms.[66]

Much of this expansion took place between 1944 and 1947 with most of the growth in women's, misses', and junior outerwear made by fifty-eight different companies. Twelve companies were making children's clothing and fourteen were making a variety of men's clothing. There were still fifteen manufacturers making military and other uniforms for police, bands, nurses, and schools.[67] Garments made in Kansas City were sold in all forty-eight states and Hawaii, Alaska, and

Canada; however, most retailers that sold Kansas City goods were in the states stretching from the Mississippi River westward, with the exception of the three Pacific Coast states. Most of the retailers were "mom and pop" stores in small towns throughout this area.[68]

The coat companies that were established during the 1920s continued to thrive, but many other companies were established, including the Nat Nast Company, a sport shirt manufacturing company that opened in 1946. According to Nast's wife, he didn't know a thing about manufacturing but was a born salesman who kept his company alive by going on the road and selling the shirts himself. The business took off after a serendipitous encounter with an unknown man who was eating lunch at Tallman's

Grill, one of the meeting places of those who owned and worked in Kansas City's garment district. The unknown man said that instead of sport shirts Nast should be making bowling shirts since league bowling was such a popular sport.[69] Nast took the stranger's advice and shifted the business to designing and manufacturing rayon shirts, often in bright color-blocks, that were decorated with chain stitch embroidery bearing the name of the bowling group on the back and the name of the bowler on the front. His daughter Patty Nast Canton described Nast as "the guy who designed the original action-back shirt" consisting of inverted pleats on each side of the back. Nast sold his company, which was renamed Swingster, in 1971. That company was sold again and is now American Identity, a Kansas City company that sells promotional products including jackets and caps.[70] Many of the products of that company are still designed in Kansas City, but they are manufactured in other countries. The Nat Nast label has been brought to life again by Nast's daughters Barbara and Patty, who work and live in Connecticut. They have revived their father's original designs, created others with the Nat Nast aesthetic, and sold to celebrities and others who enjoy the 1950s vintage appeal.[71]

The Liberty Garment Company, run by the Jacobs brothers, Phil, Eddie, and Jake, succeeded in another specialty segment of the apparel industry—maternity clothing. The first dress happened almost by accident in 1946 when one of the Jacobs's cousins wanted a nice-looking maternity dress. They made one and then began mass manufacturing them after they sent a flier illustrating their maternity dresses to J.C.

Penney Company. The company even held a patent for an adjustable maternity skirt. Jacobs described the business as the Ford of maternity wear, eventually selling dresses to Sears and Roebuck and Montgomery Ward under the catalogue companies' labels. At one time they had 20 percent of the maternity wear market nationwide. The Liberty Garment Company had thirteen salesmen who traveled throughout the United States, selling maternity wear that was sewn in six plants, all but one in or near Kansas City. Their designer created 135 sample garments for each of the four seasons but cut only seventy-five styles once they knew which designs were selling to retailers. Most of the pattern makers were originally from Europe, but the sewing machine operators were from the small communities where the plants were located. Liberty's market declined during the 1960s when loose shift dresses reduced the need for specialized maternity clothing and when fashion changed again; competition from overseas manufacturing was already having an effect.[72]

The Quality Hill Dress Company, opened by Harry Zarr and his sons Ben and Ralph, manufactured two-piece dresses that met a real need in the marketplace after World War II when "women had paychecks and wanted to spend them."[73] The dresses, which consisted of a skirt with a matching top in colorful cotton and silk prints, made fitting a variety of figures easier. This company made only five or six styles each season, depending on reorders, to keep their fifty employees busy. Bullock's department store, a major chain in California, had a standing order with Quality Hill Dress Company of two hundred dresses per

Curtsy Coats was one of Brand and Puritz's labels, ca. 1961. The coat was designed in such a way that the sleeves could be turned back and then let down as a child grew, a style feature that made it appealing to a broad market.

Courtesy Howard Wilson.

286 WARDS ᴾᴱᴰ

COATS on these two pages mailed from Kansas City. Pay postage only from Wards Mail Order House nearest you.

Curtsy Coats label.

Courtesy Howard Wilson.

month since this two-piece style fit a variety of body types unlike the cinch-waist dresses also fashionable during the 1950s. The Zarr brothers enjoyed the garment business, which produced a comfortable living until sack dresses came into fashion. In a 2005 interview, they talked of missing the comradeship within the industry, which Ben described as a "big warm family, everyone got along."[74]

One of the most compelling stories of the Kansas City garment industry belongs to designer Eugene Lebovitz, mentioned earlier in the chapter, who was a Holocaust survivor. He was just sixteen years old in 1940 when the Nazis "invited" the Jews of Hungary to labor camps where they were put to work. Lebovitz learned tailoring from his father, who told him that "all you need is a thimble and a needle," so he was assigned to make uniforms for the Gestapo. He described his sewing skills as "the thing that really saved my life." In the labor camps he had to do perfect work, and he learned to recognize design details and copy them precisely. He attributes sewing these uniforms to providing him with skills he would put to work in America. Lebovitz said, "God bless the soul of my father for teaching me a trade, it shaped my life forever."[75]

He and his wife, Kate, also a Holocaust survivor, emigrated from Italy to New York on July 20, 1946, and four days later Lebovitz began work in the New York garment industry. He credits his success in New York's garment industry to his ability to speak Italian, a language he learned during the year he spent in an Italian displaced persons camp after the war. He said that 50 percent of the employees in the New York garment industry were Jewish and 50 percent were Italian. After three years Lebovitz became head designer for Leslie Junior, where he worked until 1959 when Youthcraft, a Kansas City ladies' coat and suit company owned by Leon Karosen, recruited him to be their head designer. Lebovitz worked for that company for over five years, but after a serious disagreement with Karosen he decided to work for Henry Present of Fashionbilt, another ladies' coat and suit company, where he worked until his retirement in 1983.[76] There is no doubt that Lebovitz was one of the most skilled designers in Kansas City. Ann Brownfield, who learned the trade at Stephens College in Columbia, Missouri, and was a designer for Brand and Puritz, called Lebovitz a "designer's designer."[77]

In 1969, Brownfield opened Ann L. Company. Much of her business centered on manufacturing private-label garments for Jones Store as well as producing custom jobs for a variety of retailers. She said that she started with "four machines and $400" and stayed in business for twelve years.[78] According to Brownfield, when she first began her business, some of the old-timers would ask, "Still in business?" When she was still in business after five years, they asked, "How's business?"[79]

Decline of the Garment Industry

The peak of the Kansas City garment industry generally occurred in the 1950s and early 1960s when a variety of factors changed the industry. One of the most important was that styles were becoming more casual as lifestyles shifted from a dress for each time of day and social occasion to less formal clothing that was considered suitable for a variety of occasions. This reduced the number of garments that women purchased. It was also more difficult to find employees who were willing to sit at sewing machines all day. The machine operators of the 1940s and 1950s used their incomes to send their children to college, and college graduates went into different lines of work. Unions also made demands that made it extremely difficult to sustain a profitable business since the profit margin in the apparel industry was so low. The union required companies to pay a guaranteed salary for a thirty-five-hour week, and this put many companies out of business. The Frances Gee Manufacturing company, owned by Milton Gordon and his son Marshall, tried opening plants in Puerto Rico and Japan in the 1970s but found that it was difficult to maintain quality.[80]

Some manufacturers were able to extend their business by capitalizing on new trends. The Fried–Siegel Company was among the last of the manufacturers because they made sportswear, career apparel, and uniforms. They are still open in a small way—making VFW caps for this niche market. Stern, Slegman, and Prins made car coats that were popular during the late 1960s and 1970s but closed their factory in the 1970s. Archie Bercu's Maurice Coat and Suit closed in 1969, but he and his daughter opened Lan-Mar Manufacturing in 1972 and made Little League uniforms and Kansas City Royals' warm-up jackets in addition to other sport garments until 1988.

A number of the manufacturers blamed the union for the eventual failure of garment manufacturing in Kansas City. Seymour Weiner, of Krest Originals (dresses), cited inflexibility in rules, which forced some owners to pay overtime to employees whose eight-hour shifts began later, but whose hours extended beyond 5:00 p.m.[81] Other manufacturers complained about union demands but did not feel that the union was in any way responsible for the demise of a thriving Kansas City garment industry.

The real decline of the Kansas City garment industry is tied to the consolidation of agriculture across the nation. According to Harvey Fried, 27 percent of the population made a living in agriculture in 1930, but by 1990 only 2 percent of the population was engaged in agriculture.[82] The agricultural industry began to consolidate during the 1950s when specialized farm machinery began to replace human labor, but much of the collapse of agriculture occurred in the 1980s when the farm crisis, as it was called, forced the closure of thousands of "mom and pop" stores that once did business in small towns where Kansas City manufacturers once sold their goods. In addition, department stores, including J.C. Penney, Walmart, and Sears and Roebuck, consolidated their buying, demanding lower prices and causing even smaller profit margins for manufacturers already suffering from too narrow profit margins. Finally, cheap imports that were manufactured in the Far East and Central America dealt the final blow when retailers, pressured by consumers desiring lower prices, decided to buy their goods outside the United States. A once-lively garment manufacturing industry, third among Kansas City industries in the late 1940s, had largely disappeared by the late 1980s.

Interpretation

Although the garment industry in Kansas City did well for many years, especially during its golden age, it could not withstand changes in economic forces. In its early years of development Kansas City's real estate brokers wrote that "Kansas City is a metropolitan city of wonderful resources and activities. Its population is from every section of our country, with no one dominant element to rule in their own interest."[83] Gaw reiterated that sentiment about sixty years later when he explained why eastern entrepreneurs were relocating from the East Coast to Kansas City to take advantage of a more abundant labor supply and an environment more tolerant and open. "Manufacturers, it is said, were wanting to make a fresh start away from old traditions. They were looking also for a different type of labor supply, more stable and less bound by prejudice and tradition."[84]

Kansas City was, indeed, a place where Jewish companies could grow and prosper. The influence of Jewish ownership in the Kansas City garment industry is undeniable since Jewish entrepreneurs established so many of the large and small companies. Yet, the garment industry was integrated in terms of ethnicity, religion, and race. The workforce was a mixture of newcomers to America from all parts of the globe and native-born Americans including whites and African Americans. Much of the sales force that carried sample garments to small-town stores was non-Jewish but working for Jewish and Gentile companies. Although there was apparent anti-Semitism like that concerning efforts to unionize the Donnelly Garment Company, there was also cooperation between Jewish and Gentile companies such as the partnership between Milton Gordon and Sarah Gernes.[85] The garment industry provided a means of living for immigrants from across the globe. The industry enabled them to educate the next generation, many of whom are involved in professions such as law, medicine, education, and research and who continue to contribute to the intellectual, cultural, and social life of Kansas City.

Postscript

The Kansas City Garment Industry History Museum would not exist without Ann Brownfield, who once worked for the Brand and Puritz Company and later established her own company. As garment factories were being converted to other uses, Brownfield diligently rescued garment company records and artifacts. Harvey Fried, owner of Fried–Siegel Company and president of the Historic Garment District Group, works with Brownfield to preserve the history of Kansas City's garment industry. The Kansas City Garment Industry Museum exhibits equipment, photographs, written materials, and garments produced by a number of companies that once operated in Kansas City. Tours of the museum and the garment district are conducted by appointment.

Most of the people who were involved in the Kansas City garment industry speak of their experiences with affection. There was friendly competition but also assistance when needed. Even though Sherman Dreiseszun said that the garment industry "was a terrible business, everyone complaining all the time," he was proud of the contribution that Vic-Gene Manufacturing made and said that the company made enough for him to "get started on other stuff."[86] This was also true of other manufacturers, many of whom went into real estate development. Some converted the buildings, once occupied by garment manufacturing companies, into offices and artists' and residential lofts, while others helped to create a growing Kansas City by developing empty land into a variety of uses.

13 From Seventh Avenue to Hollywood: Fashioning Early Cinema, 1905–1935

MICHELLE TOLINI FINAMORE

Introduction

In the early part of the twentieth century, the fashion and film industries evolved on a parallel course, reflecting changes in mass production and marketing as well as broader social and cultural trends. The stories of these two industries would not be complete without investigating the unique link between Jewish film pioneers and the New York garment trade. Many of the early filmmakers responsible for putting the dressed body on film had, at some point in their careers, been involved in dressing the off-screen body as well. While the careers of a number of film entrepreneurs would provide apt case studies for this connection between fashion and film, Samuel Goldwyn's career trajectory in particular exemplifies changes taking place within the women's garment industry between 1905 and 1935. During this thirty-year period, ready-to-wear apparel and films became increasingly more accessible, contributing to the rise of the power of Hollywood and the potency of its images. As art and fashion historian Anne Hollander has observed, "Dressing is always picture making."[1]

While many scholars have addressed the connection between these two industries in the post-1935 golden age of Hollywood, the groundwork was already being laid in the silent film period. This time frame encompasses the transition of the movie business from New York to Hollywood and the simultaneous shift in film narratives from those that addressed the actual production of ready-made garments to those that emphasized their consumption. From approximately 1905 to 1915, large numbers of documentary, fictional, and social problem films addressed the day-to-day life of the mill worker, the factory seamstress, and the at-home pieceworker. Such films reflected the immigrant, working-class origins of both the film creators and the moviegoers.[2] High fashion could be presented to audiences in the form of newsreels, but when it was the actual subject of film, it was often parodied. In this era, the notion of a costume designer was still relatively new and actors were required to provide their own wardrobe, much of which they purchased from New York–based dressmakers. Although fashion was often used for promoting particular movies in the nascent days of film, it was not until the 1920s and the rise of the corporate studio system that special marketing strategies were developed to sell film fashion to the consumer. As the film industry grew, film producers and exhibitors continually sought to broaden their audience, and plots evolved to have broader appeal to middle-class viewers. The creation of a distinctive Hollywood fashion idiom by studio designers coincided with Hollywood's heightened awareness of the power of moving pictures to sell fashion. The viewer as an avid consumer rather than a creator of garments resulted in motion picture promotion that encompassed commercial tie-ins with department stores, pattern makers, and wholesale garment producers.

The New York Garment Industry in Film, 1900–1915

Between 1882 and 1920, large numbers of eastern European Jews immigrated to New York City and played a vital role in the development of the ready-to-wear clothing industry in America. In fact, the immigrant population was largely responsible for the period of its greatest growth.[3] Many settled on the Lower East Side of New York City and were involved in manufacture for the wholesale market, contract work in the ready-to-wear trade, and retail. A large number of the movie moguls who shaped America's film industry started their careers in the field of fashion. Samuel Goldwyn was a glove salesman, Louis B. Mayer worked as a used-clothing dealer, Carl Laemmle operated a retail clothing establishment, Adolph Zukor was a furrier, Marcus Loew was employed as a traveling salesman for a clothing company, William Fox cut linings for men's suits, Jessy Lasky was the son of a shoe salesman, and Harry Cohn was the son of a tailor.[4] Many of these future film producers had profited from the garment business and thus had some initial money to invest in the burgeoning film industry. In the early twentieth century, New York City was the center of both industries and opportunities arose for these men through various familial and business connections. In addition, lessons learned from the world of fashion could be applied to the medium of film. Not only did they understand merchandising and how to attract customers, but they were also attuned to the shifts in popular taste. It is perhaps this intimate knowledge of the garment industry that encouraged producers such as Goldwyn to eventually use fashion to "sell the ladies."

By the end of the nineteenth century, ready-to-wear clothing was so well-constructed and readily available in department stores or by mail order that a kind of sartorial democracy existed in the United States. Even the newest immigrants could afford to be relatively well-dressed, a phenomenon that was the subject of commentary by numerous contemporary observers. Abraham Cahan, a social realist writer who chronicled Jewish New York, noted this blurring of social and class distinction in his book *The Rise of David Levinsky*. This fictional account of a young man's rise within the garment industry reflected Cahan's own experience as a Russian immigrant. The main character, Levinsky, notes upon his arrival in America:

The great thing was that these people were better dressed than the inhabitants of my town. The poorest-looking man wore a hat (instead of a cap), a stiff collar and a necktie, and the poorest woman wore a hat or a bonnet.[5]

In film, evidence that high fashion was becoming more available to a broad segment of the population is seen in early shorts such as *Her Exclusive Hat* (1911). In this photoplay, the main character, Mrs. Aitkens, purchases what she believes is a grand creation from such fashionable streets of Paris as the *rue de la Paix* or the "Place Ven Dome [sic]." By the 1910s, the cachet of the Paris label was well entrenched and the ready-to-wear market ably reproduced the latest in haute couture, purporting to be authentic creations from the Paris salons.[6] Mrs. Aitkens proudly flaunts her forty-dollar bonnet until she sees an Ethiopian woman wearing the same hat. Her dismay at seeing an African and, it is implied, lower-class woman in her bonnet prompts her to tear the ersatz millinery creation to pieces.[7] As illustrated in this film, by the 1910s, when Cahan was writing his novel, the democratization of fashion had increased exponentially.

One of the best examples of a truly democratic garment in the early part of the twentieth century is the shirtwaist, which was produced on a large scale and was a frequent subject of early film. Edna Woolman Chase, who eventually became editor of *Vogue*, wrote in her memoirs that the separate shirtwaist and street-length skirt were the essential uniform of the working

girl and that women of virtually all classes were wearing ready-to-wear versions of the latest styles.[8] Not only were vast numbers of women wearing these ready-made garments, but their actual production involved a large portion of the working-class population. Chase also wrote of the so-called Pig Market, or area of labor exchange where immigrants would wait to be hired by a contractor in need of workers.[9] Pig Market or Pig Alley encompassed Essex and Hester Streets on the Lower East Side of New York City, a neighborhood not only heavily populated by Jews but also the site of the largest concentration of movie houses in the city.[10] The term *Pig Alley* has various derivations, with some contemporary writers expounding that it was coined by Christians because everything with the exception of pork could be purchased there, while others have described the name as an Americanization of the French *Pigalle*.[11] Whatever the origins, the name of this working-class neighborhood had evidently entered into the popular imagination by the 1910s.

A number of films addressed various aspects of garment manufacture, including at-home contract work. One of these films, *The Musketeers of Pig Alley* (1912), is interesting for many reasons, not the least of which is the realistic depiction of tenement life in this quarter. While this Biograph short is often cited as the first gangster film, it also provides a visual record of a vital aspect of garment production in this era. Lillian Gish plays its main female protagonist, "The Little Lady," a seamstress who does piecework at home to support her ailing mother. Such contract work was commonplace on the Lower East Side, and the work

Advertisement for embroidered shirtwaist by Bellas Hess & Co., New York City, 1909.

Private collection.

would be turned over to "inside" shops that acted as middlemen for the bigger manufactories on Broadway. Typical of such an arrangement, the seamstress would have had to supply her own sewing machine and other accoutrement needed to perform her tasks. The competition for such work was so intense that the contractors could pay very little to the pieceworkers.[12] In one lively street scene, Gish, wearing the archetypal working girl ensemble of a plain white shirtwaist and street-length skirt, is shown transporting a bundle of her piecework to her employer.

The Musketeers of Pig Alley was marketed as social exposé and is emblem-

**Still from *The Muske-
teers of Pig Alley*, 1912.**

*Courtesy George Eastman
House.*

atic of the kind of working-class films
created by producer D. W. Griffith in the
early part of his career. In such sympathetic
portrayals of the working class, Griffith was
not only drawing upon his own impoverished background, but also creating films
with which a great majority of filmgoers
could identify. In 1910, approximately 72
percent of film patrons in Manhattan came
from the working-class segment of the
population.[13] The film shares some similarities with *The Song of the Shirt* (1908),
another early Griffith short that directly
addresses the exploitation of garment workers. The plot revolves around a young
seamstress played by Florence Lawrence,
who lives in a tenement and tries to support
her sickly sister by looking for employment
at the Acme Waist Company. Like Gish's

character in *The Musketeers of Pig Alley*, she
sews shirtwaists at home. Scenes of
Lawrence working at home are contrasted
with scenes of wealthier classes indulging in
a meal at a fine restaurant or surrounded by
finery in their lavish homes. This crosscut-
ting technique is one employed often by
Griffith to garner empathy for the hard-
working protagonist.

Another film of this genre, *A Working
Girl's Romance* (1914), portrays the industry
that employed Samuel Goldwyn soon after
his arrival to the United States—glove
manufacturing. Goldwyn, née Gelbfisz,
came to New York City from Poland in
1899. After a short-lived job with a telegraph company, he learned from someone
at the American Council of Nationalities
that a large number of Polish immigrants

were moving to a town in Upstate New York that promised sure employment. Then the unrivaled center of glove production in America, Gloversville offered Goldwyn an alternative to the teeming and impoverished Lower East Side. Goldwyn joined twelve thousand other workers in the city and was first hired as a sweeper and then an apprentice cutter at Bacmo Glove Company. Much like the main character in *The Musketeers of Pig Alley* and typical of both factory and at-home employment, he was paid by the piece for his work. His involvement in the business varied, and after a failed attempt to open his own glove company, he became a foreman at the Elite Glove Company.[14]

The plot of *A Working Girl's Romance* centers on a young girl named Nell Goodwin who is employed by a silk glove manufacturer. Its storyline and imagery give some insight into Goldwyn's early employment, providing scenes of the inner workings of a glove factory and underscoring the aspirations of many of these new immigrants. Nell is engaged to another worker, but they cannot afford to get married. In a desperate attempt to change her financial situation, Nell writes a note describing her plight and slips it into one of the gloves. A spoiled heiress purchases the gloves in a department store and finds the note. She visits Nell with the intention of helping her out of her dire situation, but instead learns a lesson from Nell that money cannot buy happiness.[15]

A Working Girl's Romance follows the formula of highlighting the disparity between rich and poor that was successful for director D. W. Griffith. But while the film ends celebrating a happiness that rises

above material fulfillment, it also provides an appropriate bridge between these sympathetic portrayals of the working classes and the shift to the interests of middle-class aspirations. While Nell's home life is happy in spite of her dire poverty, the crux of the story is her attempt to move beyond her impoverished life. This type of "cross-class fantasy," as it is termed by historian Steven Ross, had become a popular theme in film.[16] Films that celebrated working-class life, in addition to other social problem films, were on the wane by the mid-1910s for a number of reasons, including increasing pressure from film censors and the public's lack of interest in "blatant sermonizing."[17] In addition, while working conditions within the garment industry remained less than ideal, the labor movement had made great strides. For example, the tragedy of the Triangle Shirtwaist Fire of 1911, in which 146 young workers perished, figured prominently in various films and became a rallying cry for factory reform.[18]

The demographic of the film viewer of the mid- to late 1910s was also undergoing change. While the blue-collar classes remained a vital and important constituency, the middle class was considered to be a crucial target market for an industry with aspirations of continued growth. To that end, both film companies and exhibitors began to "clean up" their act by offering more morally uplifting or educational films in dedicated movie spaces that were cleaner and had better ventilation. As noted in one 1913 publication, "five years ago, attending a motion picture was a slumming expedition," but now "wives, mothers, sisters and daughters of the best classes in America are the most devoted patrons."[19] Women were regarded as moral guideposts, and in addition to what were thought of as more respectable films, fashion was considered a natural attraction for female viewers. Subsequently, the kind of garments shown, the way they were presented, and who made clothing decisions all began to undergo transformation.

While the main focus here is on fashion within film narrative, it is worthwhile to briefly address the newsreels that were venues for featuring high fashion. These newsreels, which date to the earliest days of film, served as animated fashion plates by bringing the haute couture creations of Paris designers such as Paul Poiret and Callot Soeurs to a very wide audience. The success of the fashion component within the weekly newsreels spawned serial dramas that revolved around the presentation of the latest modes set within the context of a very simple storyline. Designers like Lucile, or Lady Duff Gordon as she was also known, effectively used serials such as *The Perils of Pauline* (1914) and *Our Mutual Girl* (1914) to promote their business. Gradually, filmmakers found that feature films with added fashion shows ensured a successful promotional angle and drew the female audience. And in the oft-repeated words of Goldwyn, "pictures are for entertainment, messages should be delivered by Western Union."[20]

Potash and Perlmutter

Goldwyn was already well aware of the power of such fashion appeal by the time he made his first film as an independent producer. At this point in his career, Goldwyn had found success as a salesman with Elite, and his work there had drawn him back to Manhattan. He continued working in the glove industry until 1913 when the pending threat of the repeal of import duties convinced him that the industry was not destined to survive. Goldwyn decided to try his hand in the burgeoning film industry and began his career in film with the Jesse Lasky Play Company (which eventually became Famous Players-Lasky and finally evolved into Paramount Pictures), where he worked until 1916. In 1917, he formed a partnership with the Selwyn family of theatrical players, and together they formed Goldwyn Pictures, from which he took his name. Metro pictures bought Goldwyn's shares in 1922 (eventually becoming the conglomerate Metro-Goldwyn-Mayer), and he used his experience and connections to operate as an autonomous producer.

The first film that Goldwyn produced drew inspiration from his time in Gloversville and employment in the garment industry. *Potash and Perlmutter* (1923) derives its plot from a fiction serial by Montague Glass that was published in popular periodicals such as the *Glover's Review* and the *Saturday Evening Post* from 1909 through 1913. The storyline revolves around two American Jews who become business partners in a successful cloak and suit company in New York. After its initial publication, the story was produced for the Broadway stage in 1913, and Goldwyn purchased the rights to the story to turn it into a film in 1923. The adaptation of popular fiction to stage and then screen was common practice in this period and proved a profitable formula for the film industry.

Potash and Perlmutter, with its ethnic subject matter, was perceived as a risky endeavor. Goldwyn, however, saw the value in bringing to the screen what *Moving Picture World* described as a "comedy of long-standing reputation."[21] Goldywn, who had by now learned that high production values could result in high returns, hired established writer Frances Marion to create the scenario and well-known actors Barney Bernard and Alexander Carr to play the title characters in the film. The essence of the plot is a comedic drama about Abe Potash's (played by Bernard) daughter Irma and her suitors, set against a backdrop of Potash and Perlmutter's business escapades in the garment industry. In the original Glass story, Morris (or "Mawruss" as he is often called) Perlmutter is a self-made garment industry man who, like Goldwyn, worked his way up from entry-level hard labor to management and manufacturing. Perlmutter is described as a "fine business man" and a "swell dresser" in the story, a description that could also be applied to Goldwyn, who was noted for both his business savvy and his elegant attire.[22]

The review of the film for *Moving Picture World* noted, "Other features in which the screen particularly excels have been added. These include an effective dash of melodrama and a fashion parade."[23] When fashion is specifically singled out as "an appeal for the women," it often takes the form of a fashion show set within a storyline that may or may not be related to

fashion per se.[24] This ensured that even if a title did not appear to be of interest to the female viewer it could still draw a large number of women viewers. In *Potash and Perlmutter*, the fashion show featured couture finery by Madame Frances, Madame Stein, Madame Blaine, and Evelyn McHorter, all of whom would have been recognizable entities to fashion-conscious filmgoers. In all probability, Madame Stein and Madame Blaine refer to the New York dress shop Stein & Blaine, where a woman by the name of Miss E. M. A. Steinmetz worked as an in-house designer. Located at 13–15 West 57th Street, the design house was in business from the 1910s through at least the 1950s.

Like many New York–based fashion salons at this time, the firm of Stein & Blaine imported French couture and retailed custom-made clothing created by their own designers, including Steinmetz. As an arbiter of American style, the house was frequently featured in the pages of *Harper's Bazaar* and recommended by *Vogue* as a shopping destination. In the film, the fashion parade of Stein & Blaine clothing was modeled by experienced mannequins, and one of the surviving stills from the film depicts Rosie Potash (played by Vera Gordon) longingly viewing the display of haute couture finery. Inspired by the elegant presentation, Rosie dons one of these high-fashion garments and affects an exaggerated runway walk. In the comedic scene that follows, her lack of experience and poise almost results in Abe Potash losing his customer.

Small design houses, including establishments such as Henri Bendel, Madame Frances, Frances Clyne, Thurn, Bonwit

Fashion sketch, Stein & Blaine, New York, ca. 1913.

Courtesy Special Collections, Gladys Marcus Library at the Fashion Institute of Technology.

Teller, and J.M. Gidding (who employed Evelyn McHorter, another designer on the film), have received insufficient attention, but were important forces within American garment industry history.[25] J.M. Gidding was located on Fifth Avenue at 46th Street and boasted shops in Paris, Washington, Cincinnati, and Duluth. Not only did these small houses offer a challenge to the hegemony of Paris haute couture, but they were also a strong presence within films that thousands of filmgoers viewed every week. Both stage and screen actresses wore and promoted clothing by these New York–based designers and retailers. The firms were also incubators for important American talents such as Germaine Monteil, Mollie Parnis, and Muriel King, all of whom worked at Stein & Blaine at some point in their careers.[26]

Goldwyn's prediction that *Potash and Perlmutter* would appeal to the immigrant population is confirmed by the film's success and the positive reviews it received in numerous periodicals. It must have appealed to an even broader audience because Goldwyn produced a sequel entitled *In Hollywood with Potash and Perlmutter* the following year. This film is yet again loosely adapted from the Montague Glass play. Mirroring Goldwyn's personal story and that of many other Jewish film producers, this film chronicles the adventures of Potash and Perlmutter

Still from *Potash and Perlmutter*, 1923.

Courtesy George Eastman House.

when they leave the apparel industry to produce films. It also illustrates two shifts that occurred within the world of film: the start of the move to Hollywood in the mid-1910s and the rise of the in-house studio designer.

The reviews of *In Hollywood with Potash and Perlmutter* were again very positive, with papers such as the *New York Times* writing that it was "one of the funniest farces it has been our lot to view on screen," and a "pictorial gem."[27] It is fitting that Potash and Perlmutter shift their

attention to California by 1924 because from approximately World War I onward, the West Coast played a more important and vital role in both the film and fashion industries. Hollywood became the center of world film production and distribution, and the California garment industry, inspired by film fashion, started to have a more pronounced influence on American fashion in general. The film industry was evolving into big business and was increasingly backed by Wall Street financiers. Consequently, the pressure was more intense to create so-called KOs (knock-outs) that would bring in large numbers of moviegoers and result in a high profit margin. While films were now much more expensive to create and production values were higher, the actual process of making a film had been streamlined and lessons learned from mass production had been incorporated.

In the movie, the first film that Potash and Perlmutter produced is called *The Fatal Murder*. Rosie Potash is again employed for comic relief in a scene that involves her personal attire. As Abe's wife, she is allowed to play a small role in the partners' movie and wears a "glittering gem" even though her character is supposedly destitute. Rosie's wearing of inappropriate dress for her scene was a commonplace occurrence in the earlier days of film, when actors were required to supply their own wardrobe for their films. With their then low salaries, it was quite difficult to accommodate the wardrobe requirements of the various films and scenes within films. For example, it was recommended that prospective actors provide all of the following: a street suit, a one-piece day dress, an office ensemble, an afternoon gown, sportswear, a motoring outfit, and an evening dress.[28] Some contracts actually specified the type and quality of clothing required, and there are numerous accounts of actors complaining of the high cost of furnishing their own costumes. Madge Bellamy, who first came to Hollywood from New York in 1920, revealed in an interview that she hadn't noticed the small print in the contract that read "furnish your own costumes." She recalled that "Mr. Ince insisted on the very finest and he'd look at the label on my

dresses. My mother learned to take the label off one dress and put it on another dress so that I was always wearing a Patou or a Mainbocher, but he could have kept me broke wearing expensive clothes."[29] It was not unusual to see an actress wear one dress throughout an entire film, an evening dress during a day scene, or the same dress in multiple films.

There was some improvement, however, by the mid- to late 1910s, prompting one film reviewer to write, "by now they are no longer wearing silk and chiffon gowns for breakfast scenes and they are not saving old clothes for the pictures; clothing is now an important part of the picture."[30] In lieu of the inappropriate and ill-fitting ensembles of the early 1910s, more and more filmmakers were making an effort to "costume" a picture, and instead of the "remains of a discarded studio curtain," leading ladies were now "harmoniously gowned from slipper to bandeau."[31] The story also mentions that by this date the larger studios were beginning to hire head designers, although many stars were still using their own modistes. When they could afford custom-made clothing, the higher paid and more successful movie stars patronized local New York dressmakers such as Stein & Blaine and J.M. Gidding for both their on- and off-screen dressing.

The mid- to late 1910s was thus a transitional period in costume design as Hollywood began to realize the benefit of promoting in-house costume designers whose work could be tied to various commercial products. With the increasing disjuncture between what Paris created and how Hollywood wanted to dress its stars, the divide between "real" clothing and

**Advertisement for J.M.
Gidding and Co., 1920.**

Private collection.

Hollywood artifice was in ascendancy. One such example of this disengagement is evident in a 1922 article in *Picture Play*, an early fan magazine, which opens with "Paris wants skirts long, Hollywood wants them short." Paramount wardrobe designer Ethel Chaffin is interviewed in the article and complains about the sophisticated styles being shown in Paris, which are "simply not suited to the wholesome, all-American girl image" epitomized by stars such as Mary Pickford. Instead, the article endorses flowered and ruffled dresses for the "sweet young girl full of whimsicalities and dainty mannerisms; the frocks should be as delicate as moonlight." Chaffin explained that viewers want young-looking girls on the screen, and "they won't look young if we dress them in those long skirts."[32]

Chaffin was one of the earliest recognized designers from this period and was head of the wardrobe department at Paramount from 1919 through 1925 before moving to Metro-Goldwyn-Mayer. By the late 1910s, some of the major movie studios, most of which had bases on the West Coast, began hiring in-house designers. Jane Lewis was at Vitagraph, Peggy Hamilton Adams was at Triangle, Mrs. Frank Farrington was at Thanhouser Film Corporation, Irene Duncan was at Universal, and Alpharetta Hoffman was at Lasky Studios. While there was active promotion of California-based designers by figures such as Peggy Hamilton Adams (who became a fashion columnist and stylist), there is a remarkable dearth of information pertaining to their careers, and they are rarely, if ever, credited on the screen. Bess Schlank, the wife of producer Morris R. Schlank, for example, was a custom dressmaker based in Los Angeles from the mid-1920s through 1956. Even with such a long history of fashion involvement on the West Coast, only one film seems to credit her as the designer—a 1926 Tiffany production entitled *Souls for Sables.*

Goldwyn, Chanel, and the Rise of the Studio Designer

Not until the mid-1920s, with the hiring of Adrian at MGM and Howard Greer at Paramount Pictures, is the professional and credited designer in ascendancy. Contemporaneously, the American garment business was the eleventh top manufacturing industry in the country, with turnover of over one billion dollars a year. With the help of Hollywood, the Los Angeles women's-wear industry was now being recognized as a competent player on a national level. The notion that moving pictures could be employed to promote new products and stimulate trade can be summed up in the words of the United States Department of Commerce: "trade follows the motion pictures."[33]

It is within this context that commercial tie-ins between specific films and consumer goods became part of the exploitation strategies for movie producers. To this end, Goldwyn invited Coco Chanel, a famous French couturière, to Hollywood to design for his films between 1930 and

1932, approximately one year after the Wall Street market crash. The Great Depression had acutely affected the film industry as hundreds of Hollywood businesses filed for bankruptcy by the end of 1931. So too, the French couture suffered as its exports fell each year, decreasing a dramatic 70 percent by 1933. It seemed a stronger relationship between Hollywood and haute couture would therefore benefit both industries. As an added incentive, Goldwyn viewed his collaboration with Chanel as a way to ensure the international appeal of American films at a time when talkies, or sound film, were emerging as the future of the industry and, in the process, threatening the cross-cultural accessibility provided by silent films. While companies such as Paramount opened up studios in the suburbs of Paris in an effort to maintain their audience, Goldwyn brought Paris haute couture to Hollywood.

As with *Potash and Perlmutter*, Goldwyn once again drew some inspiration from stage successes. Biographer Scott Berg notes that Goldwyn learned much from productions such as the Ziegfeld Follies, particularly that "women enjoyed looking at beautiful women in beautiful clothes, the glorification of their gender."[34] In a very well-publicized campaign, Goldwyn presented Chanel with a one-million-dollar contract for work on three films. He claimed that this collaboration represented "a new era in the movies" as he would be the first producer to show advanced styles from the runway "six months before they are being stolen by copyists."[35] The copyists to which he referred were the illustrators and designers hired by Seventh Avenue manufacturers to transform high fashion into wearable design. The American designer Elizabeth Hawes, for example, offers a lively account of her experience as an illicit copyist for an American knock-off house in her book *Fashion Is Spinach*. Businesses, such as Berley Studios, offered a subscription fashion forecasting service with the most up-to-date reports from American and Parisian design houses and were essential to the success of the garment industry. Operated by Ethel Rabin and located at 9 East 48th Street, Berley was in business from 1919 through at least 1935. While they did not intentionally operate as a copy house, their sketches were detailed enough to provide design inspiration for many fashion companies.

Marketing and public relations vehicles enthusiastically heralded Chanel's arrival in Hollywood. In a *Collier's* magazine article, she claimed to be very excited by the notion that her clothing would be seen in "every small village of the world, in every city, in every country!"[36] She evidently was aware of the power of film, and Hollywood film in particular, to reach a much wider audience for her business and also firmly believed she could teach Hollywood how to dress. Chanel looked at the creations of "star" designers such as Adrian with disdain, calling them "costumes" and "artificial creations." Chanel dressed three films for Goldwyn: *Palmy Days* (1931), *Tonight or Never* (1931), and *The Greeks Had a Word for Them* (alternatively titled *Three Broadway Girls*). One source quotes a figure of $100,000 for the thirty ensembles she produced for the last film, which was distributed in 1932.[37] The press pages for this film emphasized the Chanel clothing

Illustration from Berley Studios, 1921.
Private collection.

over the film content, which considered somewhat risqué. The simple plot revolves around three gold-digging, cocktail-swigging stage girls looking for sugar daddies. The actresses, Joan Blondell, Ina Claire, and Madge Evans, wore clothing that was more subtle than most Hollywood creations. The attention paid to the wardrobe in the film is evident in the frequent pans up and down the bodies of the actresses, full body shots and poses, and the attention paid to details such as the double fold cuffs and satin lounging pajamas that the studio deemed press worthy.

While Goldwyn believed he was producing something entirely new in showing advance runway styles from one of the premiere couturières from Paris, none of the films was very successful. Goldwyn actually admitted to a member of the Hays Commission, which monitored film content, that he was somewhat ashamed of *The Greeks Had a Word for Them*, and there appear to be numerous reasons the collaboration was ineffective, not the least of which was the volatile state of both the film and couture industries at that time. One could also argue that the rise of the Hollywood

Still from *The Greeks Had a Word for Them (Three Broadway Girls)*, 1931.

Courtesy Margaret Herrick Library, Academy of Motion Picture Arts and Sciences.

designer and the establishment of a unique Hollywood aesthetic played a role in the failure. Chanel's "poverty de luxe" did not translate well for a film audience that had by then adjusted to fantasy. In addition, while Chanel evidently was aware of the power of Hollywood to promote fashion, Goldwyn neglected to realize that it was the escapism of Hollywood artifice that viewers were looking to purchase.

The costume designer Howard Greer, who started working with Famous Players-Lasky in 1924 (later Paramount), wrote of the ineffectiveness of using Paris couture at this point in Hollywood's history and spoke to the divergence in style that had evolved:

New York and Paris disdainfully looked down their august noses at the dresses we designed in Hollywood. Well maybe they *were* vulgar, but they *did* have imagination. If they were gaudy, they but reflected the absence of subtlety which characterized all early motion pictures. [Over-emphasis], as it applied to acting techniques and story treatments, was essential. If a lady in real life wore a train one yard long, her prototype in reel life, wore it three yards long. . . . The most elegant Chanel dress of the early twenties was a wash out on the screen. When you strip color and sound and the third dimension from a

moving object, you have to make up for the loss with dramatic black-and-white contrasts and enriched surfaces.[38]

While it is unclear if he was directly referring to Chanel's work on the Goldwyn films, it is evident that he was speaking to the emergence of a distinctive Hollywood design idiom. Greer also realized the potency of the Hollywood image and had opened his own couture shop, Greer Inc., in Los Angeles in 1927. What Goldwyn had

failed to consider was that the American apparel industry, and Hollywood fashion in particular, could now directly compete with Paris. In an August 1924 newspaper article, the popular film flapper Colleen Moore proclaimed "Los Angeles the Paris of America" because many of the seamstresses and dressmakers that now lived on the West Coast were trained in Paris and the screen had replaced the fashion magazine as an authority on the latest styles.[39]

Still from *Madam Satan* (MGM, 1930) with costumes designed by Adrian.

Private collection.

Conclusion

Although the stock market crash and Depression interrupted the progress of the California clothing industry, it had largely recovered by 1932; by 1936, the Combined Market Week trade fairs in Los Angeles boasted 185 women's clothing manufacturers and drew over ten thousand buyers.[40] This was a marked difference from its position at the turn of the twentieth century, when only one clothing manufacturer was in business. The motion picture industry is often credited with the success of the West Coast apparel industry. The connections between the two industries that were forged in New York City in the nascent days of film remained strong and mutually supportive throughout the 1930s and 1940s, but the emphasis had fully shifted to California-based designers and retailers. In the late 1930s, for example, Helen Wilson, the wardrobe shopper for David Selznick, recalled how her first assignment was to buy clothing and material for stars such as Mae Murray, Eleanor Boardman, Billie Dove, Colleen Moore, and Fay Wray. She shopped primarily in the Los Angeles department stores, which were by now stocked with clothing by California-based designers.[41] In addition, the "exploitation" strategies of film companies now effectively promoted California design with various types of commercial tie-ins. The MGM press books suggested to exhibitors that for the 1930 film *Our Blushing Brides* they should promote the bathing revue sequence of the film by conducting fashion shows at local department stores featuring bathing suits by the California firm Catalina. And while numerous scholars have explored the relationship between film and fashion in the golden age, it is worth noting past research such as Charles Eckert's examination of Bernard Waldman's Modern Merchandising Bureau, organized in 1930 to create ready-to-wear versions of screen styles. Waldman's agency, like the aforementioned copy houses, acted as a middleman between the major studios and manufacturers who would then sell the film-inspired garments in department stores.[42]

In terms of costume design, Adrian's work, although disparaged by designers such as Chanel, best encapsulates what Hollywood had become. Adrian's insistence that he be credited with "Gowns by" rather than "Wardrobe by" illustrates the new status of these high-profile designers. Adrian considered himself a couturier and fashion authority who had effectively replaced the Paris runway with a distinctive American style. By establishing such a reputation, Hollywood was able to avoid the pitfalls of the vagaries of haute couture. Abe Potash aptly sums up the problem in the original version of Glass's story. While dining with Morris Perlmutter, Potash is squirted in the eye by a pickle and observes, "Dill pickles is uncertain like Paris fashions. . . . You could never tell what they would do next."[43] To bring the Hollywood story full circle, one can return to David Levinsky, who claimed, "The average American woman is the best-dressed average woman in the world, and the Russian Jew has had a good deal to do with making her one."[44] Levinsky is obviously referring to garment industry pioneers, yet there was another important group of businessmen who were also responsible for this achievement: the Hollywood moguls who successfully popularized and sold the American ready-to-wear market to filmgoers.

Notes

Chapter 1 Sewn Together:
The Garment Industry and American Jewry

1. www.yumuseum.org/APerfectFit/resources.html.

Chapter 2 Jewish Immigrants and the Garment
Industry: A View from London

1. Andrew Godley, *Jewish Immigrant Entrepreneurship in New York and London, 1880–1914* (New York: Palgrave, 2001). Chapter 5 details the patterns of Jewish migration during the period.
2. Andrew Godley, *The Emergence of Ethnic Entrepreneurship* (Princeton, NJ: Princeton University Press, 2012). Chapter 4 focuses on Jewish upward social mobility.
3. Samuel Joseph, *Jewish Immigration to the United States from 1881 to 1910* (n.p.: New York, 1914), 193, Table LXII.
4. For a very similar pattern of developments in Paris, see Chapter 3.
5. Godley, *Jewish Immigrant Entrepreneurship*, 67–89.

Chapter 3 Jewish Immigrants and the Garment
Industry: A View from Paris

1. Emile Levasseur, *L'Ouvrier américain* (Paris: L. Larose, 1898), 2:32, 37; and more generally 2:32–40, and 1:50–51.
2. Nancy L. Green, *Ready-to-Wear and Ready-to-Work: A Century of Industry and Immigrants in Paris and New York* (Durham, NC: Duke University Press, 1997).
3. Levasseur had already published a major multivolume study on French workers, *Histoire des classes ouvrières en France depuis la conquête de Jules César jusqu'à la révolution*, 2 vols. (Paris: Guillaumin, 1859); and *Histoire des classes ouvrières en France depuis 1789 jusqu'à nos jours*, 2 vols. (Paris: Hachette, 1867), but he did not "see" the immigrant workers who had already begun to arrive.

4. David H. Weinberg, *A Community on Trial: The Jews of Paris in the 1930s* (Chicago: University of Chicago Press, 1977); Paula E. Hyman, *From Dreyfus to Vichy: The Remaking of French Jewry* (New York: Columbia University Press, 1979); Nancy L. Green, *The Pletzl of Paris: Jewish Immigrant Workers in the Belle Epoque* (New York: Holmes & Meier, 1986).
5. Roger Ikor, *Les fils d'Avrom: Les Eaux mêlées* (Paris: Albin Michel, 1955), 159, 161.
6. Wolf Speiser, *Kalendar* (Paris, 1910), 78–80.
7. Michel Roblin, *Les Juifs de Paris* (Paris: A. et J. Picard, 1952), 99–100; Joseph Klatzmann, *Le travail à domicile dans l'industrie parisienne du vêtement* (Paris: Armand Colin, 1957), 81–82.
8. Roblin, *Les Juifs*, 115.
9. Ibid., 114.

Chapter 4 American Jewish Identity and the
Garment Industry

1. Nahum Gross, ed., *Economic History of the Jews* (New York: Schocken Books, 1975), makes amply clear the deep and widespread roots of Jewish involvement in garment making.
2. Hasia R. Diner, *A Time for Gathering: The Second Migration* (Baltimore: Johns Hopkins University Press, 1992), 75.
3. Quoted in Rudolf Glanz, "German Jews in New York City in the 19th Century," in *Studies in Judaica Americana* (New York: KTAV Publishing, 1970), 127.
4. Clyde Griffin and Sally Griffin, *Natives and Newcomers: The Ordering of Opportunity in Mid-Nineteenth-Century Poughkeepsie* (Cambridge, MA: Harvard University Press, 1978), 121.
5. Quoted in Nancy L. Green, *Ready-to-Wear and Ready-to-Work: A Century of Industry and Immigrants in Paris and New York* (Durham, NC: Duke University Press, 1997), 33.
6. Jesse Pope, *The Clothing Industry in New York* (Columbia: University of Missouri Press, 1905).

7. Diner, *A Time for Gathering*, 158.

8. Lynn Weiner, *From Working Girl to Working Mother: The Female Labor Force in the United States, 1820–1980* (Chapel Hill: University of North Carolina Press, 1985).

9. Thomas Kessner, "Jobs, Ghettoes, and the Urban Economy, 1880–1935," *American Jewish History* 71, no. 2 (December 1981): 224.

10. Gerald Sorin, *A Time for Building: The Third Migration, 1880–1924* (Baltimore: Johns Hopkins University Press, 1992), 74.

11. Daniel E. Bender, *Sweated Work, Weak Bodies: Anti-Sweatshop Campaigns and Languages of Labor* (New Brunswick, NJ: Rutgers University Press, 2004).

12. On the preference of Jewish women for the big, modern factories, which paid better and where they felt less vulnerable to sexual harassment, see Susan Glenn, *Daughters of the Shtetl: Life and Labor in the Immigrant Generation* (Ithaca, NY: Cornell University Press, 1990).

13. This pattern played itself out in, for example, the Jewish baking industry and in butchering, which saw some of the most explosive strikes in the Jewish immigrant communities. See Hasia R. Diner, *Hungering for America: Italian, Irish, and Jewish Foodways in the Age of Immigration* (Cambridge, MA: Harvard University Press, 2001).

14. William Graham Sumner, *What Social Classes Owe to Each Other* (New Haven, CT: Yale University Press, 1925). First published 1883.

Chapter 5 The Birth of the Clothing Industry in America, 1815–1860

1. Information in this and the next paragraph is taken from a variety of sources, including D. T. Valentine, *Manual of the Corporation of the City of New York for 1864* (New York: New York Common Council, 1864), 753–54; *New York Post*, July 13, 1819; Catharine Street store ledger, 1822, box 03, Brooks Brothers Archive, Chantilly, VA; A.3, book 2A, Brooks Brothers Archive; sales book, 1824–29, box 03, A.3, Brooks Brothers Archive; and "Report on the Founding," box 01, BB.1, F10, Brooks Brothers Archive; William R. Bagnall, *Sketches of Manufacturing Establishments in New York City, and of Textile Establishments in the United States* (North Andover, MA: Merrimack Valley Textile Museum, 1977), 344–46; *Longworth's American Almanac, New-York Register and City Directory, 1806–1819* (New York: David Longworth, 1806–19).

2. Alexander Stuart, "Anniversary Address before the American Institute of the City of New-York" (New York, 1844), 19; see also Adam Smith, *An Inquiry into the Nature and Causes of the Wealth of Nations* (Indianapolis: Bobbs-Merrill Educational Publishing, 1961), 11–13.

3. Carole Shammas, *The Pre-Industrial Consumer in England and America* (Oxford: Clarendon Press, 1990); Adrienne D. Hood, *The Weaver's Craft: Cloth, Commerce, and Industry in Early Pennsylvania* (Philadelphia: University of Pennsylvania Press, 2003); Rolla Milton Tryon, *Household Manufactures in the United States, 1640–1860* (1917; repr., New York: Augustus M. Kelley, 1966); Michael Zakim, "Sartorial Ideologies: From Homespun to Ready-Made," *American Historical Review* 106, no. 5 (December 2001).

4. *Hunt's Merchant's Magazine*, January 1849, 116.

5. On the rise of an American market, see Robert Greenhalgh Albion, *The Rise of New York Port, 1815–1860*, with the collaboration of Jennie Barnes Pope (New York: Charles Scribner's Sons, 1939); George Rogers Taylor, *The Transportation Revolution, 1815–1860* (New York: Rinehart & Co., 1951); Douglass C. North, *The Economic Growth of the United States, 1790–1860* (New York: W. W. Norton, 1966); D. W. Meinig, *The Shaping of America: Continental America, 1800–1867* (New Haven, CT: Yale University Press, 1993). On the clothing trade's place in industrial revolution, see Michael Zakim, "A Ready-Made Business: The Birth of the Clothing Industry in America," *Business History Review* 73 (Spring 1999): 61–90.

6. Lillian Schlissel et al., *Far From Home: Families of the Westward Journey* (New York: Schocken Books, 1989), 39; *Wilson's Business Directory of New York City, 1860* (New York, 1860); *New Trade Directory for New York, 1800* (New York, 1800); Chamber of Commerce of New York, *Annual Report* (1858), 38–40.

7. "Tom, Dick, and Harry" from James M. Edney, of New York, NY, to Francis H. Cooke, of Augusta, Georgia, April 22, 1837, letter book, 1835–1837, Special Collections, Rutgers University, New Brunswick, NJ; Linton Wells, *The House of Seligman* (typescript, New-York Historical Society, 1931), 1–56; Jesse Seligman, *In Memorium* (printed for private circulation, 1894), 9–14, 131–32; Leslie Meyers Zomalt, "An Exercise in Caution: The Business Activities of the Joseph Seligman Family in the 19th Century American West" (PhD diss., University of California, Santa Barbara, 1979), 8–9, 21–27, 30–31, 36–40; New York County, New York, vol. 198, pp. 130, 137, 167; Green County, Alabama, vol. 11, p. 255, R.G. Dun & Co. Collection, Baker Library, Harvard University Graduate School of Business Administration, Cambridge, MA; Chauncey M. Depew, ed., *One Hundred Years of American Commerce, 1795–1895* (New York: D.O. Haynes, 1895), 562.

8. *New York Tribune*, June 16, 1849; *Hunt's Merchant's Magazine*, January 1849, 116; biographical facts in Devlin's obituary in *New York Times*, February 23, 1867; *Wilson's Illustrated Guide to the Hudson River, 1849* (New York, 1848); "Eights Millions" from *Sheldon & Company's Business or Advertising Direc-*

tory (New York: John F. Trow & Co., 1845); William E. Devlin, "Shrewd Irishmen: Irish Entrepreneurs and Artisans in New York's Clothing Industry, 1830–1880," in *The New York Irish*, ed. Ronald H. Bayor and Timothy J. Meagher (Baltimore: Johns Hopkins University Press, 1996), 184.

9. New York County, New York, vol. 365, p. 123; Green County, Alabama, vol. 198, p. 196, R.G. Dun & Co. Collection, Baker Library, Harvard University Graduate School of Business Administration, Cambridge, MA; Hone quoted in Philip Hone, *Diary of Philip Hone, 1828–1851*, ed. Allan Nevins (1850; repr., New York: Kraus Reprint Co., 1969); *Putnam's Monthly: A Magazine of Literature, Science, and Art*, February 1853, 124–35; *Putnam's Monthly*, April 1853, 353–68, quote is on 357. On the significance of men's suits in modern life in general, see Michael Zakim, *Ready-Made Democracy: A History of Men's Dress in the American Republic, 1760–1860* (Chicago: University of Chicago Press, 2003).

10. On standardized sizes, see Michael Zakim, "Customizing the Industrial Revolution: The Reinvention of Tailoring in the Nineteenth Century," *Winterthur Portfolio* 33, no. 1 (Spring 1998): 41–58; quotes on Brooks and Devlin in *Boyd's Pictorial Directory of Broadway, 1859* (New York: Andrew Boyd, 1859); illustration of Grand Street store, box 01, BB.1, F6, Brooks Brothers Archive; "New York Daguerreotyped," *Putnam's Monthly*, February 1853, 128; *New York Illustrated News*, September 1, 1860; George Templeton Strong, *The Diary of George Templeton Strong, Young Man in New York, 1835–1849*, ed. Allan Nevins (New York: Macmillan, 1952); William Hancock, *An Emigrant's Five Years in the Free States of America* (London: T. Cautley Newby, 1860), 36; *Hunt's Merchant's Magazine*, January 1849, 116.

11. *New York Herald*, April 18, 1852; all quotes from Devlin advertisement in *Carroll's Directory* (New York, 1859).

12. *Mirror of Fashion*, November 1, 1849; July 2, 1849, 50; New York County, New York, vol. 3 (new series, 1855), 21–22; vol. 364, p. 69; vol. 365, p. 102. Also see vol. 211, p. 274; vol. 365, p. 105; vol. 212, p. 377; Green County, Alabama, R.G. Dun & Co. Collection, Baker Library, Harvard University Graduate School of Business Administration, Cambridge, MA.

13. *New York Herald*, May 7, 1836; Nathaniel Whittock, *The Complete Book of Trades* (London: John Bennett, 1837), 432; Sarah Levitt, "Cheap Mass-Produced Men's Clothing in the Nineteenth and Early Twentieth Centuries," *Textile History* 22, no. 2 (1991): 183–84; Ava Baron and Susan E. Klepp, "'If I Didn't Have My Sewing Machine . . .': Women and Sewing Machine Technology," in *A Needle, a Bobbin, a Strike: Women Needleworkers in America*, ed. Joan M. Jensen and Sue Davidson (Philadelphia: Temple University Press,

1984), 29; H. L. Eades, *Instruction Book, 1847–8*, Library of Congress Manuscript Collection; Alison Beazeley, "The 'Heavy' and 'Light' Clothing Industries, 1850–1920," *Costume*, no. 7 (1973): 55; Jesse Eliphant Pope, *The Clothing Industry in New York* (Columbia: University of Missouri Press, 1905), 22–23; *Clothier and Hatter*, August 15, 1873.

14. First three quotations from Caroline Cowles Richards, *Village Life in America, 1852–1872* (London: T. Fisher Unwin, 1912), 73–74; *Niles' National Register*, August 30, 1817.

15. United States, Seventh U.S. Census (1850), Products of Industry, raw data, New York County, New York, in National Archives, Washington, DC; *Hunt's Merchant's Magazine*, March 1849, 348; Duncan Bythell, *The Sweated Trades: Outwork in Nineteenth-Century Britain* (New York: St. Martin's Press, 1978), 158, 182, 192, 194; Richard B. Stott, *Workers in the Metropolis: Class, Ethnicity, and Youth in Antebellum New York City* (Ithaca, NY: Cornell University Press, 1990), 23.

16. *New York Tribune*, August 14, 1845; Charles Burdett, *The Elliott Family; or, the Trials of New-York Seamstresses* (New York: E. Winchester, New World Press, 1845), 75; quotes from Chas. P. Neill, *Woman and Child Wage-Earners in the United States, vol. II: Men's Ready-Made Clothing*, 61st Cong. S. Doc. No. 645, at 226, 242; Society of Relief of Widows, *Report* (New York, 1859).

17. Virginia Penny, *The Employments of Women: A Cyclopaedia of Woman's Work* (Boston: Walker, Wise, 1863), 352–55.

18. *New York Daily Sentinel*, February 17, 1831; March 5, 1831; quotes from Philip S. Foner, *Women and the American Labor Movement: From the First Trade Unions to the Present* (New York: Free Press, 1982), 1–6; "Unfeminine" in Helen Sumner, *History of Women in Industry in the United States*, 61st Cong. S. Doc. No. 645, vol. 94, at 36.

19. *New York Tribune*, July 19, 1850; July 23, 1850; July 26, 1850; July 31, 1850; August 2, 1850; August 6, 1850; *New York Herald*, July 25, 1850; July 26, 1850; July 31, 1850; August 5, 1850; August 6, 1850; *New York Post*, July 25, 1850; *New York Morning Express*, July 21, 22, 25, 1850; Carl N. Degler, "Labor in the Economy and Politics of New York City, 1850–1860: A Study of the Impact of Early Industrialism" (PhD diss., Columbia University, 1952), 81.

20. Penny, *Employments of Women*, 113–14, 355; *New York Tribune*, July 29, 1850; November 15, 1845; *Mirror of Fashion*, September 2, 1850, 65; Mark Seltzer, *Bodies and Machines* (New York: Routledge, 1992), 26; James A. Schmiechen, *Sweated Industries and Sweated Labor: The London Clothing Trades, 1860–1914* (Urbana: University of Illinois Press, 1984), 17; *New York Herald*, October 21, 1857; Christine Stansell, "The Origins of the Sweatshop: Women and Early Industrialization in New York City," in *Working-Class America: Essays on*

Labor, Community, and American Society, ed. Michael H. Frisch and Daniel J. Walkowitz (Urbana: University of Illinois Press, 1983), 84–85; Foster quoted in George Foster, *New York Naked* (New York: De Witt & Davenport, 185–), 137–38.

21. *New York Herald*, October 21, 1857; Bythell, *The Sweated Trades*, 184–85; Jesse Thomas Carpenter, *Competition and Collective Bargaining in the Needle Trades, 1910–1967* (New York: New York State School of Industrial and Labor Relations, Cornell University, 1972), 107–8; Maxine Berg, "Small Producer Capitalism in Eighteenth-Century England," *Business History* 35, no. 1 (January 1993): 22–23; Ben Fine and Ellen Leopold, *The World of Consumption* (London: Routledge, 1993), 94; Steven Fraser, "Combined and Uneven Development in the Men's Clothing Industry," *Business History Review* 57 (Winter 1983); Carol Groneman Pernicone, "The 'Blody Ould Sixth,' A Social Analysis of a New York City Working-Class Community in the Mid-Nineteenth Century" (PhD diss., University of Rochester, 1973), 105; Penny, *Employments of Women*, 310–11.

22. United States, *Manufactures of the United States in 1860; compiled from the original returns of the eighth census* (Washington, DC: Government Printing Office, 1865), lxiv; Fred Mitchell Jones, *Middlemen in the Domestic Trade of the United States, 1800–1860* (Urbana: University of Illinois, 1937), 13; Warshaw Collection, Men's Clothing, box 11; Samuel Terry, *How to Keep a Store* (New York: Fowler & Wells, 1891), 75; Edwin T. Freedley, *Leading Pursuits and Leading Men: A Treatise on the Principal Trades and Manufactures of the United States* (Philadelphia: Edward Young, 1854), 90; Joseph H. Appel, *The Business Biography of John Wanamaker, Founder and Builder* (New York: Macmillan, 1939), 4–46; "Wants of Clothiers" in *United States Economist and Dry Goods Reporter*, November 6, 1852; see also May 8, 1852; June 12, 1852; July 31, 1852; August 14, 1852; February 26, 1853; May 7, 1853; May 28, 1853; January 7, 1854; January 14, 1854; August 12, 1854; September 2, 1854; *New York Herald*, October 21, 1857; "Pass Through" in Arthur Harrison Cole, *The American Wool Manufacture* (Cambridge, MA: Harvard University Press, 1926), 272, 286, 294–95.

Chapter 6 German Jews in the Early Manufacture of Ready-Made Clothing

1. Hasia Diner has noted that Jewish scholars have divided American Jewish history into three periods based on immigrations: the Sephardic era from 1654 to 1820, the German era from 1820 to 1880, and the eastern European era from 1880 to 1920. She believes this scheme is too simplistic. The Jews who immigrated between 1820 and 1880 included a majority from "German lands with smaller numbers from Bohemia, Moravia, Alsace and even parts of Russia and Lithuania." The national origins of Jewish immigrants from this period were more diverse than is generally recognized and their experience in America was not homogenous. Hasia Diner, *A Time for Gathering: The Second Migration 1820–1880* (Baltimore: Johns Hopkins University Press, 1992), 1. While most of the Jews who became clothing manufacturers before 1880 were from German lands, the group also included some from eastern Europe. In this chapter, I am using the popular term *German Jews* to focus the lens on a particular historical period, during which the majority but not all Jewish immigrants hailed from German lands.

2. Michael Zakim, *Ready-Made Democracy: A History of Men's Dress in the American Republic, 1760–1860* (Chicago: University of Chicago Press, 2003), 71, 84–95, 130–38, 141–54; Claudia B. Kidwell and Margaret C. Christman, *Suiting Everyone: The Democratization of Clothing in America* (Washington, DC: Smithsonian Institution Press, 1974), 39–47.

3. Zakim, *Ready-Made Democracy*, 109–26.

4. "Manufacture of Ready-Made Clothing," transcript in pencil, 1857, clothing vertical file, box 1, folder 32, Warshaw Collection of Business Americana, Archives Center, National Museum of American History, Smithsonian Institution, Washington, DC.

5. Kidwell and Christman, *Suiting Everyone*, 47–53.

6. Ibid., 52.

7. Bruce S. Bazelon and William F. McGuinn, *A Directory of American Military Goods Dealers & Makers 1785–1915 Combined Edition* (n.p.: Bruce S. Bazelon and William F. McGuinn, 1999), 317–18.

8. Harry A. Cobrin, *The Men's Clothing Industry: Colonial Through Modern Times* (New York: Fairchild Publications, 1970), 46.

9. Diner, *A Time for Gathering*, 8.

10. *Encyclopaedia Judaica* (Jerusalem: Keter Publishing House Ltd., 1971), vol. 15, s.v. "tailoring," 705–6.

11. For occupational affinity and immigrant enterprise, see Roger Waldinger, *Through the Eye of the Needle: Immigrants and Enterprise in New York's Garment Trades* (New York: New York University Press, 1986), 5–16, 27, 41, 51. Jews were also early manufacturers in Berlin. A history of fashion in Berlin notes that twelve firms were making fashionable ready-made outerwear clothing for women in Berlin by the 1830s. Six of the twelve firms were Jewish-owned. Christine Waidenschlager, *Berliner Chic: Mode von 1820 bis 1990* (Berlin: Stiftung Stadtmuseum, 2001), 11.

12. *Encyclopaedia Judaica*, s.v. "tailoring," 704–5.

13. Mark Kishlansky, Patrick Geary, Patricia O'Brien, and R. Bin Wong, *Societies and Cultures in World History* (New York: HarperCollins College Publishers, 1995), 258–59.

14. *Encyclopaedia Judaica*, s.v. "tailoring," 705.

15. Ibid., 705.

16. Diner, *A Time for Gathering*, 11.

17. Abraham Kohn, a clothier in Chicago, described ped-

dling in his diary as quoted in Kenneth Libo and Irving Howe, *We Lived There, Too: In Their Own Words and Pictures, Pioneer Jews and the Westward Movement of America, 1630–1930* (New York: St. Martin's/Marek, 1984), 36. For clothiers who started as peddlers, see Jonathan D. Sarna and Nancy H. Klein, *The Jews of Cincinnati* (Cincinnati: Hebrew Union College, 1989), 36–37.

18. The popular notion that Jews were primarily involved in the clothing industry as secondhand dealers is connected to the historic roots of that trade on Chatham Street. Because Jews were considered the most numerous secondhand dealers on that street, they became identified with that trade. The firms may also have sold cheap ready-mades.

19. *Asmonean* (for the week ending October 21, 1853), 9, no. 1: 2. The Jewish Collection, New York Public Library.

20. Ibid., 2.

21. Bazelon and McGuinn, *Directory of American Military Goods*, 23.

22. For American mills focused on lower-end fabrics, see Egal Feldman, *Fit for Men: A Study of New York's Clothing Trade* (Washington, DC: Public Affairs Press, 1960), 19.

23. Cobrin, *Men's Clothing Industry*, 82.

24. Ibid., 82.

25. Cynthia Amneus, *A Separate Sphere: Dressmakers in Cincinnati's Golden Age, 1877–1922* (Cincinnati: Cincinnati Art Museum and Texas Tech University Press, 2003), 68–77.

26. Sarna and Klein, *Jews of Cincinnati*, 181.

27. Ibid., 3.

28. Ibid., 6.

29. Ibid., 6.

30. S. G. Mostov, "A 'Jerusalem' on the Ohio," quoted in Sarna and Klein, *Jews of Cincinnati*, 38.

31. Ibid., 38.

32. Cobrin, *Men's Clothing Industry*, 39.

33. Cincinnati's Jews supplied great coats, trousers, sack coats, and caps. For a more complete list see Bazelon and McGuinn, *Directory of American Military Goods*, 317–18.

34. Bazelon and McGuinn, *Directory of American Military Goods*, 82.

35. "Fechheimer Bros. Co. A 150 Year Old Legacy," in The Jacob Rader Marcus Center of American Jewish Archives, Cincinnati; Fechheimer Brothers is still in business and can be found at www.fechheimer.com.

36. "Editorial," *Gazette*, September 17, 1881, in the Fechheimer Collection in the Jacob Marcus Center of the American Jewish Archives, Hebrew Union College, Cincinnati.

37. Henry L. Feingold, *Zion in America: The Jewish Experience from Colonial Times to the Present* (Mineola, NY: Dover Books, 2002), 100–101; Elizabeth Blackmar, "The Congregation and the City," in *Congregating and Consecrating at Central Synagogue: The Building of a Religious Fellowship and Public Ceremonies*, ed. Elizabeth Blackmar and Arthur A. Goren (New York: Central Synagogue, 2003), 4.

38. For the business basis of nineteenth-century American congregational life, see Blackmar and Goren, *Congregating and Consecrating*, 7–11.

39. Feingold, *Zion in America*, 101.

40. Ibid., 101.

41. "Phoenix Club Celebrates 75th Anniversary—Original Constitution Was Printed in German," *Times-Star*, November 4, 1931, in the Phoenix Club Collection, Cincinnati Historical Society Library at the Cincinnati Museum Center.

42. "Last Members Join Cincinnati Club in Body," *Times-Star*, July 22, 1942, in the Phoenix Club Collection, Cincinnati Historical Society Library at the Cincinnati Museum Center.

43. Eric Homberger, *Mrs. Astor's New York: Money and Social Power in a Gilded Age* (New Haven, CT: Yale University Press, 2002), 1–7.

44. Jonathan D. Sarna and Nancy H. Klein, quoted in John Higham, *Send These to Me*, 2nd ed. (Baltimore: Johns Hopkins University Press, 1984), 142–43.

45. *1887–1987—A Centennial Celebration*, brochure (n.p.: Hartmarx Corporation, 1987).

46. Joan M. Jensen and Sue Davidson, eds., *A Needle, a Bobbin, a Strike: Women Needleworkers in America* (Philadelphia: Temple University Press, 1984), 117.

47. *The Clothing Designer and Manufacturer* 3, no. 1 (October 1914) in The Harry Simons Collection, The Costume Institute Library, The Metropolitan Museum of Art.

48. *The Clothing Designer and Manufacturer* 3, no. 4 (January 1915) in The Harry Simons Collection, The Costume Institute Library, The Metropolitan Museum of Art.

49. Kidwell and Christman, *Suiting Everyone*, 135.

50. Caroline Rennolds Milbank, "Ahead of the World: New York City Fashion," in *Art and the Empire City: New York, 1825–1861*, ed. Catherine Hoover Voorsanger and John K. Howat (New Haven, CT: Yale University Press and the Metropolitan Museum of Art, 2000), 243–57.

51. Quoted in Milbank, "Ahead of the World," 244.

52. Milton M. Gottesman, *Hoopskirts and Huppas: A Chronicle of the Early Years of the Garfunkel-Trager Family in America, 1856–1920* (New York: The American Jewish Historical Society, 1999).

53. Strouse-Adler and the Royal Worcester Company were among the earliest companies to manufacture corsets. "Manufacturer's Association Speech, D.L.J.," transcript lent by Bernard Smith (1949). The Strouse-Adler firm became the Smoothie brand and the firm was in business through the 1980s.

54. *Jordan Marsh Illustrated Catalog of 1891* (1891; repr., New York: Athenaeum of Philadelphia and Dover Publications, 1991), 93–115.

55. M. D. C. Crawford, *The Ways of Fashion* (New York: G. P. Putnam's Sons, 1941), 100–101, 104–16.

56. Ibid., 104.

57. Ibid., 109.

58. After Meyer retired from A. Beller & Co. in 1929, he worked under President Franklin Roosevelt for the National Recovery Act (NRA) and helped found the Fashion Institute of Technology in 1944.

Chapter 7   The Ready-Made Menswear Industry of Rochester, New York, 1848–1900

1. Blake McKelvey, "The Men's Clothing Industry in Rochester's History," *Rochester History* 22 (July 1960): 1–32; Stuart E. Rosenberg, *The Jewish Community in Rochester, 1843–1925* (New York: American Jewish Historical Society and Columbia University Press, 1954), 3–50.

2. Blake McKelvey, *Rochester: The Flower City, 1855–90* (Cambridge, MA: Harvard University Press, 1949), 14, 103–4; Rosenberg, *The Jewish Community in Rochester*, 10; Egal Feldman, *Fit for Men: A Study of New York's Clothing Trade* (Washington, DC: Public Affairs Press, 1960); Michael Zakim, "A Ready-Made Business: The Birth of the Clothing Industry in America," *Business History Review* 73 (Spring 1999): 61–90.

3. Hasia R. Diner, *The Jews of the United States, 1654–2000* (Berkeley: University of California Press, 2004), 99–107.

4. Rosenberg, *The Jewish Community in Rochester*, 5–6; Isaac A. Wile and Isaac M. Brickner, *The Jews of Rochester* (Rochester, NY: Historical Review Society, 1912), 7–21, 49, 55, 67–69, 87, 89, 105, 107; "Sigmund Stettheimer," *Jewish Tidings*, August 31, 1888, 6; "Death of Julius Wile," *Jewish Tidings*, November 6, 1891, 6.

5. Rosenberg, *The Jewish Community in Rochester*, 7–13, 20–24, 32; Peter Eisenstadt, *Affirming the Covenant: A History of Temple B'rith Kodesh Rochester, New York, 1848–1998* (Rochester, NY: Temple B'rith Kodesh, 1999), 1–36.

6. McKelvey, "The Men's Clothing Industry in Rochester's History," 2–3; McKelvey, *Rochester: The Flower City*, 14, 167. McKelvey estimates that Jews accounted for one-quarter of Rochester's German immigrant population during the 1860s.

7. Paul Johnson, *A Shopkeepers Millennium: Society and Revivals in Rochester, New York, 1815–1837* (New York: Hill and Wang, 1977).

8. Alan H. Gleason, "The History of Labor in Rochester, 1820–1880" (master's thesis, University of Rochester, 1941), 7–8, 25–27, 65–66.

9. Ibid., 75–79, 89–90.

10. Rosenberg, *The Jewish Community in Rochester*, 14; McKelvey, *Rochester: The Flower City*, 69, 76–79; Gleason, "The History of Labor," 134–36, 174–78, 197.

11. Gary L. Bunker and John Appel, "Shoddy, Anti-Semitism and the Civil War," *American Jewish History* 82 (Autumn 1994): 43–72.

12. Jesse Eliphalet Pope, *The Clothing Industry in New York* (Columbia: University of Missouri, 1905); Foreign and Domestic Commerce Bureau, Department of Commerce, Miscellaneous Series #34, *The Men's Factory Made Clothing Industry—Report on the Costs of Production of Men's Factory-Made Clothing in the U.S.* (Washington, DC: Government Printing Office, 1916); Foreign and Domestic Commerce Bureau, Department of Commerce, Miscellaneous Series #34, *The Shirt and Collar Industries* (Washington, DC: Government Printing Office, 1916); *History of the Men's Wear Industry, Men's Wear 60th Anniversary Issue* (New York: Fairchild Publications, 1950), 195–209; Harry A. Cobrin, *The Men's Clothing Industry, Colonial Through Modern Times* (New York: Fairchild Publications, 1970), 13–79.

13. Walter Licht, *Industrializing America: The Nineteenth Century* (Baltimore: Johns Hopkins University Press, 1995). Licht offers a succinct account of general economic developments during this time.

14. A number of major clothing firms emerged in other cities in the late-nineteenth and early-twentieth century. For a theoretical and historical account of this process, see Steven Fraser, "Combined and Uneven Development in the Men's Clothing Industry," *Business History Review* 57 (Winter 1983): 522–47.

15. "Some Centers of Clothing Manufacture, Rochester," *The Clothing Gazette*, July 1886, 32–38; Robert Adler, "The Rise and Decline of the Men's Clothing Industry of Rochester, New York" (unpublished manuscript, Robert M. Adler Papers, Department of Rare Books and Special Collections, University of Rochester Library, 1987); Rosenberg, *The Jewish Community in Rochester*, 54, 120–28.

16. McKelvey, "The Men's Clothing Industry in Rochester's History," 3–7; McKelvey, *Rochester: The Flower City*, 110–11, 200, 225–26, 275–77; Robert Adler, "The Rise and Decline of the Men's Clothing Industry of Rochester, New York," 120–28.

17. "Enterprise in Rochester," *The Clothing Gazette*, August 1887, 155; "Some Centers of Clothing Manufacture-IV Philadelphia," *The Clothing Gazette*, February 1888, 33–38; "Hit and Miss Chat," *The Clothing Gazette*, April 1888, 82; *The Clothing Gazette*, July 1888, 153; "Stein-Bloch & Co.," "Stein-Bloch & Co. New Building," "Rochester News and Notes," *The Clothing Gazette*, January 1889, 6–8, 35–37, 38–40. New York City was by far the largest manufacturing center in the nation, supplying all markets with all kinds of goods. Philadelphia was the second-largest center with a comparatively stronger market presence in medium-priced and less expensive goods. Boston's industry produced relatively higher-grade goods and had its niche in New England. Baltimore, Cincinnati,

and Chicago made primarily medium and cheap goods for southern and western markets. Rochester's firms serviced markets for higher- and medium-grade goods throughout the country.

18. Wile and Brickner, *The Jews of Rochester*, 55, 69, 89, 99.

19. "Death of Mark Sloman," *Jewish Tidings*, June 4, 1887, 3; "The Clothing Industry; Something About a Few Prominent Houses," *Jewish Tidings*, June 26, 1891, 7; "Brief Sketch of the Career of Henry Michaels," *Jewish Tidings*, November 18, 1892, 6; Wile and Brickner, *The Jews of Rochester*, 53–54, 113, 115.

20. Wile and Brickner, *The Jews of Rochester*, 85–86; "A Well Known Citizen; Something About the Career of Joseph Cauffman," *Jewish Tidings*, December 2, 1892, 1.

21. Wile and Brickner, *The Jews of Rochester*, 85, 109; "Called to His Final Rest; Leopold Garson Dies After a Severe Illness," *Jewish Tidings*, January 22, 1892, 6; "A Prominent Manufacturer," *Jewish Tidings*, August 12, 1892, 6; "The Late Leopold Garson," *Jewish Tidings*, January 20, 1893, 1.

22. Wile and Brickner, *The Jews of Rochester*, 51, 59, 72–74, 97–98, 105, 117; "Here Is Levi Adler," *Jewish Tidings*, December 16, 1892, 1; "Career of Abram Adler," *Jewish Tidings*, January 13, 1893, 1; "Rochester Clothing," *Gibson's Monthly Review of the Clothing and Furnishing Trades*, August 1882, 26.

23. Matthew Frye Jacobson, *Whiteness of a Different Color: European Immigrants and the Alchemy of Race* (Cambridge, MA: Harvard University Press, 1998); Nancy Cohen, *The Reconstruction of American Liberalism, 1865–1914* (Chapel Hill: University of North Carolina Press, 2002); Richard F. Bensel, *The Political Economy of American Industrialization, 1877–1900* (New York: Cambridge University Press, 2000).

24. "The Hebrews of America," *The Clothing Gazette*, March 1887, 48. It was widely known that almost all of the firms and the capital investment in the ready-made menswear industry were Jewish. For a discussion on the challenge of marketing ready-made menswear, see Rob Schorman, "Ready or Not: Custom-Made Ideals and Ready-Made Clothes in Late 19th Century America," *Journal of American Culture* 19 (Winter 1996): 111–20.

25. "All Things Considered," *Clothing and Furnishing Gazette*, September 1883, 19, 22.

26. *The Clothing Gazette*, March 1889, 37–38.

27. Ibid.

28. "The Fall Trade," *Gibson's Monthly Review of the Clothing and Furnishing Trades*, September 1882, 18.

29. "A Wholesale Slander of Jews," *The Clothing Gazette*, March 1890, 70. Huntley had begun his campaign against Jewish clothing drummers as early as March 1886. See "No Drummers Need Apply," *The Clothing Gazette*, March 1886, 41. The trade paper had already marked him to be somewhat of a con artist in March

1887. See "The Great Huntley," *The Clothing Gazette*, March 1887, 55.

30. "Despicable Act in Tacoma," *Jewish Tidings*, June 27, 1890, 1.

31. "A Wholesale Slander of Jews," *The Clothing Gazette*, March 1890, 70; "An Interesting Biography," *The Clothing Gazette*, April 1890, 29–31; "Ed L. Huntley Charged with Larceny," *The Clothing Gazette*, April 1891, 43; "More Woe for Ed L. Huntley," *The Clothing Gazette*, May 1891, 50; "Whatsoever a Man Soeth, That Shall He Also Reap," *The Clothing Gazette*, June 1891, 68; "The Bitter Bitten," *The Clothing Gazette*, January 1892, 72; "A Deserved Rebuke," *The Clothing Gazette*, May 1892, 56; "All of the Same Sort," *Jewish Tidings*, May 9, 1890, 4; "Despicable Act in Tacoma," *Jewish Tidings*, June 27, 1890, 1.

32. "Hoffenstein's Humor," *The Clothing Gazette*, August 1881, 16; "Who Sold Dot Coat," *The Clothing Gazette*, December 1881, 24; "Rube Hoffenstein on Poor Men," *The Clothing Gazette*, December 1881, 26; "Schnorrers," *The Clothing Gazette*, February 1882, 16; "Wild Animals," *The Clothing Gazette*, March 1882, 17; "Spring Poetry," *The Clothing Gazette*, March 20, 1884, 32.

33. "Men and Things," *The Clothing Gazette*, August 1888, 176.

34. "A Model to Imitate," *The Clothing Gazette*, May 1888, 106.

35. "The Jewish Traders of the South," *Gibson's Monthly Review of the Clothing and Furnishing Trades*, March 1883, 21; "Do Not Injure Your Neighbor's Credit," *Gibson's Monthly Review of the Clothing and Furnishing Trades*, November 1883, 16; "Slander," *Gibson's Monthly Review of the Clothing and Furnishing Trades*, December 1883, 15.

36. "The Latest Declaration of Independence," *The Clothing Gazette*, January 1885, 33. The names of the signers are allusions to Yiddish words and probably can be translated to mean: A. Thief, John Bankrupt and finished, Al Something for Nothing, Leo Chutzpah, Ten percent discount, the Wolf.

37. See, for example, "Self Protection," *The Clothing Gazette*, January 1885, 28.

38. "Fire Insurance," *The Clothing Gazette*, November 1884, 15; "The Clothing Trade," *The Clothing Gazette*, January 1885, 23; *The Clothing Gazette*, June 1888, 118; "A Big Clothing Fire," *The Clothing Gazette*, February 1890, 72; "A Great Fire in Providence," *The Clothing Gazette,* January 1891, 68.

39. "Warning to Property Owners," *Jewish Tidings*, November 16, 1888, 2; "Awful Calamity," *Jewish Tidings*, November 16, 1888, 6.

40. "A Protest," *Gibson's Monthly Review of the Clothing and Furnishing Trades*, January 1883, 18.

41. *The Clothing Gazette*, June 1888, 118; *The Clothing Gazette*, July 1888, 150.

42. *Jewish Tidings*, September 5, 1890, 4; "Jews and Fire Risks," *Jewish Tidings*, September 26, 1890, 4; "An Odious Calumny Refuted," *Jewish Tidings*, October 24, 1890, 8; "Absurd Discrimination," *Jewish Tidings*, May 22, 1891, 4.

43. *Jewish Tidings*, September 26, 1890, 4; *Jewish Tidings*, October 24, 1890, 8.

44. *Jewish Tidings*, May 22, 1891, 4; *Jewish Tidings*, September 26, 1891.

45. McKelvey, "The Men's Clothing Industry in Rochester's History," 7–14; Board of Mediation and Arbitration of the State of New York, *The Lockout of Cutters by the Clothiers' Exchange of Rochester* (Albany, NY: James B. Lyon, New State Printer, 1891).

46. Natalie F. Hawley, "The Labor Movement in Rochester, 1880–1898" (master's thesis, University of Rochester, 1948), 203–46; "An Association to Resist Blackmail," *The Clothing Gazette*, December 1890, 49; "Millions for Defense," *The Clothing Gazette*, January 1891, 68; "A Great Struggle Against Labor Tyranny," *The Clothing Gazette*, March 1891, 29–31; "The Great Lockout and Its Results," *The Clothing Gazette*, April 1891, 31–32, 43; "Conviction of James Hughes, The Blackmailer," *The Clothing Gazette*, June 1891, 45–47.

47. Clothiers' Exchange of Rochester, *Facts About the Clothing Industry of Rochester, N.Y.* (Rochester, NY: Clothiers' Exchange of Rochester New York, 1891), 15–16; *Jewish Tidings*, March 27, 1891, 4; "Dr. Jekyll and Mr. Hyde," *Jewish Tidings*, September 30, 1892, 4.

48. "Threatened a Boycott," *The Clothing Gazette*, May 1889, 30; "Conviction of James Hughes, The Blackmailer," *The Clothing Gazette*, June 1891, 45–47.

49. Hawley, "The Labor Movement in Rochester," 203–46; McKelvey, "The Men's Clothing Industry in Rochester's History," 7–14; "President Brickner," *Jewish Tidings*, January 15, 1892, 6; "Max Brickner's Career," *Jewish Tidings*, January 6, 1893, 1.

50. Rabbi H. Berkowitz, *Judaism and the Social Question* (New York: John B. Alden Publisher, 1888); "Announcement of Lectures by Henry Berkowitz on 'Judaism and the Social Question,'" *Jewish Tidings*, January 20, 1888, 2; "Talmudic Labor Laws. Relations of the Old Hebrew Capitalist and His Employees," *Jewish Tidings*, September 26, 1890, 1.

51. *Jewish Tidings*, October 22, 1887, 2; "Nihilism Among Jews," *Jewish Tidings*, October 12, 1888, 1; "Hebrew Anarchists," *Jewish Tidings*, January 3, 1890, 4; "A Hurtful Tendency," *Jewish Tidings*, May 15, 1891, 4.

Chapter 8 Fitting In: Advertising, Clothing, and Social Identity Among Turn-of-the-Century Jewish Immigrants

1. Annie de Montaigu, "Fashion, Fact and Fancy," *Godey's Magazine*, January 1896, 97.

2. Isabel Mallon, "Coats to Be Worn This Season," *Ladies' Home Journal*, November 1891, 25.

3. Isabel Mallon, "Costumes of Early Autumn," *Ladies' Home Journal*, October 1892, 21.

4. Charles Beezley, *Our Manners and Social Customs* (Chicago: Elliot and Beezley, 1891), 307.

5. *The Manners That Win* (Minneapolis: Buckeye Publishing, 1880), 375.

6. "Notes About Women," *Yiddishes Tageblatt*, December 12, 1898, 8.

7. Rogers, Peet & Co. advertisement, *New York Times*, October 19, 1897, 12.

8. James Wilde Jr. & Co. advertisement, *Chicago Tribune*, June 12, 1897, 4.

9. Aurora Corset Company advertisement, *Chicago Dry Goods Reporter*, October 12, 1895, 26 (italics added).

10. Although the distinction between men's ready-made clothing and women's custom-made clothing was real, it is a somewhat simplistic formulation. The development of both sectors of the clothing industry was considerably more complicated than this implies, as were the dynamics by which men and women's gender roles continually formed and reformed during this period. These issues, along with others discussed in this essay, are examined in more detail in Rob Schorman, *Selling Style: Clothing and Social Change at the Turn of the Century* (Philadelphia: University of Pennsylvania Press, 2003).

11. Good overviews of this period can be found in John Whiteclay Chambers II, *The Tyranny of Change: America in the Progressive Era, 1890–1920*, 2nd ed. (New Brunswick, NJ: Rutgers University Press, 2000); Steven Diner, *A Very Different Age: America in the Progressive Era* (New York: Hill and Wang, 1998); and Mark Summers, *The Gilded Age, Or, A Hazard of New Functions* (Upper Saddle River, NJ: Prentice-Hall, 1997).

12. On sack suits, see Jo Barraclough Paoletti, "Changes in the Masculine Image in the United States 1880–1910: A Content Analysis of Popular Humor about Dress" (PhD diss., University of Maryland, 1980); Jo Barraclough Paoletti, "Ridicule and Role Models as Factors in American Men's Fashion Change, 1880–1910," *Costume* 19 (1985): 121. On the evolution of men's suits, see David Kuchta, *The Three-Piece Suit and Modern Masculinity* (Berkeley: University of California Press, 2002); and Anne Hollander, *Sex and Suits* (New York: Kodansha International, 1994).

13. Daniel Pope, *The Making of Modern Advertising* (New York: Basic Books, 1983); Richard Ohmann, *Selling Culture: Magazines, Markets and Class at the Turn of the Century* (London: Verso, 1996); and Ellen Gruber Garvey, *The Adman in the Parlor: Magazines and the Gendering of Consumer Culture, 1880s to 1910s* (New York: Oxford University Press, 1996).

14. Gail Bederman, *Manliness and Civilization* (Chicago: University of Chicago Press, 1995), 12–19, 170–215;

Michael Kimmel, *Manhood in America: A Cultural History* (New York: Free Press, 1996), 81–100, 135–41, 181–87; Anthony Rotundo, *American Manhood: Transformations in Masculinity from the Revolution to the Modern Era* (New York: Basic Books, 1993), 279–83; John Higham, "The Reorientation of American Culture in the 1890s," in *The Origins of Modern Consciousness*, ed. John Weiss (Detroit: Wayne State University Press, 1965), 27–33; Arnaldo Testi, "The Gender of Reform Politics: Theodore Roosevelt and the Culture of Masculinity," *Journal of American History* 84, no. 1 (March 1995): 1509–33.

15. Charles Austin Bates, "Advertising for Retailers," *Printers' Ink* (July 1894): 38; Nicoll the Tailor advertisement, *Chicago Tribune*, May 5, 1897, 6; Stein-Bloch Co., *Smartness* (n.p.: Rochester, NY, 1903); Charlotte P. Gilman, "Symbolism in Dress," *Independent*, June 8, 1905, 1297.

16. Charlotte P. Gilman, "Modesty: Feminine and Other," *Independent*, June 29, 1905, 1448.

17. Brown, Durrell & Co. advertisement, *The Trade Monthly* (April 1895): 41.

18. Claudia Brush Kidwell, "Gender Symbols or Fashionable Details?" in *Men and Women, Dressing the Part*, ed. Claudia Brush Kidwell and Valerie Steele (Washington, DC: Smithsonian Institution Press, 1987), 126–29; Valerie Steele, *Fashion and Eroticism: Ideals of Feminine Beauty from the Victorian Era to the Jazz Age* (New York: Oxford University Press, 1985), 52–53.

19. Mary W. Blanchard, "Boundaries and the Victorian Body: Aesthetic Fashion in Gilded Age America," *American Historical Review* 100, no. 1 (February 1995): 48–50.

20. Bederman, *Manliness and Civilization*, 170–96; Emily Rosenberg, *Spreading the American Dream: American Economic and Cultural Expansion, 1890–1945* (New York: Hill and Wang, 1982), 38–42; Gerald F. Linderman, *The Mirror of War: American Society and the Spanish-American War* (Ann Arbor: University of Michigan Press, 1974).

21. Sam Whitmire, "War-Time Advertising," *Fame* (July 1898): 275; Arlington Mills advertisement, *Chicago Dry Goods Reporter* (June 4, 1898): 11; Carson Pirie Scott & Co. advertisement, *Ladies' Home Journal*, September 1898, 27; "Dress Accessories," *Standard Designer* (October 1898): 57–59.

22. Quoted in Elizabeth Ewen, *Immigrant Women in the Land of Dollars: Life and Culture on the Lower East Side, 1890–1925* (New York: Monthly Review Press, 1985), 68.

23. Abraham Cahan, "All Right! Hurry Up!" in *Grandma Never Lived in America: The New Journalism of Abraham Cahan*, ed. Moses Rischin (Bloomington: Indiana University Press, 1985), 143–44.

24. Quoted in Barbara A. Schreier, *Becoming American Women: Clothing and the Jewish Immigrant Experience, 1880–1920* (Chicago: Chicago Historical Society, 1994), 4.

25. Mary Antin, *The Promised Land* (Boston: Houghton Mifflin, 1912), 187.

26. John Higham, *Strangers in the Land*, 2nd ed. (New York: Atheneum, 1969), 68–105; John Higham, *Send These to Me*, rev. ed. (Baltimore: Johns Hopkins University Press, 1984), 95–116; Leonard Dinnerstein, *Antisemitism in America* (New York: Oxford University Press, 1994), 35–77.

27. Walter R. Houghton, *American Etiquette and Rules of Politeness* (Indianapolis: A. E. Davis Publisher, 1882), 258.

28. Edward Bok, "What Makes a Gentleman," *Ladies' Home Journal*, July 1898, 14.

29. Viola Paradise, "The Jewish Immigrant Girl in Chicago," *Survey* (September 6, 1913): 704.

30. "Advice to Working Women," *Yiddishes Tageblatt*, December 2, 1898, 8; immigrant Ida Richter quoted in Sydelle Kramer and Jenny Masur, eds., *Jewish Grandmothers* (Boston: Beacon Press, 1976), 130; Andrew Heinze, *Adapting to Abundance: Jewish Immigrants, Mass Consumption and the Search for American Identity* (New York: Columbia University Press, 1990), 101.

31. Abraham Cahan, *Yekl and the Imported Bridegroom and Other Stories of Yiddish New York* (New York: Dover, 1970), 34, 83. In the story, Gitl adopts a role that combines elements of Americanization as well as more traditional behaviors. Cahan's own opinion of assimilation, on the evidence of his fiction, was quite ambivalent.

32. Cahan, "All Right! Hurry Up!," 144–45; the 1898 *Tageblatt* editorial is quoted in Barbara Schreier, "Becoming American: Jewish Immigrant Women 1880–1920," *History Today* 44, no. 3 (March 1994): 28; "The Fashions," *Yiddishes Tageblatt*, August 31, 1898, 8.

33. Hutchins Hapgood, *The Spirit of the Ghetto*, ed. Moses Rischin (Cambridge, MA: Harvard University Press, 1967), 180; Heinze, *Adapting to Abundance*, 156. I owe special thanks to Sven-Erik Rose for his help in translating material from the *Tageblatt* and for his insights into the linguistic characteristics of its text.

34. "Jewish Patriotism," *Yiddishes Tageblatt*, May 3, 1898, 8.

35. M. Yachnin advertisement, *Yiddishes Tageblatt*, May 4, 1898, 2. The advertisement appeared in every issue until August 19—a full week after the peace protocol that ended the war had been signed in Washington, DC.

36. "At the Hub," *Printers' Ink* (May 25, 1898): 39.

37. Gage-Downs advertisement, *Chicago Dry Goods Reporter* (November 25, 1899): 40; "The Fashions," *Yiddishes Tageblatt*, May 3, 1898, 8.

Chapter 9 From Division Street to Seventh Avenue:
The Coming of Age of American Fashion

1. "America Comes to Seventh Avenue," *Fortune* 20, no. 1 (July 1939): 123.
2. Claudia Kidwell and Margaret Christman, *Suiting Everyone: The Democratization of Clothing in America* (Washington, DC: Smithsonian Institution: Press, 1974), 87. While immigration figures vary widely, Daniel Boorstin claimed, "Among the four hundred thousand Jewish immigrants in the first decade of the twentieth century, more than half were in the needle trades." See Daniel Boorstein, *The Americans: The Democratic Experience* (New York: Random House, 1973), 100.
3. Irving Howe, *World of Our Fathers* (New York: Harcourt Brace Jovanovich, 1976), 155.
4. Quoted in ibid., 80–81.
5. Jessica Daves, *Ready-Made Miracle* (New York: Putnam, 1967), 41–42.
6. Much of the information concerning Fred Pomerantz, Maurice Rentner, and Abe Schrader is from oral histories in the Special Collections in the library of the Fashion Institute of Technology in New York City as well as a number of mentions in contemporary fashion publications.
7. Abraham Cahan, *The Rise of David Levinsky* (1917; repr., New York: Modern Library Edition, 2001), 432.
8. "Garment Trade Removal," *New York Times,* February 8, 1920, W12.
9. "New Garment Centre," *New York Times,* June 19, 1921, 32.
10. "America Comes to Seventh Avenue," 122.
11. Ibid., 122.
12. Ibid., 183.
13. Americana Issue, *Vogue* (February 11, 1938): 86.
14. Excerpt from report by Alice Hughes to the executive director of the Fashion Group, regarding the manner in which garments were being manufactured.
15. *The Fashion Group Bulletin* 6, no. 3 (April, 1940): 12. The Fashion Group was founded in 1930 to advance the role of women in the fashion industry. Mayor LaGuardia, seeing an opportunity created by wartime and the absence of Paris fashion, was promoting the idea of New York as the new world fashion center.
16. "America Comes to Seventh Avenue," 183.
17. "American Dress Designer Nettie Rosenstein," *Life,* December 14, 1937, 23.
18. Phyllis Lee Levin, *The Wheels of Fashion* (Garden City, NY: Doubleday, 1965), 212.
19. Daves, *Ready-Made Miracle,* 146.
20. Elizabeth Hawes, *Fashion Is Spinach* (New York: Random House, 1938), 194. Hawes claimed that promoting American designers was a Lord & Taylor press stunt and quoted Shaver's remarks to the *World-Telegram* of April 13, 1932.
21. H. Stanley Marcus, "Future of Fashion," *Fortune* 22, no. 5 (November 1940): 81.
22. Levin, *Wheels,* 199.
23. The statuette, nicknamed the "Winnie," was created by the noted sculptor Malvina Hoffman, a one-time pupil of Auguste Rodin. When Norman Norell received the award he was with the firm of Traina-Norell, established in 1941.
24. New York Dress Institute advertisement, *Women's Wear Daily,* April 8, 1942.
25. "Adam Smith on Seventh Avenue," *Fortune* (August 1949): 76.
26. Bettina Ballard, *In My Fashion* (New York: David McKay, 1960), 285.
27. Jeannette Jarnow, Miriam Guerreiro, and Beatrice Judelle, eds., *Inside the Fashion Business,* 4th ed. (New York: Macmillan, 1987), 133.
28. Cahan, *The Rise of David Levinsky,* 433.

Chapter 10 Labor Relations and the Protocol of
Peace in Progressive Era New York

1. This chapter was originally presented as a paper to the History of Labor Management Relations Conference at California University of Pennsylvania in 2002. I thank those who provided feedback. A fuller account can be found in my book, *The Triangle Fire, the Protocols of Peace, and Industrial Democracy in Progressive Era New York* (Philadelphia: Temple University Press, 2005).
2. Steve Fraser, "Dress Rehearsal for the New Deal," in *Working-Class America,* ed. Michael H. Frisch and Daniel J. Walkowitz (Champaign: University of Illinois Press, 1983), 212, 220–21.
3. Stanley Vittoz, *New Deal Labor Policy and the American Industrial Economy* (Chapel Hill: University of North Carolina Press, 1987), 36 (emphasis is mine).
4. New York City's share of production grew steadily during these years. In 1899 it stood at 64 percent of production; by 1909, it rose to 69 percent; and by 1921, it rose to 74 percent. See U.S. Bureau of the Census, *Census of Manufacturers* (Washington, DC: Government Printing Office, 1931), 325–26.
5. Daniel E. Bender, *Sweated Work, Weak Bodies: Anti-Sweatshop Campaigns and Languages of Labor* (New Brunswick, NJ: Rutgers University Press, 2003).
6. Daniel J. Walkowitz, *Working with Class: Social Workers and the Politics of Middle-Class Identity* (Chapel Hill: University of North Carolina Press, 1999).
7. Greenwald, *The Triangle Fire.*
8. Robert H. Wiebe, *The Search for Order, 1877–1920* (New York: Hill and Wang, 1967).
9. See Arthur Goren, *New York Jews and the Quest for Community: The Kehillah Experiment, 1980–1922* (New York: Columbia University Press, 1970).
10. The original 1910 Protocol in the suit and cloak sector

was soon applied to virtually all sectors of the industry. Therefore, there were multiple protocols. Since most shared core features, I refer to the collective efforts as the Protocols of Peace.

11. U.S. Bureau of the Census, *Census of Manufacturers* (Washington, DC: Government Printing Office, 1931), 325–26.

12. The literature on the 1909 strike is voluminous. For an introduction see Annelise Orleck, *Common Sense and a Little Fire: Women and Working-Class Politics in the United States, 1900–1965* (Chapel Hill: University of North Carolina Press, 1995).

13. Abraham Rosenberg, *Memoirs of the Cloakmakers and Their Union* (New York: Local 1, ILGWU, 1920), 202–26; B. Hoffman, *Fifty Years Cloak Operators' Union* (New York: Local 117, 1936), 182–85; *Jewish Daily Forward*, July 7, 1910, 1, 9.

14. Rosenberg, *Memoirs*, 207–9; *New York Times*, July 8, 1910, 1; on the number of strikers, the *New York Times* reported sixty thousand workers. Yet as John Bryce McPherson showed there were at least fifteen thousand allied workers in support trades, reefer, and raincoats who also joined the cloak makers. See John Bryce McPherson, "The New York Cloakmakers' Strike," *Journal of Political Economy* 19 (March 1911): 154–55.

15. Goren, *New York Jews and the Quest for Community*, 186–213.

16. See Hyman Berman, "Era of the Protocol: A Chapter in the History of the International Ladies' Garment Workers' Union, 1910–1916" (PhD diss., Columbia University, 1956), 126–27. For the Brandeis quote see L. D. Brandeis to J. H. Cohen, July 24, 1910 in Berman, "Era of the Protocol," 127; also see Alpheus Thomas Mason, *Brandeis: A Free Man's Life* (New York: Viking Press, 1946), 292.

17. *New York World*, August 21, 1910, 4; *New York Times*, August 26, 1910, 16; *McClure's Magazine*, 1910, 36, no. 712; Meyer Bloomfield to A. Lincoln Filene, August 21, 1910, as quoted in Berman, "Era of the Protocol," 143–44.

18. See letter from Meyer London to John P. Mitchell, September 1, 1910, in the *New York Times*, September 2, 1910, 5.

19. "Outcome of the Cloakmakers' Strike," *Outlook* 96 (September 17, 1910): 99–101; Hoffman, *Fifty Years*, 207–8; Rosenberg, *Memoirs*, 245.

20. *New York Times*, September 3, 1910, 1; *Jewish Daily Forward*, September 3, 1910, 1.

21. *New York Times*, September 6, 1910, 9; *Jewish Daily Forward*, September 4, 1910, 1; *Jewish Daily Forward*, September 5, 1910, 1; *Jewish Daily Forward*, September 6, 1910, 1.

22. Benjamin Stolberg, *Tailor's Progress: The Story of a Famous Union and the Men Who Made It* (Garden City, NY: Doubleday, Doran, and Company, 1944), 73–74.

23. Julius Henry Cohen, *Law and Order in Industry: Five Years' Experience* (New York: Macmillan Company, 1916), 91.

24. For a similar point, see Colin Gordon, *New Deals: Business, Labor, and Politics in America, 1920–1935* (New York: Cambridge University Press, 1994).

25. Louis D. Brandeis to Ray Stannard Baker, February 26, 1912, in Melvin I. Urofsky, ed., *The Letters of Louis D. Brandeis*, vol. 2 (Albany: State University of New York Press), 562–63.

26. The most obvious place to see this is Osmond K. Fraenkel, ed., *The Curse of Bigness: Miscellaneous Papers of Louis D. Brandeis* (New York: Viking Press, 1934); useful sources to help place Brandeis within the larger Progressive movement include Melvin I. Urofsky, *A Mind of One Piece: Brandeis and American Reform* (New York: Scribner's, 1971); *Louis D. Brandeis and the Progressive Tradition* (Boston: Little, Brown, 1981); "To Guide by the Light of Reason: Mr. Justice Brandeis—An Appreciation," *American Jewish History* 81 (spring/summer 1994): 365–93; and Phillipa Strum, *Brandeis: Beyond Progressivism* (Lawrence: University of Kansas Press, 1994).

27. For a full discussion of "Civilization" during the Progressive Era, see Gail Bederman, *Manliness and Civilization: A Cultural History of Gender and Race in the United States, 1880–1917* (Chicago: University of Chicago Press, 1995).

28. Brandeis to Paul Kellogg, December 19, 1911, in Urofsky, *Letters*, vol. 2, 522; and Brandeis to Lawrence Fraser Abbott, September 6, 1910, in Urofsky, *Letters*, vol. 2, 371–72.

29. On the inner workings of the machinery of the Protocol, see Charles H. Winslow, *Conciliation, Arbitration and Sanitation in the Cloak, Suit and Skirt Industry of New York City, Bulletin of the United States Bureau of Labor Statistics no. 98* (Washington, DC: Government Printing Office, 1912).

30. See Winslow, *Conciliation*, 225–27; "Rules and Plan of Procedure Adopted by the Board of Grievances, Approved by the Board of Arbitration, Clauses 4 and 11," n.d., but most likely March 1911, Abelson Papers.

31. See Charles H. Winslow, *Industrial Court of the Cloak, Suit and Skirt Industry of New York City, Bulletin of the U.S. Bureau of Labor Statistics no. 144* (Washington, DC: Government Printing Office, 1914): 8–22.

32. Ibid., 24–27; see also John A. Dyche, "Report of the Secretary-Treasurer, ILGWU," in *Report of the Proceedings, 12th Convention* (Cleveland, ILGWU, June 1–14, 1914), 57–59; as well as Brandeis to Moskowitz, March 25, 1912, Brandeis to Hillquit, March 28, 1912, and Brandeis to Holt, March 28, 1912, in Urofsky, *Letters*, 569–72.

33. See Brandeis to Ray Stannard Baker, February 26, 1912, in Urofsky, *Letters*, 563.

34. Any discussion of industrial democracy must start with the work of the British Fabian Socialists, Sidney and

Beatrice Webb, *Industrial Democracy* (1897; repr., New York: Augustus M. Kelley Booksellers, 1965).

35. The literature on the 1910 cloak makers' strike and the Protocol is vast. A good starting point would be Melvyn Dubofsky, *When Workers Organize: New York City in the Progressive Era* (Amherst: University of Massachusetts Press, 1968), 58–68; Jesse Thomas Carpenter, *Competition and Collective Bargaining in the Needle Trades, 1910–1967* (Ithaca, NY: Cornell University ILR Press, 1972), 1–54; Greenwald, *The Triangle Fire.*

36. See Alan Brinkley, *The End of Reform: New Deal Liberalism in Recession and War* (New York: Knopf, 1998).

Chapter 11 Acclimatizing Fashion: Jewish Inventiveness on the Other (Pacific) Coast, 1850–1940

1. Paul H. Nystrom, *Economics of Fashion* (New York: Ronald Press Company, 1928), 409. Nystrom notes that the Gold Rush was among the first events to create a large demand for men's ready-made clothing.

2. William Issel and Robert W. Cherny, *San Francisco, 1865–1932: Politics, Power and Urban Development* (Berkeley: University of California Press, l986), 29, note Levi Strauss's prominent building in 1880; Alfred L. Lomax, "Oregon City Woolen Mill," *Oregon Historical Quarterly* 32 (September 1931): 240–61; Harold Hirsch interview, 1977, Jewish Historical Society of Oregon, Portland.

3. William Toll, "The Jewish Merchant and Civic Order in the Urban West," *Jewish Life in the American West,* ed. Ava Kahn (Los Angeles: Autry Museum of Western Heritage, 2002), 100–104.

4. Thomas Schatz, *The Genius of the System: Hollywood Film Making in the Studio Era* (New York: Pantheon Books, 1988), 4–7.

5. Harry Carr, *Los Angeles, City of Dreams* (New York: Grossett & Dunlap, 1935), 245.

6. Toll, "Jewish Merchant," 83–97.

7. Issel and Cherny, *San Francisco, 1865–1932,* 23–24.

8. On the elite role of Jews in the history of San Francisco see Earl Raab, "There's No City Like San Francisco," *Commentary* (October 1950): 369–70; Gustave A. Danziger, "The Jews in San Francisco," *Overland Monthly* 25 (April 1895): 381–410.

9. The alternate use of both a putting-out system for completing production and the acquisition of new equipment and hiring of women to work in the Levi Strauss factory illustrates how the technology and labor economics of the garment industry remained in flux. See Joseph Buckman, *The Immigrants and the Class Struggle: The Jewish Immigrant in Leeds, 1880–1914* (Manchester, UK: Manchester University Press, 1983), 13, 29–30, 38–40.

10. Hasia R. Diner, *A Time for Gathering: The Second Migration, 1820–1880* (Baltimore: Johns Hopkins University Press, 1992), 28–32.

11. Lomax, "Oregon City Woolen Mill," 249.

12. Ben Selling to "Uncle," July 4, 1886, letter book, Ben Selling Papers, Oregon Historical Society, Portland.

13. Lomax, "Oregon City Woolen Mill," 252, 260–61; E. Kimbark MacColl, *Merchants, Money and Power, the Portland Establishment, 1843–1913* (Portland: Georgian Press, 1988), 150, 235.

14. "Founder Biography," on Levi Strauss & Company Web site, http://www.levistrauss.com/about/history/founder.htm.

15. Molly Cone, Howard Droker, and Jacqueline Williams, *Family of Strangers: Building a Jewish Community in Washington State* (Seattle: Washington State Jewish Historical Society, 2003), 53.

16. "California Firm Celebrates Golden Jubilee," *California Stylist* (May 1939): 15.

17. "1846–1946 Los Angeles—A Century of Growth and Progress Under the U.S. Flag," *California Stylist* (1946).

18. Hirsch interview; Dorothy L. Wallis, *The Jantzen Story* (n.p.: Fairchild Publications, 1959), 8–10, 13.

19. Oral histories, city directories, and biographies attest to the Jewish pioneer legacy of political prominence. For a summary, see Harriet Rochlin and Fred Rochlin, *Pioneer Jews: A New Life in the Far West* (Boston: Houghton Mifflin, 1984), 141–67. See also interviews with Bailey Gatzert, 1887, and Bernard Goldsmith, November 29, 1889, Hubert Howe Bancroft Papers, Bancroft Library, University of California, Berkeley.

20. Alvin Auerbach, "San Francisco's South of Market District, 1850–1950: The Emergence of a Skid Row," *California Historical Quarterly* 52 (Fall 1973): 204; William Toll, *The Making of an Ethnic Middle Class: Portland Jewry Over Four Generations* (Albany: State University of New York Press, 1982), 110–17.

21. Jenna Weissman Joselit, *A Perfect Fit: Clothes, Character and the Promise of America* (New York: Henry Holt & Company, 2001), 4–5. Joselit argues that ready-to-wear loosened the hold of social class on Americans and gave rise to "the democracy of beauty."

22. For a complex discussion see Steven J. Ross, *Working Class Hollywood, Silent Film and the Shaping of Class in America* (Princeton, NJ: Princeton University Press, 1998), 3–12.

23. Hyman Kirshner, interview, June 13, 1974, Oregon Jewish Historical Society, Portland.

24. Rose Pessota, *Bread Upon the Waters*, ed. John Nicols Beffel (Ithaca, NY: ILR Press, 1987), 76. On the Maloufs, Zukin, DiGesu, and Breitstein, see the *San Francisco City Directory*, 1927, and the *Los Angeles City Directory*, 1938.

25. See Table 1 for the rapid expansion of the Los Angeles clothing industry between 1919 and 1929. "Cloak and Suit," *Fortune* (June 1930): 94, notes that "the largest plants in the industry are small."

26. "Cloak and Suit," 95, provides a good description of the equally compact, but much larger, Manhattan garment district.

27. Max Vorspan and Lloyd P. Gartner, *History of the Jews of Los Angeles* (San Marino, CA: Huntington Library, 1970), 125, notes only sporadic Amalgamated Clothing Workers' locals from 1900 through the mid-1920s.

28. Pesotta, *Bread Upon the Waters*, 19, estimated that 75 percent of the workers were Mexican women. The rest were Italians, Russian Jews, and Americans. The Los Angeles city directories for 1919 and 1929 show that the hundreds of independent dressmakers who met clientele face to face were overwhelmingly "Anglo."

29. "America Comes to Seventh Avenue," *Fortune* (July 1939): 186.

30. *Los Angeles: A Guide to the City and Its Environs*, WPA American Guide Series (New York: Hastings House, 1941), 169; Wendy Elliott, "The Jews of Boyle Heights, 1900–1950: The Melting Pot of Los Angeles," *Southern California Quarterly* 78, no. 1 (1996): 1–10.

31. Carr, *Los Angeles, City of Dreams*, 246.

32. For temple locations, see *B'nai B'rith Messenger*, January 6, 1928, 20–21.

33. Charles Higham, *Warner Brothers* (New York: Charles Scribner's Sons, 1975), 85–94; Schatz, *Genius of the System*, 136; Leo B. Rosten, *Hollywood, The Movie Colony, The Movie Makers* (New York: Harcourt, Brace, 1941), 3–4, 73, provides data on the movie industry.

34. Charles Eckert, "The Carole Lombard in Macy's Window," *Quarterly Review of Film Studies* 3, no. 1 (Winter 1978): 7.

35. Eleanor Kinsella McDonnell believed on the contrary that Paris couturiers were influenced to lower hemlines by Hollywood movies; see Eleanor Kinsella McDonnell, "Fashion and the Hollywood Handicap," *The Saturday Evening Post*, May 18, 1935, 11.

36. The expansion of occasions considered appropriate for casual wear and the role of motion pictures in promoting these changes is explained in Charles S. Goodman, *The Location of Fashion Industries, With Special Reference to the California Apparel Market*, Michigan Business Studies, vol. 10, no. 2 (Ann Arbor: University of Michigan Press, 1948), 9–10.

37. Warner, "Americanization of Fashion," 92–93.

38. Edith Head and Paddy Calistro, *Edith Head's Hollywood* (New York: Dutton, 1983), 40.

39. Warner, "Americanization of Fashion," 84–85.

40. Excerpts from an "Address by Milo Anderson Given at Market Week Style Clinic," *California Stylist* (February 1939): 7.

41. "Los Angeles' Little Cutters," *Fortune* (May 1945): 134, 186, 188.

42. Warner, "America Comes to Seventh Avenue," 187.

43. Data collected from the city directories, and in some cases for 1938 especially, includes multiple members from several families, such as Malouf, Saba, Ghiz, Kotzin, Vogel, Normandie.

44. "Los Angeles' Little Cutters," 136, 185.

45. Those manufacturers persisting from 1927 to 1937 have been traced through city directories.

46. The manufacturers are those listed for men's and women's garments in the *Los Angeles City Directory*, 1938.

47. Interview with Dr. Phelon J. Malouf, December 3, 1974, is cited as the source for the connection between the Maloufs of Salt Lake City and Mode O'Day, in Utah State Historical Society, "From Babylon to Babylon: Immigration from the Middle East," http://historytogo.utah.gov/people/ethnic_cultures/the_peoples_of_utah/immigrationfromthemiddleeast.html.

48. O. J. Meinhardt, "Permanency," *California Stylist* (November–December 1938): 15, provides a list of the members of the Associated Apparel Manufacturers of Los Angeles.

49. Vorspan and Gartner, *History of the Jews of Los Angeles*, 203–4, cites the survey of Los Angeles Jewry by Samuel C. Kohs and Louis H. Blumenthal conducted for the National Jewish Welfare Board and published in 1942.

50. H. Stanley Marcus, "America Is in Fashion," *Fortune* 22 (November 1940): 142.

51. Eloyse, "Studios Must Be Right," *California Stylist* (January 1939): 42.

52. Eckert, "The Carole Lombard in Macy's Window," 9.

53. "Los Angeles Becomes Style Center," *Business Week*, September 14, 1940, 42; "Los Angeles' Little Cutters," 134.

54. "Los Angeles' Little Cutters," 134.

55. *California Stylist* (January 1938): 11, carries a Paramount Dress Company advertisement, and notes those exhibiting at the St. Louis Market Week, January 31 to February 9, 1938.

56. Entries in *Who's Who in American Jewry*, 1938–1939 (New York: National News Association Incorporated, 1939), for cities in Southern California list hundreds of men and women connected to the motion picture industry, but no clothing manufacturers. Nor were clothing manufacturers listed for San Francisco, Seattle, or Portland.

Chapter 12 Kansas City's Garment Industry

1. Frank J. Adler, *Roots in a Moving Stream: The Centennial History of Congregation B'Nai Jehudah of Kansas City 1870–1970* (Kansas City, MO: Spangler Printers, 1972), 5.

2. Henry C. Haskell and Richard B. Fowler, *City of the Future: A Narrative History of Kansas City, 1850–1950* (Kansas City, MO: Frank Glenn Publishing, 1950), 28; Darrell Garwood, *Crossroads of America: The Story of Kansas City* (New York: W. W. Norton, 1948), 47.

3. Adler, *Roots in a Moving Stream*, 8. The uniforms were made in Baltimore.

4. Haskell and Fowler, *City of the Future*, 48.

5. Adler, *Roots in a Moving Stream*, 8.

6. Ibid., 19.

7. Adler, *Roots in a Moving Stream*, 18. The remaining B'nai Jehudah members' occupations included four tobacconists, three dry goods store owners, one liquor wholesaler, one owner of a butcher store, one saloon keeper, and twelve that were store clerks, bookkeepers, or cigar-makers. *Kansas City Directory* (1871).

8. Yeshiva University Museum, *A Perfect Fit: The Garment Industry and American Jewry 1860–1960* (New York: Yeshiva University, 2005), 18.

9. Adler, *Roots in a Moving Stream*, 87–88. Although it is possible that these girls went to work for garment manufacturers since some apparel manufacturing was being done in Kansas City during this time, it cannot be confirmed.

10. Ibid., 48–50; A. Theodore Brown and Lyle W. Dorsett, *K.C.: A History of Kansas City, Missouri* (Boulder, CO: Pruett Publishing, 1978), 187.

11. *The Missouri State Gazetterier and Business Directory* (St. Louis, MO: Sutherland & McEvoy, Publishers and Compilers, 1860), 141; "The Kansas City Directory and Reference Book with a Business Directory," Bulletin Book and Job Office, 1870.

12. Woolf Brothers Company Records, Jewish Community Archives, Western Historical Manuscript Collection—Kansas City; Adler, *Roots in a Moving Stream*, 338. The Woolf Brothers were best known for the retail stores that operated until 1992.

13. Haskell and Fowler, *City of the Future*, 79.

14. Jeannette Terrell and Patricia Zimmer, *The Economic Base of Greater Kansas City* (Kansas City, MO: Economic Research Department, Federal Research Bank,1949), 25.

15. Nancy Hipsh, interview by Gary Swanson, May 25, 2005, *Kansas City Garment Industry History Project.*

16. Bureau of the Census, *Thirteenth Census of the United States Taken in the Year 1910* (Washington, DC: Government Printing Office, 1913), 711. The only detail included in this report is the number of establishments, salaried employees, and the number of wage earners.

17. Bureau of the Census, *Thirteenth Census of the United States*, 711.

18. Terrell and Zimmer, *The Economic Base of Greater Kansas City*, 80.

19. Frances I. Gaw, *The Garment Industry of Greater Kansas City*, Industrial and Agricultural Analysis, Kansas City, MO, Research and Information Department, City Hall, November 28, 1945, 5.

20. Lee Company, *American History: Lee Jeans 101* (Kansas City, MO: Lee Company, 2000), 7.

21. Ibid.

22. VF Corporation, *VF Corporation*, 2004, accessed February 7, 2008, http://www.vfc.com/sub_pages/headquarters.php.

23. A *Mother Hubbard* was a loose-fitting, cotton housedress commonly worn from the 1880s through the 1910s by women doing heavy housework.

24. Terence Michael O'Malley, *Nelly Don: A Stitch in Time* (Kansas City, MO: Covington Group, 2006), 2.

25. Ibid., 90.

26. A *wash dress* is another common name used for *housedress*. They were called wash dresses because they were made of easily washed fabrics.

27. David Lipke, "Manufacture of Women's Wash Dresses—Production Factors More Favorable Than in the East," *Daily News Record*, April 3, 1927.

28. "Carroll Dorn Company Increases Its Capacity 50 Percent in Planning for 1929," *Kansas City Star*, January 20, 1929.

29. "In Lofty-Ceilinged, Pretentious Room Electric Knives Cut High Piled Cloth and 50 Power Machines Dash Off Stitches," *Kansas City Star*, June 9, 1929.

30. "Missouri Garment Company Developing Output of 800 Wash Dresses Daily Becomes Factor in City's Prominence in That Line," *Kansas City Star*, June 19, 1927.

31. This particular report did not include statistics concerning men's employment.

32. The only category in the report was for men's clothing and shirts. There were several companies that were making women's clothing, but those were not cited in the report.

33. Bureau of Labor Statistics, State of Missouri, *Labor Statistics* (Jefferson City, MO: Missouri Bureau of Labor Statistics, 1922), 1016.

34. Bob Slegman, interview by Gary Swanson, October 23, 2007, *Kansas City Historic Garment History Project.*

35. DeSaux Gernes, interview by Gary Swanson, c. 2004, *Kansas City Garment Industry History Project.*

36. Gaw, *The Garment Industry of Greater Kansas City*, 3.

37. Kansas City Historic Garment District Museum, n.d.

38. "Brand and Puritz Firm Employs 135 Workers in Making Women's Garments for Central Western Market," *Kansas City Star*, September 30, 1928.

39. Ben Zarr and Ralph Zarr, interview by Gary Swanson, January 26, 2005, *Kansas City Garment Industry History Project.*

40. "Stern-Slegman-Prins Company Will Make More Than 1,200 Coats a Week and Will Provide Steady Employment for 100 Workers," *Kansas City Star*, May 15, 1927.

41. Slegman, interview.

42. Eugene Lebovitz, interview by Gary Swanson, January 4, 2005, *Kansas City Garment Industry History Project.*

43. Ibid.

44. Gerald L. Baliles, ed., *Life Before the Presidency*,

accessed December 17, 2007, http://www.millercenter
.virginia.edu/academic/americanpresident/truman/
essays/biography/2.

45. Rose Stolowy, interview by Gary Swanson, February
3, 2005, *Kansas City Garment Industry History Project*.
The referenced newspaper article was framed and
displayed on the wall over Rose Stolowy's head during
the interview. She pointed it out when asked about her
husband's friendship with Truman.

46. Sherman Dreiseszun, interview by Gary Swanson,
October 5, 2004, *Kansas City Garment Industry History
Project*.

47. Terrell and Zimmer, *The Economic Base of Greater
Kansas City*, 114.

48. Chamber of Commerce Industrial Department, *Kansas
City for the Manufacture of Afternoon and Street Dress
and House Aprons* (Kansas City, MO: Chamber of
Commerce, 1930), 8.

49. Terrell and Zimmer, *The Economic Base of Greater
Kansas City*, 116.

50. Harvey Fried, interview by Laurel Wilson, November
17, 2007.

51. Dale Rice, interview by Gary Swanson and Ann
Brownfield, August 23, 2005, *Kansas City Garment
Industry History Project*.

52. David Boutros, interview by Laurel Wilson, February
14, 2008, Western Historical Manuscripts, University
of Missouri–Kansas City. The records end in 1915,
and it is probable that the United Garment Workers of
America union in Kansas City did not survive after that
time.

53. Judy Ancel, "Talk for Kansas City Labor History
Tour," *Kansas City Star*, October 17, 1992, 3–6.

54. Ibid., 6.

55. O'Malley, *Nelly Don*, 69–70, 90.

56. It is unknown what this device was since the only
record shows it as "a special device."

57. Fried, interview.

58. Ann Brownfield, interview by Laurel Wilson,
August 30, 2005.

59. Lee Company, *American History*, n.p.

60. Slegman, interview.

61. Gaw, *The Garment Industry of Greater Kansas City*, 1.

62. Ibid., 13.

63. Ibid., 15.

64. Slegman, interview.

65. Gaw, *The Garment Industry of Greater Kansas City*, 38.

66. Terrell and Zimmer, *The Economic Base of Greater
Kansas City*, 21.

67. Ibid.

68. Fried, interview; Terrell and Zimmer, *The Economic
Base of Greater Kansas City*, 20. The manufacturers'
representatives were usually Gentiles selling goods to
non-Jewish stores that dotted the plains.

69. Alice Nast Stratland, interview by Barbara Bloch and

Ann Brownfield, c. 2006, *Kansas City Garment Industry
History Project*.

70. Michael Quintanilla, "Enthusiasm Can't Be Curbed,"
Los Angeles Times, December 3, 2002, E11.

71. David Lipke, "Nat Nast," *Daily News Record*, December 31, 2001, 70.

72. Eddie Jacobs, interview by Gary Swanson, January 6,
2005, *Kansas City Garment Industry History Project*.

73. Zarr and Zarr, interview.

74. Ibid.

75. Lebovitz, interview.

76. Ibid.

77. Brownfield, interview.

78. Ann Brownfield, e-mail message to author, March 10,
2008.

79. Brownfield, interview, 2007.

80. Marshall Gordon, interview by Gary Swanson,
August 4, 2005, *Kansas City Garment Industry History
Project*.

81. Seymour Weiner, interview by Gary Swanson and
Ann Brownfield, May 20, 2005, *Kansas City Garment
Industry History Project*.

82. Fried, interview.

83. Samuel Sexton and Frank B. Bracking, *Kansas City: An
Illustrated Review of Progress and Importance* (Kansas
City, MO: Enterprise Publishing Company, May
1886), introduction.

84. Gaw, *The Garment Industry of Greater Kansas City*, 5.

85. Gernes, ca. 2004.

86. Dreiseszun, interview.

Chapter 13 From Seventh Avenue to Hollywood:
Fashioning Early Cinema, 1905–1935

1. Anne Hollander, *Seeing Through Clothes* (Berkeley:
University of California Press, 1975), 311.

2. While the class status of film viewers in the early
history of film has been debated, I am using recent
research outlined in Ben Singer's chapter "Manhattan
Nickelodeons: New Data on Audiences and Exhibitors" in *The Silent Cinema Reader*, ed. Lee Grieveson
and Peter Krämer (London: Routledge, 2004), that
questions revisionist thinking about the middle-class
film attendance and provides evidence that the audiences in question were primarily drawn from the blue-
collar sector. For further discussion, see also Michelle
Tolini Finamore, *Fashioning Early Cinema: Dress and
Representation in American Film, 1905–1930* (New
York: Bard Graduate Center, 2010).

3. Claudia B. Kidwell and Margaret C. Christman,
*Suiting Everyone: The Democratization of Clothing in
America* (Washington, DC: Smithsonian Institution
Press, 1974), 87.

4. This information has been gathered from a variety of

sources, including Peter Wollen, "Strike a Pose," *Sight and Sound* 5, no. 3 (March 1995): 14.

5. Abraham Cahan, *The Rise of David Levinsky* (New York: Harper Brothers, 1917), chap. 2, accessed January 10, 2005, http://www.eldritchpress.org/cahan/rdl.htm.

6. This information is supported by an article that was originally published in the March 1913 issue of *Ladies' Home Journal* entitled "The Dishonest Paris Label: How American Women Are Being Fooled by a Country Wide Swindle," by Samuel Hopkins Adams. The article recounts how rolls of fake Paris couture were being sold by the yard to millinery and dress manufacturers.

7. "Her Exclusive Hat," *Moving Picture World* 10, no. 2 (October 24, 1911): 144.

8. Edna Woolman Chase and Ilka Chase, *Always in Vogue* (New York: Doubleday & Company, 1954), 53.

9. Ibid., 52. See also Louis Levine, *The Women's Garment Workers* (New York: International Ladies' Garment Workers' Union, 1924; New York: Arno and the *New York Times*, 1969), 15.

10. Singer, "Manhattan Nickelodeons," 122.

11. The name *Pig Alley* as it refers to pork was noted by William Dean Howells in "An East Side Ramble," *Impressions and Experiences* (New York: Harpers & Brothers, 1896), 127–49, which records a visit he took to the Lower East Side in 1896. Howells was another popular realist writer and he promoted the work of Abraham Cahan.

12. Levine, *The Women's Garment Workers*, 16.

13. Steven J. Ross, *Working-Class Hollywood: Silent Film and the Shaping of Class in America* (Princeton, NJ: Princeton University Press, 1999), 19.

14. Goldwyn's biographical information drawn from A. Scott Berg, *Goldwyn: A Biography* (New York: Ballantine Books, 1990).

15. "A Working Girl's Romance," *Moving Picture World* 9 (February 28, 1914): 1162.

16. Ross, *Working-Class Hollywood*, 175.

17. Richard Koszarski, *An Evening's Entertainment: The Age of the Silent Feature Picture, 1915–1928* (Berkeley: University of California Press, 1994), 187.

18. After the Triangle fire, slides of the incident were shown at the Virginian Theater in Washington, DC, and there were a number of films that included factory fires in their storyline including *That's Happiness* (1911) about a sweatshop seamstress who becomes a hero during a fire.

19. Eustace Hale Ball, *The Art of the Photoplay* (New York: Veritas, 1919), 117.

20. Tim Cavanaugh, "Shoot the Messenger: Hollywood Calls Western Union Again—Message Movies," *Reason* (May 2002), accessed December 2004, http://www.reason.com.

21. Mary Kelly, "Potash and Perlmutter," *Moving Picture World* 64, no. 4 (September 22, 1923): 352.

22. Montague Glass, *Potash and Perlmutter: Their Copartnership Ventures and Adventures* (New York: Grosset & Dunlap, 1911); repr. *American Jewish Archives* 27, no. 1 (April 1985): 168.

23. Kelly, "Potash and Perlmutter," 352.

24. Ibid.

25. Caroline Milbank, *New York Fashion: The Evolution of American Style* (New York: Harry Abrams, 1989), 90.

26. Ibid., 125–26.

27. "Abe and Mawruss, Producers," *New York Times*, September 30, 1924, 27.

28. Jean Bernique, *Motion Picture Acting for Professionals and Amateurs* (Chicago: Producers Service Company, 1916), 182.

29. Quoted in William Drew, *Speaking of Silents: Ladies of the Screen* (Vestal, NY: Vestal Press, 1989), 15.

30. Grace Kingsley, "Clothes," *Photoplay* (n.d.), ca. 1915 clipping in Mary Pickford Scrapbook, 1914–16, Margaret Herrick Library, Academy of Motion Picture Arts and Sciences, Beverly Hills.

31. Madame Therese Lavoisier, "The Latest Fashions in Moving Pictures: A Review of Dainty Gowns Worn by Studio Stars," *Motion Picture Magazine* 9, no. 6 (July 1915): 117–20.

32. "Bebe's Way," *Picture Play* 15, no. 5 (January 1922): 60.

33. Anne Massey, *Hollywood Beyond the Screen: Design and Material Culture* (Oxford, UK: Berg, 2000), 35.

34. Berg, *Goldwyn: A Biography*, 201.

35. Laura Mount, "Designs on Hollywood," *Collier's* (April 1931): 21–22.

36. Ibid., 21.

37. Elizabeth Leese, *Costume Design in the Movies* (Isle of Wight, UK: BCW Publishing, 1976), 14.

38. Howard Greer, *Designing Male* (New York: G. P. Putnam's Sons, 1951), 219.

39. Colleen Moore, "Fashions Set by the Screen: Some Practical Advice," *Evening News*, December 20, 1924, Colleen Moore Scrapbooks, Margaret Herrick Library, Academy of Motion Picture Arts and Sciences, Beverly Hills, CA.

40. Charles Eckert, "The Carole Lombard in Macy's Window," in *Fabrications: Costume and the Female Body*, ed. Jane Gaines and Charlotte Herzog (New York: Routledge, 1990), 108.

41. Information taken from radio segment documented in Russell Birdwell Selznick International Pictures File, Culver City, CA, May 1938, Margaret Herrick Library, Academy of Motion Picture Arts and Sciences, Beverly Hills.

42. Eckert, "The Carole Lombard in Macy's Window," 106.

43. Glass, *Potash and Perlmutter*, 169.

44. Cahan, *The Rise of David Levinsky*, chap. 7.

Contributors

Phyllis Dillon has an MA in anthropology from New York University. She has worked in the field of costume history/textile studies and museums as a textile conservator, curator, and museum director. Her publications include conservation and costume history/textile studies topics. She was the consulting associate curator of the exhibition *A Perfect Fit: The Garment Industry and American Jewry, 1860–1960* at Yeshiva University Museum. She is associate producer of the documentary film *Dressing America: Tales from the Garment District.*

Hasia Diner is the Paul and Sylvia Steinberg Professor of American Jewish History at New York University, with a joint appointment in the department of history and the Skirball Department of Hebrew and Judaic Studies. She is the director of the Goldstein-Goren Center for American Jewish History. A specialist in immigration and ethnic history, American Jewish history, and the history of American women, she is the author of numerous published books including *In the Almost Promised Land: American Jews and Blacks, 1915–1935* (1977; reissued 1995); *Erin's Daughters in America: Irish Immigrant Women in the Nineteenth Century* (1984); *A Time for Gathering: The Second Migration, 1820–1880*, which was the second volume in the Johns Hopkins University Press series *Lower East Side Memories: The Jewish Place in America* (2000); and *The Jews of the United States*, a synthetic history of American Jewry in a series on the histories of modern Jewish communities.

Michelle Tolini Finamore holds her PhD in the history of decorative arts, design, and material culture from the Bard Graduate Center in New York City. She is currently employed as a Curatorial Research Associate in the department of Textile and Fashion Arts at the Museum of Fine Arts, Boston. She has also worked in a curatorial capacity at a number of major museums, including the Costume Institute at the Metropolitan Museum of Art, and as a fashion specialist at Sotheby's auction house. She has taught courses on fashion, design, and film history at the Rhode Island School of Design and Massachusetts College of Art. She most recently co-authored a book on the history of studio jewelry, *Jewelry by Artists: In the Studio, 1940–2000*, and is working on a forthcoming book on fashion in silent film (Palgrave). She has written numerous articles for both the scholarly and popular press, including *Fashion Theory*, *Architecture Boston*, and *Gastronomica.*

Andrew Godley is a reader in business history at the University of Reading Business School. He has authored several books and more than fifty articles and chapters, including *Jewish Immigrant Entrepreneurship in New York and London, 1880–1914* (New York: Palgrave, 2001) and *The Emergence of Ethnic Entrepreneurship* (Princeton, NJ: Princeton University Press, 2005).

Jessica Goldring received her BA from Smith College magna cum laude and an MA degree from University of Missouri, Kansas City, in Voice Performance and Theater History. She has extensive experience as a freelance editor and translator in Germany and the United States, and worked as a research assistant for the Kansas City Garment Industry History

Project in Kansas City, Missouri. In 2007 she was awarded a Fulbright grant to study in Berlin, Germany, after which she returned to New York City and began her work on the *A Perfect Fit* project at Yeshiva University Museum. Since 2010, Ms. Goldring has been on the staff of Macklowe Gallery in New York City, where she served as curator of *Dynamic Beauty: Sculpture of Art Nouveau Paris*—a landmark exhibition featuring nearly 300 bronze sculptures from Paris 1900.

Gabriel M. Goldstein served as Exhibition Curator and Project Director of the *A Perfect Fit* exhibition at Yeshiva University Museum. A specialist in Jewish art and material culture, he is an Adjunct Professor of Art History at Yeshiva University and a museum curator and consultant. He worked for more than two decades at Yeshiva University Museum in New York City, most recently as their Associate Director for Exhibitions and Programs. He was previously employed at the Jewish Museum in New York and the Royal Ontario Museum in Toronto, Canada. Gabe also serves as the Adjunct Curator of Judaica at the North Carolina Museum of Art in Raleigh. Gabe studied at Yeshivat Hamivtar in Jerusalem, the University of Toronto, and the Bard Graduate Center in New York. He has undergraduate and graduate degrees in multiple disciplines: history, fine art history, Judaism, decorative arts, design history, and material culture. He recently was awarded an MPhil degree at Bard, where he is completing his doctoral dissertation on visuality, materiality, and belief in Jewish ceremonial objects.

Nancy L. Green is directrice d'études (professor) at the École des Hautes Études en Sciences Sociales in Paris. Her publications include *The Pletzl of Paris: Jewish Immigrant Workers in the Belle Epoque* (New York: Holmes & Meier, 1986); *Ready-to-Wear and Ready-to-Work: A Century of Industry and Immigrants in Paris and New York* (Durham, NC: Duke University Press, 1997); *Jewish Workers in the Modern Diaspora* (Berkeley: University of California Press, 1998); and *Repenser les migrations* (Paris: Presses Universitaires de France, 2002).

Elizabeth E. Greenberg served as Assistant Curator and Exhibition Coordinator on the 2005–2006 exhibition *A Perfect Fit: The Garment Industry and American Jewry, 1860–1960* at Yeshiva University Museum, and previously worked at the Museum at FIT and the Costume Institute at the Metropolitan Museum of Art. Following *A Perfect Fit*, she served as head archivist at Fairchild Publications, publisher of *Women's Wear Daily, Footwear News,* and *W* magazine. Trained as a fashion historian, Elizabeth received an MA in Art History (History of Dress) from the Courtauld Institute of Art; an MA in Museum Studies (Costume and Textiles) from the Fashion Institute of Technology; and a BA in History from Dartmouth College. She is currently the Curator of Fine Arts at Siena College in Loudonville, New York.

Richard A. Greenwald, a professor of history and social sciences, is Dean at St. Joseph's College in New York. He is the author of *The Triangle Fire, the Protocols of Peace and Industrial Democracy in Progressive Era New York* (2005), coeditor of *Sweatshop USA: The American Sweatshop in Global and Historical Perspective* (2003), and editor of *Exploring America's Past: Essays in Social and Cultural History* (1996). His current projects include *The Death of 9–5: Permanent Freelancers, Empty Offices and the New Way America Works* (2012), and two books with Daniel Katz (New Press), a coedited collection on the future of work in America entitled *Labor Rising: The Past and Future of the American Working Class* and a coauthored history of the needle unions, entitled *Woven Together for Justice.*

Sylvia Axelrod Herskowitz was the Director of Yeshiva University Museum for the *A Perfect Fit* exhibition. She was Director of Yeshiva University Museum for thirty-three years. During that time she initiated and directed such major exhibitions as *Lights/Orot* (1982); *Ashkenaz: The German Jewish Heritage* (1988); *The Sephardic Journey* (1990-92); *Sacred Realm: The Emergence of the Synagogue in the Ancient World* (1996); and *Printing the Talmud* (2005). She studied at Hunter College, the Herzliah Hebrew Institute, and Bank Street College. Under her leadership, the Museum became a world-class institution, exhibiting works by artists from around the world, and organizing exhibitions on Jewish history and culture, including numerous major exhibitions from Jewish museums in Israel, Austria, Germany, and Poland, as well as North America. She has been president of the Council of American Jewish Museums, a reviewer for the National Endowment for Humanities, and still serves as a board member of the Memorial Foundation for Jewish Culture. In 2009 she retired from the Museum and was awarded an Honorary Doctorate by the University. She is now Director Emerita.

JoAnne Olian is curator emeritus of the costume department of the Museum of the City of New York, where her exhibitions included *The House of Worth: The Gilded Age* and *Ladies' Mile: Emporia and Entertainments.* She has lectured and published widely on the history of French and American fashion. Among her publications is the series *Everyday Fashions of the Teens, Forties, Fifties and Sixties as Pictured in Sears Catalogs.* Ms. Olian holds a master of arts from the Institute of Fine Arts at New York University.

Rob Schorman is associate professor of history and regional associate dean for academic affairs at Miami University, Ohio. His book *Selling Style: Advertising and Social Change at the Turn of the Century* appeared in 2003. More recently, he has published essays examining the work of leading advertising practitioners in the late nineteenth and early twentieth centuries.

Bernard Smith is an associate professor of economics at Drew University in Madison, New Jersey. He earned a BSBA degree at the University of Florida and a PhD at Yale University. He is an economic historian with research interests in late-nineteenth-century industrial history and labor relations.

William Toll received his PhD in American history from the University of California at Berkeley and currently teaches American Jewish history at the University of Oregon. He has written several books, including *The Making of an Ethnic Middle Class: Portland Jewry Over Four Generations* (1982), *Women, Men and Ethnicity: Essays on the Structure and Thought of American Jewry* (1991), and with Ellen Eisenberg and Ava Kahn, *Jews of the Pacific Coast, Reinventing Community on America's Edge* (2010).

Mary Vens served as Exhibition Curatorial Associate for the 2005–2006 exhibition *A Perfect Fit: The Garment Industry and American Jewry, 1860–1960* at Yeshiva University Museum. Mary specializes in twentieth-century art history, and following *A Perfect Fit,* she continued to pursue her graduate studies. She has taught classes as an adjunct lecturer at several colleges and universities, most recently Baruch College. She holds an MPhil degree in Art History from The Graduate Center, City University of New York, an MA in Art History from the Institute of Fine Arts, New York University, and a BA in English from Georgetown University.

Laurel Wilson is professor in the Department of Textile and Apparel Management at the University of Missouri. She earned her BS at Montana State University and her PhD at the University of North Carolina–Greensboro. She is best known for her research concerning the dress of the American West.

Michael Zakim is the author of *Ready-Made Democracy: A History of Men's Dress in the American Republic, 1760–1860,* and of the forthcoming *Accounting for Capitalism: The World the Clerks Made.* He teaches history at Tel Aviv University.

Bibliography

Books

Albion, Robert Greenhalgh. *The Rise of New York Port, 1815–1860.* In collaboration with Jennie Barnes Pope. New York: Charles Scribner's Sons, 1939.

Amneus, Cynthia. *A Separate Sphere: Dressmakers in Cincinnati's Golden Age, 1877–1922.* Cincinnati: Cincinnati Art Museum/Texas Tech University Press, 2003.

Appel, Joseph H. *The Business Biography of John Wanamaker, Founder and Builder.* New York: Macmillan Company, 1939.

Bagnall, William R. *Sketches of Manufacturing Establishments in New York City, and of Textile Establishments in the United States.* North Andover, MA: Merrimack Valley Textile Museum, 1977.

Ball, Eustace Hale. *The Art of the Photoplay.* New York: Veritas, 1919.

Bayor, Ronald H., and Timothy J. Meagher. *The New York Irish.* Baltimore: Johns Hopkins University Press, 1996.

Bazelon, Bruce S., and William F. McGuinn, eds. *A Directory of American Military Goods Dealers and Makers 1785–1915.* Printed by the authors, 1999.

Bederman, Gail. *Manliness and Civilization: A Cultural History of Gender and Race in the United States, 1880–1917.* Chicago: University of Chicago Press, 1995.

Bender, Daniel E. *Sweated Work, Weak Bodies: Anti-Sweatshop Campaigns and Languages of Labor.* New Brunswick, NJ: Rutgers University Press, 2004.

Bensel, Richard F. *The Political Economy of American Industrialization, 1877–1900.* New York: Cambridge University Press, 2000.

Berg, A. Scott. *Goldwyn: A Biography.* New York: Ballantine Books, 1990.

Bernique, Jean. *Motion Picture Acting for Professionals and Amateurs.* Producers Service Company, 1916.

Blackmar, Elizabeth, and Arthur A. Goren. *Congregating and Consecrating at Central Synagogue: The Building of a Religious Fellowship and Public Ceremonies.* New York: Central Synagogue, 2003.

Boorstein, Daniel. *The Americans: The Democratic Experience.* New York: Random House, 1973.

Brinkley, Alan. *The End of Reform: New Deal Liberalism in Recession and War.* New York: Knopf, 1998.

Buckman, Joseph. *Immigrants and the Class Struggle: The Jewish Immigrant in Leeds, 1880–1914.* Manchester, UK: Manchester University Press, 1983.

Bythell, Duncan. *The Sweated Trades: Outwork in Nineteenth-Century Britain.* New York: St. Martin's Press, 1978.

Cahan, Abraham. In *Grandma Never Lived in America: The New Journalism of Abraham Cahan,* edited by Moses Rischin. Bloomington: Indiana University Press, 1985.

———. *The Rise of David Levinsky.* 1917. Reprint, New York: Modern Library Edition, 2001.

———. *Yekl and the Imported Bridegroom and Other Stories of Yiddish New York.* New York: Dover, 1970.

Carpenter, Jesse Thomas. *Competition and Collective Bargaining in the Needle Trades, 1910–1967.* Ithaca, NY: Cornell University ILR Press, 1972.

Carr, Harry. *Los Angeles, City of Dreams.* New York: Grossett & Dunlap, 1935.

Chambers, John Whiteclay, II. *The Tyranny of Change: America in the Progressive Era, 1890–1920.* 2nd ed. New Brunswick, NJ: Rutgers University Press, 2000.

Chase, Edna Woolman, and Ilka Chase. *Always in Vogue.* New York: Doubleday & Company, 1954.

Cobrin, Harry A. *The Men's Clothing Industry, Colonial Through Modern Times.* New York: Fairchild Publications, 1970.

Coffin, Judith G. *The Politics of Women's Work: The Paris Garment Trades, 1750–1915.* Princeton, NJ: Princeton University Press, 1996.

Cohen, Nancy. *The Reconstruction of American Liberalism, 1865–1914.* Chapel Hill: University of North Carolina Press, 2002.

Cole, Arthur Harrison. *The American Woolen Manufacture.* Cambridge, MA: Harvard University Press, 1926.

Cone, Molly, Howard Droker, and Jacqueline Williams. *Family of Strangers: Building a Jewish Community in Washington State.* Seattle: Washington State Jewish Historical Society, 2003.

Crawford, M. D. C. *The Ways of Fashion.* New York: G. P. Putnam's Sons, 1941.

Daves, Jessica. *Ready-Made Miracle*. New York: Putnam, 1967.

Diner, Hasia R. *Hungering for America: Italian, Irish, and Jewish Foodways in the Age of Immigration*. Cambridge, MA: Harvard University Press, 2001.

———. *The Jews of the United States, 1654–2000*. Berkeley: University of California Press, 2004.

———. *A Time for Gathering: The Second Migration*. Baltimore: Johns Hopkins University Press, 1992.

Diner, Steven. *A Very Different Age: America in the Progressive Era*. New York: Hill and Wang, 1998.

Dinnerstein, Leonard. *Antisemitism in America*. New York: Oxford University Press, 1994.

Drew, William. *Speaking of Silents: Ladies of the Screen*. Vestal, NY: Vestal Press, 1989.

Dubofsky, Melvyn. *When Workers Organize: New York City in the Progressive Era*. Amherst: University of Massachusetts Press, 1968.

Eisenstadt, Peter. *Affirming the Covenant: A History of Temple B'rith Kodesh Rochester, New York, 1848–1998*. Rochester, NY: Temple B'rith Kodesh, distributed by Syracuse University Press, 1999.

Encyclopaedia Judaica. Jerusalem, Israel: Keter Publishing House, 1971.

Ewen, Elizabeth. *Immigrant Women in the Land of Dollars: Life and Culture on the Lower East Side, 1890–1925*. New York: Monthly Review Press, 1985.

Feingold, Henry L. *Zion in America: The Jewish Experience from Colonial Times to the Present*. Mineola, NY: Dover Publications, 2002.

Feldman, Egal. *Fit for Men: A Study of New York's Clothing Trade*. Washington, DC: Public Affairs Press, 1960.

Fine, Ben, and Ellen Leopold. *The World of Consumption*. London: Routledge, 1993.

Foner, Philip S. *Women and the American Labor Movement: From the First Trade Unions to the Present*. New York: Free Press, 1982.

Fraenkel, Osmond K., ed. *The Curse of Bigness: Miscellaneous Papers of Louis D. Brandeis*. New York: Viking Press, 1934.

Frisch Michael H., and Daniel J. Walkowitz, eds. *Working-Class America: Essays on Labor, Community, and American Society*. Urbana: University of Illinois Press, 1983.

Gabler, Neal. *An Empire of Their Own: How the Jews Invented Hollywood*. New York: Crown Publishers, 1988.

Gaines, Jane, and Charlotte Herzog, eds. *Fabrications: Costume and the Female Body*. New York: Routledge, 1990.

Garvey, Ellen Gruber. *The Adman in the Parlor: Magazines and the Gendering of Consumer Culture, 1880s to 1910s*. New York: Oxford University Press, 1996.

Glass, Montague. *Potash and Perlmutter: Their Copartnership Ventures and Adventures*. New York: Grosset & Dunlap, 1911. Reprinted, *American Jewish Archives* 27, no. 1 (April 1985): 160–70.

Glenn, Susan. *Daughters of the Shtetl: Life and Labor in the Immigrant Generation*. Ithaca, NY: Cornell University Press, 1990.

Godley, Andrew. *The Emergence of Ethnic Entrepreneurship*. Princeton, NJ: Princeton University Press, 2005.

———. *Jewish Immigrant Entrepreneurship in New York and London, 1880–1914*. New York: Palgrave, 2001.

Goodman, Charles S. *The Location of Fashion Industries: With Special Reference to the California Apparel Market, Michigan Business Studies*. Ann Arbor: University of Michigan Press, 1948.

Gordon, Colin. *New Deals: Business, Labor, and Politics in America, 1920–1935*. New York: Cambridge University Press, 1994.

Gottesman, Milton M. *Hoopskirts & Huppas: A Chronicle of the Early Years of the Garfunkel-Trager Family in America, 1856–1920*. New York: American Jewish Historical Society, 1999.

Green, Nancy L. *The Pletzl of Paris: Jewish Immigrant Workers in the Belle Epoque*. New York: Holmes & Meier, 1986.

———. *Ready-to-Wear and Ready-to-Work: A Century of Industry and Immigrants in Paris and New York*. Durham, NC: Duke University Press, 1997.

Greer, Howard. *Designing Male*. New York: G. P. Putnam's Sons, 1951.

Grieveson, Lee, and Peter Krämer, eds. *The Silent Cinema Reader*. London: Routledge, 2004.

Griffin, Clyde, and Sally Griffin. *Natives and Newcomers: The Ordering of Opportunity in Mid-Nineteenth-Century Poughkeepsie*. Cambridge, MA: Harvard University Press, 1978.

Gross, Nahum, ed. *Economic History of the Jews*. New York: Schocken Books, 1975.

Hapgood, Hutchins. *The Spirit of the Ghetto*, edited by Moses Rischin. Cambridge, MA: Harvard University Press, 1967.

Hawes, Elizabeth. *Fashion Is Spinach*. New York: Random House, 1938.

Head, Edith, and Paddy Calistro. *Edith Head's Hollywood*. New York: Dutton, 1983.

Heinze, Andrew. *Adapting to Abundance: Jewish Immigrants, Mass Consumption and the Search for American Identity*. New York: Columbia University Press, 1990.

Higham, Charles. *Warner Brothers*. New York: Charles Scribner's Sons, 1975.

Higham, John. *Send These to Me*. Rev. ed. Baltimore: Johns Hopkins University Press, 1984.

———. *Strangers in the Land*. 2nd ed. New York: Atheneum, 1969.

Hoberman, J., and Jeffrey Shandler. *Entertaining America: Jews, Movies and Broadcasting*. Princeton, NJ: Princeton University Press, 2003.

Hollander, Anne. *Seeing Through Clothes*. Berkeley: University of California Press, 1975.

———. *Sex and Suits*. New York: Kodansha International, 1994.

Homberger, Eric. *Mrs. Astor's New York: Money and Social Power in a Gilded Age*. New Haven, CT: Yale University Press, 2002.

Hood, Adrienne D. *The Weaver's Craft: Cloth, Commerce, and Industry in Early Pennsylvania.* Philadelphia: University of Pennsylvania Press, 2003.

Howe, Irving. *World of Our Fathers.* New York: Harcourt Brace Jovanovich, 1976.

Hyman, Paula E. *From Dreyfus to Vichy: The Remaking of French Jewry.* New York: Columbia University Press, 1979.

Issell, William, and Robert W. Cherny. *San Francisco, 1865–1932, Politics, Power and Urban Development.* Berkeley: University of California Press, 1986.

Jacobson, Matthew Frye. *Whiteness of a Different Color: European Immigrants and the Alchemy of Race.* Cambridge, MA: Harvard University Press, 1998.

Jarnow, Jeanette, Miriam Guerreiro, and Beatrice Judelle, eds. *Inside the Fashion Business.* 4th ed. New York: Macmillan, 1987.

Jensen, Joan M., and Sue Davidson, eds. *A Needle, a Bobbin, a Strike: Women Needleworkers in America.* Philadelphia: Temple University Press, 1984.

Johnson, Paul. *A Shopkeepers Millennium: Society and Revivals in Rochester, New York, 1815–1837.* New York: Hill and Wang, 1977.

Jones, Fred Mitchell. *Middlemen in the Domestic Trade of the United States, 1800–1860.* Urbana: University of Illinois, 1937.

Joselit, Jenna Weissman. *A Perfect Fit: Clothes, Character and the Promise of America.* New York: Henry Holt & Company, 2001.

Joseph, Samuel. *Jewish Immigration to the United States from 1881 to 1910.* New York, 1914.

Kahn, Ava, ed. *Jewish Life in the American West.* Los Angeles: Autry Museum of Western Heritage, 2002.

Kidwell, Claudia Brush, and Margaret Christman. *Suiting Everyone: The Democratization of Clothing in America.* Washington, DC: Smithsonian Institution Press, 1974.

Kidwell, Claudia Brush, and Valerie Steele, eds. *Men and Women, Dressing the Part.* Washington, DC: Smithsonian Institution Press, 1987.

Kimmel, Michael. *Manhood in America: A Cultural History.* New York: Free Press, 1996.

Kishlansky, Mark, Patrick Geary, Patricia O'Brien, and R. Bin Wong. *Societies and Cultures in World History.* New York: HarperCollins College Publishers, 1995.

Klatzmann, Joseph. *Le travail à domicile dans l'industrie parisienne du vêtement.* Paris: Armand Colin, 1957.

Koszarski, Richard. *An Evening's Entertainment: The Age of the Silent Feature Picture, 1915–1928.* Berkeley: University of California Press, 1994.

Kramer, Sydelle, and Jenny Masur, eds. *Jewish Grandmothers.* Boston: Beacon Press, 1976.

Kuchta, David. *The Three-Piece Suit and Modern Masculinity.* Berkeley: University of California Press, 2002.

Lallement, Michel. *Des PME en chambre: Travail et travailleurs à domicile d'hier et d'aujourd'hui.* Paris: L'Harmattan, 1990.

Lazzarato, Maurizio, Yann Moulier-Boutang, Antonio Negri, Giancarlo et Santilli. *Des entreprises pas comme les autres: Benneton en Italie, le Sentier à Paris.* Paris: Publisud, 1993.

Leese, Elizabeth. *Costume Design in the Movies.* Isle of Wight, UK: BCW Publishing, 1976.

Levin, Phyllis Lee. *The Wheels of Fashion.* Garden City, NY: Doubleday, 1965.

Levine, Louis. *The Women's Garment Workers.* New York: International Ladies' Garment Workers' Union, 1924. Reprint, New York: Arno and the *New York Times*, 1969.

Libo, Kenneth, and Irving Howe. *We Lived There, Too: In Their Own Words and Pictures, Pioneer Jews and the Westward Movement of America, 1630–1930.* New York: St. Martin's/Marek, 1984.

Licht, Walter. *Industrializing America: The Nineteenth Century.* Baltimore: Johns Hopkins University Press, 1995.

Linderman, Gerald F. *The Mirror of War: American Society and the Spanish-American War.* Ann Arbor: University of Michigan Press, 1974.

Mason, Alpheus Thomas. *Brandeis: A Free Man's Life.* New York: Viking Press, 1946.

Massey, Anne. *Hollywood Beyond the Screen: Design and Material Culture.* Oxford, UK: Berg, 2000.

McKelvey, Blake. *Rochester: The Flower City, 1855–90.* Cambridge, MA: Harvard University Press, 1949.

Meinig, D. W. *The Shaping of America: Continental America, 1800–1867.* New Haven, CT: Yale University Press, 1993.

Milbank, Caroline. *New York Fashion: The Evolution of American Style.* New York: Harry Abrams, 1989.

Montagné-Villette, Solange. *Le Sentier: Un espace ambigu.* Paris: Masson, 1990.

North, Douglass C. *The Economic Growth of the United States, 1790–1860.* New York: W. W. Norton, 1966.

Nystrom, Paul H. *Economics of Fashion.* New York: Ronald Press Company, 1928.

Ohmann, Richard. *Selling Culture: Magazines, Markets and Class at the Turn of the Century.* London: Verso, 1996.

Orleck, Annelise. *Common Sense and a Little Fire: Women and Working-Class Politics in the United States, 1900–1965.* Chapel Hill: University of North Carolina Press, 1995.

Perrot, Philippe. *Les dessus et les dessous de la bourgeoisie.* Paris: Fayard, 1981.

Pessota, Rose. In *Bread Upon the Waters*, edited by John Nicols Beffel. Ithaca, NY: ILR Press, 1987.

Pope, Daniel. *The Making of Modern Advertising.* New York: Basic Books 1983.

Pope, Jesse Eliphalet. *The Clothing Industry in New York.* Columbia: University of Missouri Press, 1905.

Roblin, Michel. *Les Juifs de Paris.* Paris: A. et J. Picard, 1952.

Rochlin, Harriet, and Fred Rochlin. *Pioneer Jews: A New Life in the Far West.* Boston: Houghton Mifflin, 1984.

Rosenberg, Emily. *Spreading the American Dream: American Economic and Cultural Expansion, 1890–1945.* New York: Hill and Wang, 1982.

Rosenberg, Stuart E. *The Jewish Community in Rochester, 1843–1925.* New York: American Jewish Historical Society/Columbia University Press, 1954.

Ross, Steven J. *Working-Class Hollywood: Silent Film and the Shaping of Class in America.* Princeton, NJ: Princeton University Press, 1999.

Rosten, Leo B. *Hollywood, The Movie Colony, The Movie Makers.* New York: Harcourt, Brace, 1941.

Rotundo, E. Anthony. *American Manhood: Transformations in Masculinity from the Revolution to the Modern Era.* New York: Basic Books, 1993.

Sarna, Jonathan D., and Nancy H. Klein. *The Jews of Cincinnati.* Cincinnati: Hebrew Union College, 1989.

Schatz, Thomas. *The Genius of the System: Hollywood Film Making in the Studio Era.* New York: Pantheon Books, 1988.

Schmiechen, James A. *Sweated Industries and Sweated Labor: The London Clothing Trades, 1860–1914.* Urbana: University of Illinois Press, 1984.

Schorman, Rob. *Selling Style: Clothing and Social Change at the Turn of the Century.* Philadelphia: University of Pennsylvania Press, 2003.

Schreier, Barbara A. *Becoming American Women: Clothing and the Jewish Immigrant Experience, 1880–1920.* Chicago: Chicago Historical Society, 1994.

Shammas, Carole. *The Pre-Industrial Consumer in England and America.* Oxford, UK: Clarendon Press, 1990.

Sorin, Gerald. *A Time for Building: The Third Migration, 1880–1924.* Baltimore: Johns Hopkins University Press, 1992.

Steele, Valerie. *Fashion and Eroticism: Ideals of Feminine Beauty from the Victorian Era to the Jazz Age.* New York: Oxford University Press, 1985.

———. *Paris Fashion: A Cultural History.* New York: Oxford University Press, 1988.

Stolberg, Benjamin. *Tailor's Progress: The Story of a Famous Union and the Men Who Made It.* Garden City, NY: Doubleday, Doran, and Company, 1944.

Stott, Richard B. *Workers in the Metropolis: Class, Ethnicity, and Youth in Antebellum New York City.* Ithaca, NY: Cornell University Press, 1990.

Strum, Phillipa. *Brandeis: Beyond Progressivism.* Lawrence: University of Kansas Press, 1994.

Summers, Mark. *The Gilded Age, Or, A Hazard of New Functions.* Upper Saddle River, NJ: Prentice-Hall, 1997.

Taylor, George Rogers. *The Transportation Revolution, 1815–1860.* New York: Rinehart, 1951.

Toll, William. *The Making of an Ethnic Middle Class: Portland Jewry Over Four Generations.* Albany: State University of New York Press, 1982.

Urofsky, Melvin I. *A Mind of One Piece: Brandeis and American Reform.* New York: Scribner's, 1971.

Vanier, Henriette. *La mode et ses métiers: Frivolités et luttes des classes, 1830–1870.* Paris: Armand Colin, 1960.

Veillon, Dominique. *La mode sous l'occupation: Débrouillardise et coquetterie dans la France en guerre (1939–1945).* Paris: Payot, 1990.

Vittoz, Stanley. *New Deal Labor Policy and the American Industrial Economy.* Chapel Hill: University of North Carolina Press, 1987.

Voorsanger, Catherine Hoover, and John K. Howat, eds. *Art and the Empire City: New York, 1825–1861.* New Haven, CT: Yale University Press/Metropolitan Museum of Art, 2000.

Waidenschlager, Christine. *Berliner Chic: Mode von 1820 bis 1990.* Berlin: Stiftung Stadtmuseum, 2001.

Waldinger, Roger. *Through the Eye of the Needle: Immigrants and Enterprise in New York's Garment Trades.* New York: New York University Press, 1986.

Walkowitz, Daniel J. *Working with Class: Social Workers and the Politics of Middle-Class Identity.* Chapel Hill: University of North Carolina Press, 1999.

Weinberg, David H. *A Community on Trial: The Jews of Paris in the 1930s.* Chicago: University of Chicago Press, 1977.

Weiner, Lynn. *From Working Girl to Working Mother: The Female Labor Force in the United States, 1820–1980.* Chapel Hill: University of North Carolina Press, 1985.

Wiebe, Robert H. *The Search for Order, 1877–1920.* New York: Hill and Wang, 1967.

Wile, Isaac A., and Isaac M. Brickner. *The Jews of Rochester.* Rochester, NY: Historical Review Society, 1912.

Zakim, Michael. *Ready-Made Democracy: A History of Men's Dress in the American Republic, 1760–1860.* Chicago: University of Chicago Press, 2003.

Journals

Auerbach, Alvin. "San Francisco's South of Market District, 1850–1950: The Emergence of a Skid Row." *California Historical Quarterly* 52 (Fall 1973).

Beazeley, Alison. "The 'Heavy' and 'Light' Clothing Industries, 1850–1920." *Costume*, no. 7 (1973).

Berg, Maxine. "Small Producer Capitalism in Eighteenth-Century England." *Business History* 35, no. 1 (January 1993).

Blanchard, Mary W. "Boundaries and the Victorian Body: Aesthetic Fashion in Gilded Age America." *American Historical Review* 100, no. 1 (February 1995).

Bunker, Gary L., and John Appel. "Shoddy, Anti-Semitism and the Civil War." *American Jewish History* 82 (Autumn 1994): 43–72.

Cavanaugh, Tim. "Shoot the Messenger: Hollywood Calls Western Union Again—Message Movies." *Reason* (May 2002), accessed December 2004, http://www.reason.com.

Cohen, Miriam, and Michael Hanagan. "The Political Economy of Social Reform: The Case of Homework in New York and Paris, 1900–1940." *French Politics and Society* 6, no. 4 (October 1988): 31–38.

Eckert, Charles. "The Carole Lombard in Macy's Window." *Quarterly Review of Film Studies* 3, no. 1 (Winter 1978): 1–21.

Fraser, Steven. "Combined and Uneven Development in the Men's Clothing Industry." *Business History Review* 57 (Winter 1983): 522–47.

Kessner, Thomas. "Jobs, Ghettoes, and the Urban Economy, 1880–1935." *American Jewish History* 71, no. 2 (December 1981): 218–38.

McKelvey, Blake. "The Men's Clothing Industry in Rochester's History." *Rochester History* 22 (July 1960): 1–32.

McPherson, John Bryce. "The New York Cloakmakers' Strike." *Journal of Political Economy* 19 (March 1911): 153–87.

Paoletti, Jo Barraclough. "Ridicule and Role Models as Factors in American Men's Fashion Change, 1880–1910." *Costume* 19 (1985): 121–34.

Raab, Earl. "There's No City Like San Francisco." *Commentary* (October 1950): 369–78.

Schorman, Rob. "Ready or Not: Custom-Made Ideals and Ready-Made Clothes in Late 19th-Century America." *Journal of American Culture* 19 (Winter 1996): 111–20.

Schreier, Barbara. "Becoming American: Jewish Immigrant Women 1880–1920." *History Today* 44, no. 3 (March 1994): 25–31.

Testi, Arnaldo. "The Gender of Reform Politics: Theodore Roosevelt and the Culture of Masculinity." *Journal of American History* 84, no. 1 (March 1995): 1509–33.

Wollen, Peter. "Strike a Pose." *Sight and Sound* 5, no. 3 (March 1995): 10–15.

Zakim, Michael. "Customizing the Industrial Revolution: The Reinvention of Tailoring in the Nineteenth Century." *Winterthur Portfolio* 33, no. 1 (Spring 1998): 41–58.

———. "A Ready-Made Business: The Birth of the Clothing Industry in America." *Business History Review* 73 (Spring 1999): 61–90.

———. "Sartorial Ideologies: From Homespun to Ready-Made." *American Historical Review* 106, no. 5 (December 2001): 1553–86.

Unpublished manuscripts and dissertations

Adler, Robert. "The Rise and Decline of the Men's Clothing Industry of Rochester, New York." Unpublished manuscript. Department of Rare Books and Special Collections, University of Rochester Library, 1987.

Berman, Hyman. "Era of the Protocol: A Chapter in the History of the International Ladies' Garment Workers' Union, 1910–1916." PhD diss., Columbia University, 1956.

Degler, Carl N. "Labor in the Economy and Politics of New York City, 1850–1860: A Study of the Impact of Early Industrialism." PhD diss., Columbia University, 1952.

Finamore, Michelle Tolini. "Fashioning Early Cinema: Dress and Representaton in American Film, 1905–1930." PhD diss., Bard Graduate Center, 2010.

Gleason, Alan H. "The History of Labor in Rochester, 1820–1880." Master's thesis, University of Rochester, 1941.

Hawley, Natalie F. "The Labor Movement in Rochester, 1880–1898." Master's thesis, University of Rochester, 1948.

Paoletti, Jo Barraclough. "Changes in the Masculine Image in the United States 1880–1910: A Content Analysis of Popular Humor About Dress." PhD diss., University of Maryland, 1980.

Zomalt, Leslie Meyers. "An Exercise in Caution: The Business Activities of the Joseph Seligman Family in the 19th Century American West." PhD diss., University of California, Santa Barbara, 1979.

Index